UNITED STATES HISTORY

MODERN AMERICA

Adapted Reading and Note Taking Study Guide

Upper Saddle River, New Jersey   Boston, Massachusetts   Chandler, Arizona   Glenview, Illinois

ISBN-13: 978-0-13-368811-5
ISBN-10:   0-13-368811-9

5 6 7 8 9 10 V092 14 13

Contents

How to Use This Book

The **Reading and Note Taking Study Guide** will help you better understand the content of *Prentice Hall United States History.* This book will also develop your reading, vocabulary, and note taking skills. Each study guide consists of two components. The first component focuses on developing the graphic organizers that appear in your textbook.

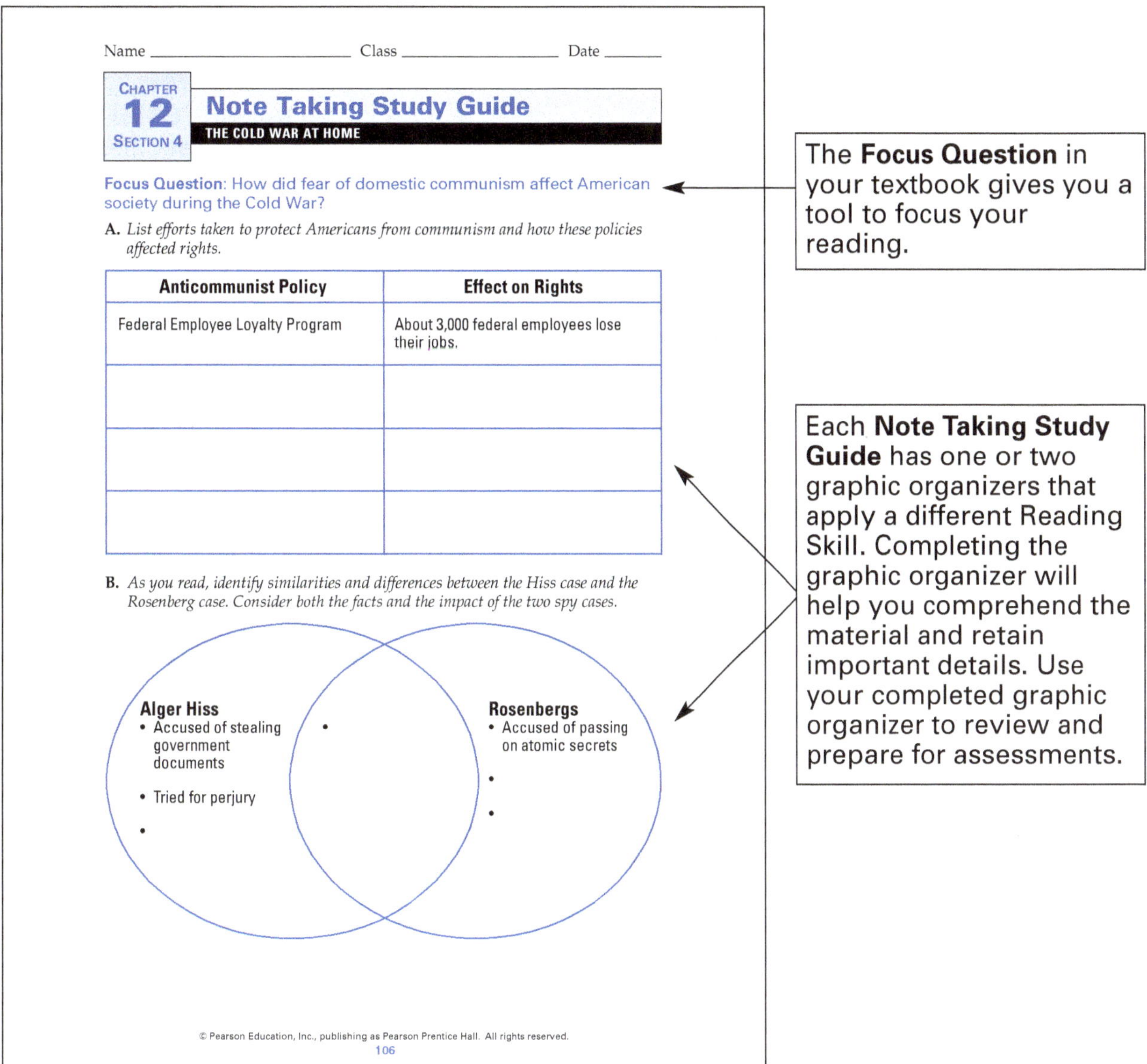

The **Focus Question** in your textbook gives you a tool to focus your reading.

Each **Note Taking Study Guide** has one or two graphic organizers that apply a different Reading Skill. Completing the graphic organizer will help you comprehend the material and retain important details. Use your completed graphic organizer to review and prepare for assessments.

The second component highlights the central themes, issues, and concepts of each section.

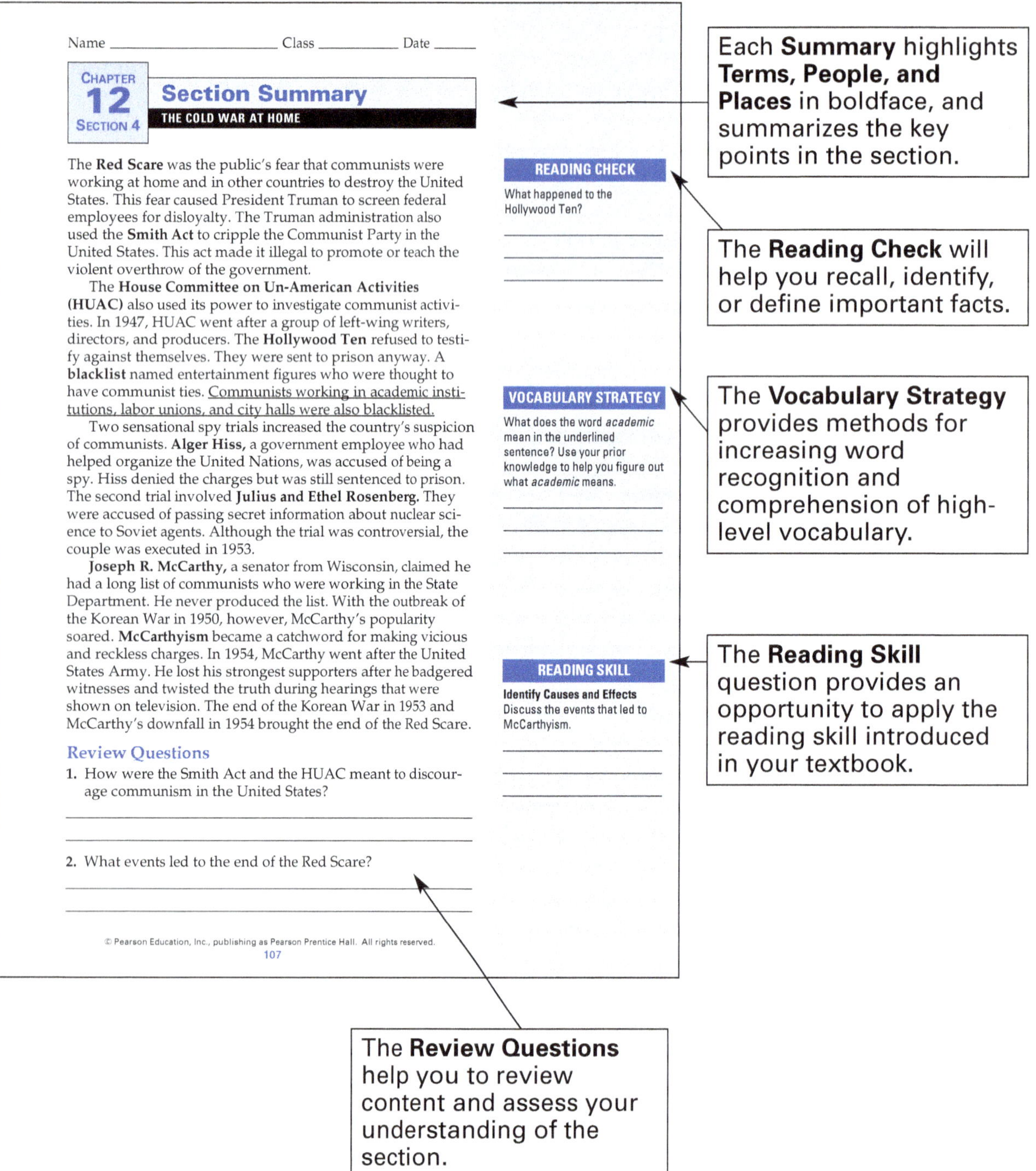

Each **Summary** highlights **Terms, People, and Places** in boldface, and summarizes the key points in the section.

The **Reading Check** will help you recall, identify, or define important facts.

The **Vocabulary Strategy** provides methods for increasing word recognition and comprehension of high-level vocabulary.

The **Reading Skill** question provides an opportunity to apply the reading skill introduced in your textbook.

The **Review Questions** help you to review content and assess your understanding of the section.

The **American Issues Journal** supports the **American Issues Connector** features found in your text. These worksheets will help you track key issues that Americans have debated throughout their history. Each worksheet covers one of the 21 recurring American issues over time.

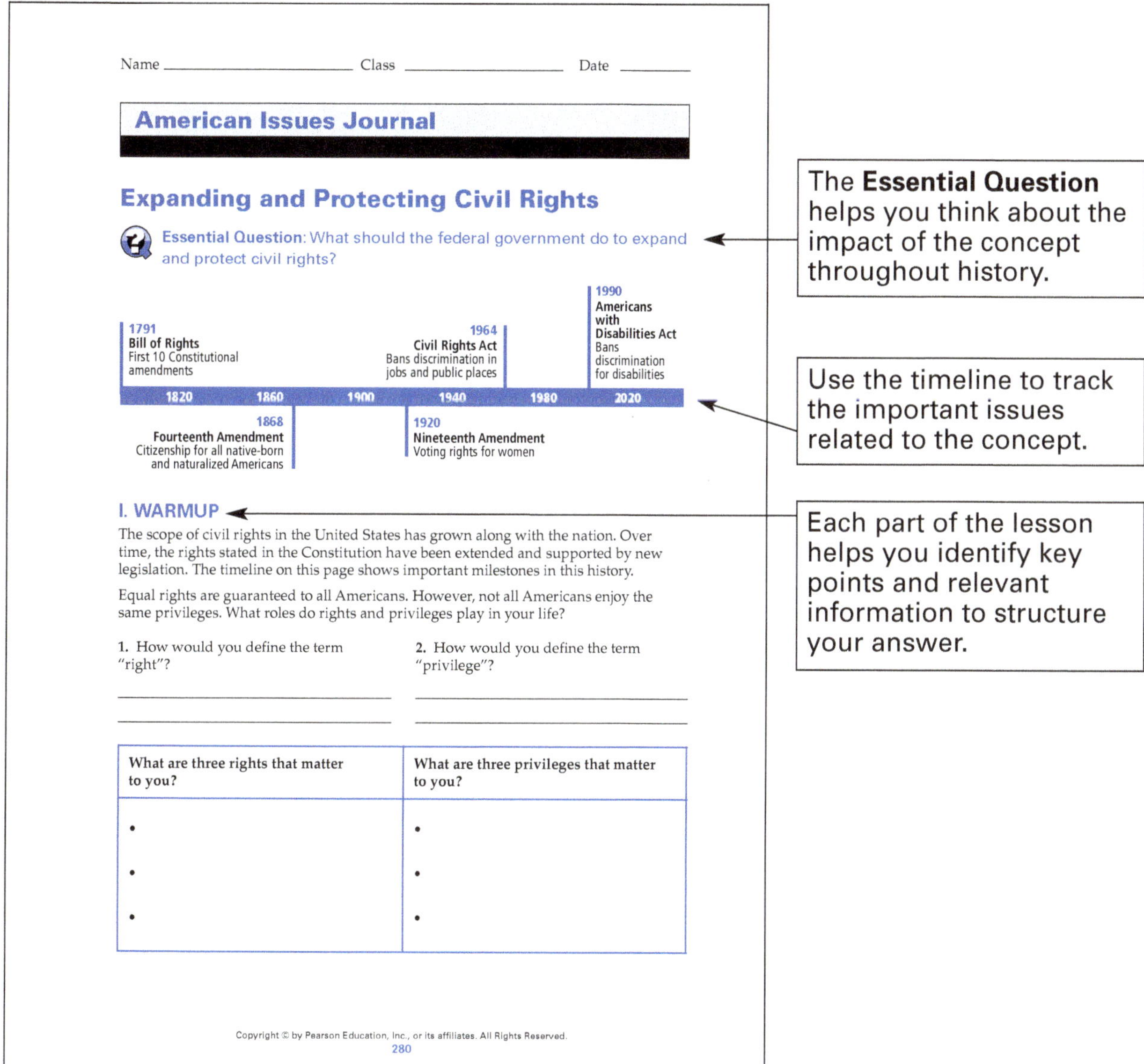

The **Essential Question** helps you think about the impact of the concept throughout history.

Use the timeline to track the important issues related to the concept.

Each part of the lesson helps you identify key points and relevant information to structure your answer.

Name ______________________ Class ________________ Date ______

CHAPTER 1 SECTION 1

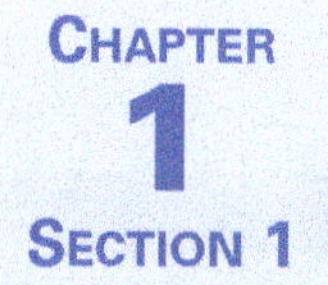

Note Taking Study Guide

MANY CULTURES MEET

Focus Question: What were the causes and effects of European arrival in the Americas?

Identify the causes and effects of European arrival in the Americas.

Effects

- Columbian Exchange
-
-

↑

Event

- Europeans arrive in the Americas.

↑

Causes

- Desire to find trade routes to Asia
- Increase in economic wealth
-
-
-
-
-

<table><tr><td>CHAPTER 1
SECTION 1</td><td><h1>Section Summary</h1>MANY CULTURES MEET</td></tr></table>

The first Americans came from northeastern Asia between 15,000 and 40,000 years ago. The American Indians expanded southward, filling the continents of North and South America. <u>They developed diverse cultures as they adapted to the different climates they inhabited.</u> However, they shared many traits. An extended family with a single ancestor became a **clan.** Several clans made up a **band** of Indians. The Indians learned how to grow crops, which expanded the food supply and allowed the population to grow.

In the fifteenth century, Europeans began to expand by sea. The Portuguese took the lead. They reached West Africa below the Sahara. There, they expanded the slave trade. After 1500, colonial plantations created a demand for slaves in the Americas. Over the next three centuries, slave traders took at least 11 million Africans across the Atlantic. The transatlantic slave trade was called the **Middle Passage.** It weakened the West African economy while making European merchants and empires rich.

In 1492, Spain sponsored a voyage by the Italian sailor **Christopher Columbus.** He hoped to reach the Indies by sailing west, across the Atlantic. He explored several Caribbean islands, thinking that he had reached the Indies.

The Spanish quickly conquered a huge empire in Central and South America. The Spanish invaders were known as **conquistadores.** The conquistadores had many advantages, including horses and steel weapons. They also carried European diseases. Native Americans had no immunity to these diseases. Indians died by the thousands. These diseases made it easier for the Europeans to conquer and colonize North and South America.

The colonizers also introduced new animals into the Americas. In addition, they took American products back to Europe. This exchange of goods and ideas between Europe and the Americas is called the **Columbian Exchange.**

Review Questions

1. Why did the American Indians develop different cultures?

____

____

2. What did Christopher Columbus hope to accomplish?

____

____

Name ______________________ Class ________________ Date ______

CHAPTER 1
SECTION 2

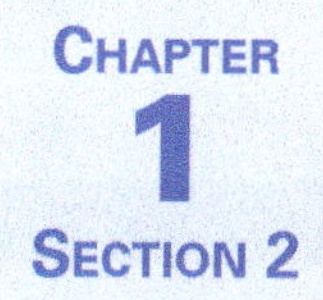

Note Taking Study Guide

THE AMERICAN REVOLUTION

Focus Question: What important ideas and major events led to the American Revolution?

Note the sequence of events that led to the American Revolution by making a series-of-events chain.

French and Indian War
↓
↓
↓
↓
↓
↓
↓
Continental Congress adopts the Declaration of Independence.

<table>
<tr><td>CHAPTER
1
SECTION 2</td><td>**Section Summary**
THE AMERICAN REVOLUTION</td></tr>
</table>

The Spanish spread from the Caribbean into Central and South America. They then claimed much of southern and southwestern North America. The French started colonies in Canada and Louisiana. In 1607, the English settled at Jamestown in Virginia. The Virginia colonists elected a legislature called the **House of Burgesses.** To the north, English settlers in New England adopted the **Mayflower Compact.** It provided a framework for self-government. The English also settled the Middle Colonies, between New England and Virginia. Another group of colonies lay south of Virginia. Plantations there increasingly relied on enslaved Africans.

The English colonists brought ideas about democracy and government to America. During the 1700s, the **Enlightenment** influenced well-educated American colonists. <u>The Enlightenment was a philosophy that applied human reason to government and religion.</u> During the 1740s, concern about these trends led to a religious movement called the **Great Awakening.** This movement led to the rise of new churches and increased tolerance of religious differences.

Between 1689 and 1763, the British and French fought a series of wars. To help pay for them, the British Parliament started to tax the colonists in the 1760s. The colonists resisted the taxes, asserting their rights as Englishmen. They cited the **Magna Carta** (1215), which limited the power of the king. They also cited the **English Bill of Rights** (1689), which blocked the king from levying taxes without Parliament's permission. The colonists did not want to pay taxes that were not levied by their elected representatives. War broke out between the colonies and the British in 1775 at Concord, Massachusetts. In 1776, **Thomas Jefferson** of Virginia wrote the Declaration of Independence, which the Continental Congress adopted. The war continued until **George Washington** led the American colonists to victory in 1783.

Review Questions

1. What two ideas influenced life in the colonies in the 1700s?

____

____

2. Why did the 13 colonies revolt against British rule?

____

____

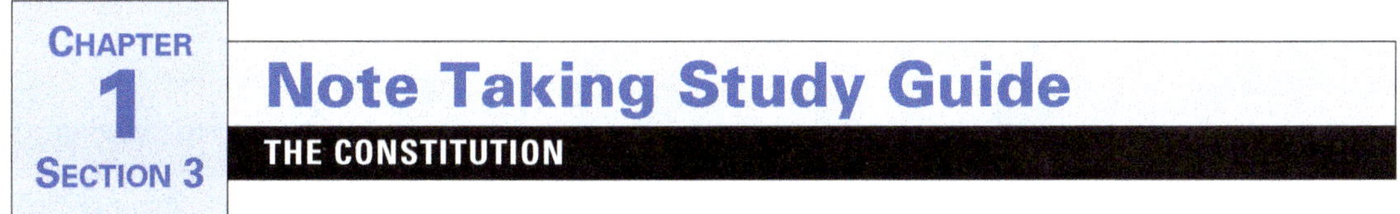

Note Taking Study Guide

CHAPTER 1 SECTION 3

THE CONSTITUTION

Focus Question: What ideas and debates led to the Constitution and Bill of Rights?

A. *Complete the timeline below with important dates that led to the formation of the U.S. government.*

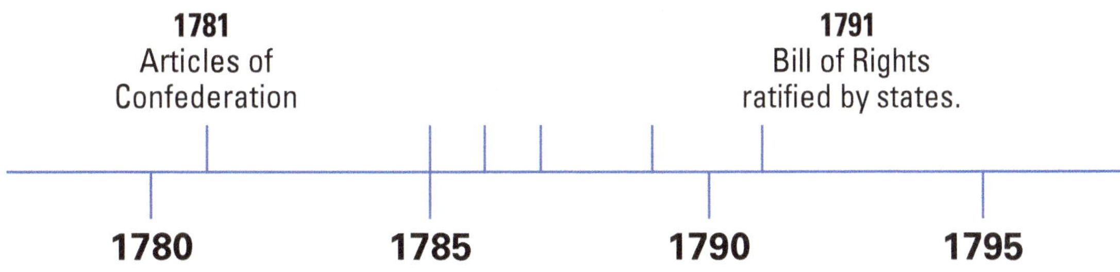

B. *As you read, identify similarities and differences between the Federalists and the Antifederalists.*

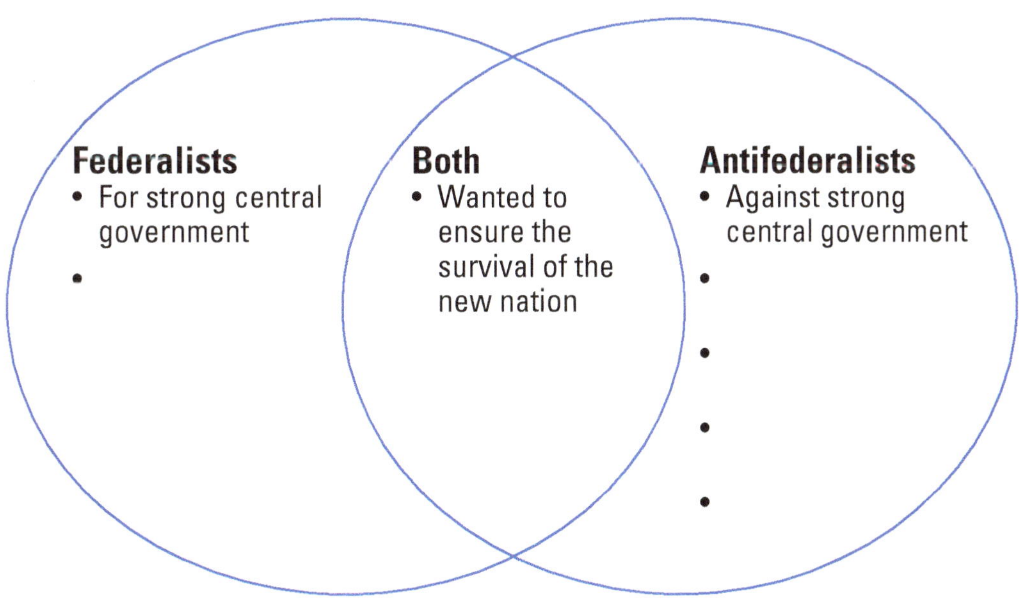

<table><tr><td>CHAPTER
1
SECTION 3</td><td># Section Summary
THE CONSTITUTION</td></tr></table>

What is federalism?

____

____

____

Find the word *constrain* in the underlined sentence. Use context clues to figure out the meaning of *constrain.*

____

____

____

Recognize Sequence Which constitution came before the current United States Constitution?

____

____

____

In 1776, the former American colonies became states. Each state created a constitution and set up a government. Most state constitutions included a **bill of rights,** which listed the freedoms guaranteed by the state government.

In 1781, the 13 states adopted the Articles of Confederation, the first federal constitution. Under the Articles, power remained with the states. Because the government could not levy taxes, it could not pay its huge war debt. It also could not defend the American frontier. <u>The Spanish tried to constrain western American settlements by closing the Port of New Orleans.</u>

In May 1787, a convention was called to change the Articles of Confederation. The small states wanted the United States to stay a loose confederation. However, **James Madison** of Virginia advocated a strong national union. The delegates compromised by creating a bicameral legislature: a House of Representatives and a Senate.

Before the new Constitution would become law, 9 of the 13 states had to **ratify,** or officially approve, it. Supporters of the Constitution were known as Federalists. They wanted to create a strong central government. Opponents of the Constitution were known as Antifederalists. The Antifederalists thought the Constitution gave too much power to the national government. They also opposed the Constitution because it did not have a bill of rights. The Federalists promised to add a bill of rights. In 1789, Congress approved the federal Bill of Rights.

The Constitution divided power between the states and the nation. This division is known as **federalism.** The Constitution defined separate executive, legislative, and judicial branches of government. This division was meant to ensure a **separation of powers.** A system of **checks and balances** prevented one branch from taking control of the government. In addition, the founders worded the Constitution to permit flexibility. The Constitution has been amended 27 times.

Review Questions

1. Describe one weakness of the Articles of Confederation.

____

____

2. Why did the Constitution define separate executive, legislative, and judicial branches of government?

____

____

Note Taking Study Guide

CHAPTER 1 SECTION 4

THE NEW REPUBLIC

Focus Question: How did the United States and its government change in the late 1700s and early 1800s?

List the major accomplishments of each President in the chart below.

President	Accomplishments
George Washington	• • • •
John Adams	• •
Thomas Jefferson	• • • • • •
James Madison	•
James Monroe	•

<table>
<tr><td>CHAPTER
1
SECTION 4</td><td># Section Summary
THE NEW REPUBLIC</td></tr>
</table>

What was the Sedition Act?

____

____

____

What does the word *compensating* mean in the underlined sentence? Look for context clues in the surrounding words, phrases, and sentences. Circle the word below that is a synonym for *compensating.*

- paying
- depriving

Categorize List at least two actions the United States took to avoid war.

____

____

____

After the Revolutionary War, Secretary of the Treasury Alexander Hamilton created a financial plan to pay off the war debt. <u>Critics from the South thought that it favored northeastern merchants by compensating them with tax dollars.</u>

The French Revolution in 1789 started a war between Britain and France. The United States declared its neutrality but continued to trade with Britain and France. The British navy then began seizing U.S. merchant ships trading with French colonies. To avoid war, John Jay negotiated Jay's Treaty between Britain and the United States. Congress then passed the Alien and Sedition acts in 1798. The **Alien Act** made it more difficult for immigrants to become citizens. The **Sedition Act** made it a crime for citizens to publicly discredit the federal government.

Jefferson was elected President in 1800. In 1803, the Supreme Court enacted **judicial review.** This was the power to decide whether federal laws were constitutional. Also in 1803, Jefferson bought the **Louisiana Purchase** territory from France. It nearly doubled the size of the United States.

The British navy started seizing American merchant ships again. They also seized sailors from U.S. ships. This practice was known as **impressment.** As a result, Jefferson asked Congress to declare an **embargo.** It would stop trade by ordering American ships to stay in port. By 1812, war with Britain could no longer be avoided. The War of 1812 ended in 1815 with a U.S. victory.

The invention of the **cotton gin,** a machine that made cotton cheaper and faster to produce, led to a surge in cotton production in the South.

In 1823, President Monroe issued the **Monroe Doctrine.** It declared that European monarchies had no business interfering with American republics. In return, the United States promised to stay out of European affairs.

Review Questions

1. What was the goal of Jay's Treaty?

____

____

2. Why did Jefferson want Congress to declare an embargo?

____

____

CHAPTER 2

SECTION 1

Note Taking Study Guide

REFORM AND WESTWARD EXPANSION

Focus Question: What trends in democratization and reform were taking shape in the United States by 1850?

As you read, outline the main ideas.

I. Democracy and the Age of Jackson

    A. More Americans can vote.

        1. Suffrage grows in the West.

        2. _______________________________________

    B. _______________________________________

    C. _______________________________________

II. Religion and Social Reform

    A. _______________________________________

    B. _______________________________________

    C. _______________________________________

        1. _______________________________________

        2. _______________________________________

III. The Antislavery Movement

    A. _______________________________________

    B. _______________________________________

    C. _______________________________________

IV. The Women's Rights Movement

    A. _______________________________________

    B. _______________________________________

        1. _______________________________________

        2. _______________________________________

V. Manifest Destiny

    A. _______________________________________

        1. _______________________________________

        2. _______________________________________

    B. _______________________________________

Section Summary
REFORM AND WESTWARD EXPANSION

READING CHECK

Who was Frederick Douglass?

____

____

____

VOCABULARY STRATEGY

What does the word *compelled* mean in the underlined sentence? The words *made* and *required* are synonyms of *compelled.* Use these synonyms to help you figure out the meaning of *compelled.*

____

____

____

READING SKILL

Identify Main Ideas Describe how the Second Great Awakening influenced social reform movements.

____

____

____

In the West, changes in the law gave most adult white men the right to vote. This new generation of voters elected **Andrew Jackson** President in 1828. Jackson's policies compelled thousands of Indians to leave their homes and endure a cruel, deadly march to Oklahoma. This march was called the Trail of Tears.

Conflicts between state and federal power increased. One conflict occurred when the federal government imposed **tariffs,** or high taxes, on imported products. Some argued that states had the right to cancel any federal law that went against their interests.

The **Second Great Awakening,** a religious movement, began in the 1820s. Many members of this movement began working for social reform. One such member was Henry David Thoreau. He was an **abolitionist,** a reformer who wanted to end slavery because he considered it morally wrong. Thoreau argued for the practice of **civil disobedience.** This was the peaceful refusal to obey laws one considered immoral. **Frederick Douglass,** an escaped slave, was another abolitionist. He became a powerful speaker in the North.

The **Missouri Compromise** of 1820 balanced power between the slaveholding South and the nonslaveholding North in Congress. It allowed Missouri to enter the union as a slave state, so long as Maine was admitted as a free state.

Meanwhile, **Elizabeth Cady Stanton** and **Susan B. Anthony** worked to achieve greater rights for women. Stanton helped organize the nation's first women's rights convention in 1848.

Manifest Destiny, the idea that God intended the United States to stretch from the Atlantic Ocean to the Pacific Ocean, brought many Americans westward. This expansion caused tension with Mexico, which owned most of this land. After a war with Mexico, a large portion of the Southwest, including California, became part of the United States.

Review Questions

1. What is civil disobedience? Who came up with this idea?

____

____

2. What is Manifest Destiny?

____

____

Name ______________________ Class ________________ Date ______

CHAPTER 2
SECTION 2

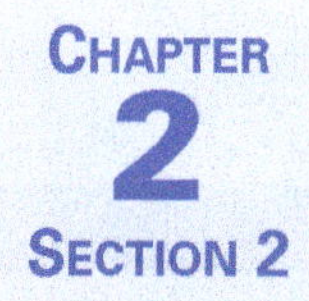

Note Taking Study Guide

THE UNION IN CRISIS

Focus Question: How did the issue of slavery divide the Union?

As you read, trace the sequence of events that led to the division of the Union.

1820: Missouri Compromise keeps balance between slave states and free states
↓
↓
1854: Kansas-Nebraska Act divides Nebraska Territory into Kansas and Nebraska; slavery to be decided by popular sovereignty
↓
↓
↓
↓
1860: Abraham Lincoln elected President and South Carolina secedes, followed by ten other states

CHAPTER 2

SECTION 2

Section Summary

THE UNION IN CRISIS

After the Mexican-American War, slavery became a major issue. The **Wilmot Proviso,** which stated that slavery would not be allowed in the territory won from Mexico, was defeated. It led to the creation of the antislavery **Free-Soil Party.**

The **Compromise of 1850** admitted California to the Union as a free state. In other territories acquired by Mexico, the voters would decide the issue of slavery. This approach was known as **popular sovereignty.** Another provision of the Compromise was the Fugitive Slave Act. This law required citizens to apprehend runaway slaves. <u>Northern opponents of the law mounted an intense resistance.</u> **Harriet Beecher Stowe** further stirred opposition to slavery with her novel *Uncle Tom's Cabin.*

In 1854, Congress passed the **Kansas-Nebraska Act.** This law divided the Nebraska Territory into Kansas and Nebraska. Voters in each territory would decide the issue of slavery. After much violence, Kansas entered the Union as a free state in 1861.

In 1857, the Supreme Court widened the growing divisions over slavery. In *Dred Scott* **v.** *Sandford,* the Court ruled that African Americans were not citizens. The Court also ruled that the government could not ban slavery, which made the Missouri Compromise unconstitutional.

In 1859, abolitionist **John Brown** and a small band of followers tried to start an antislavery revolt by seizing a federal arsenal in Harpers Ferry, Virginia. He failed and was executed.

Republican **Abraham Lincoln** was elected President in 1860. To southerners, the election was a sign that the free states would take control of national politics. South Carolina **seceded,** or broke away from, the Union. Ten other states joined South Carolina to establish the Confederate States of America. On April 11, 1861, Confederate troops fired on Union troops at Fort Sumter. The Civil War had begun.

Review Questions

1. Why did the election of Abraham Lincoln as President lead to the secession of South Carolina?

____

____

2. What major decisions about slavery were made in the *Dred Scott* v. *Sandford* case?

____

____

CHAPTER 2 · SECTION 3 — Note Taking Study Guide

THE CIVIL WAR

Focus Question: What factors and events led to the Union victory in the Civil War?

A. *As you read, identify the events and developments that led to the final Union victory in the Civil War.*

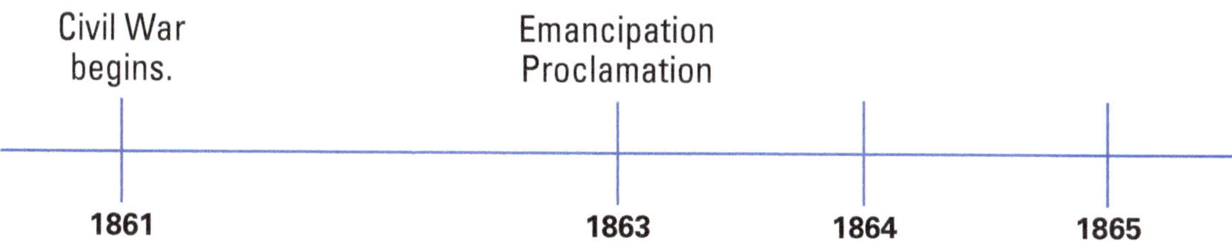

B. *As you read, note effects of the war on the North and South.*

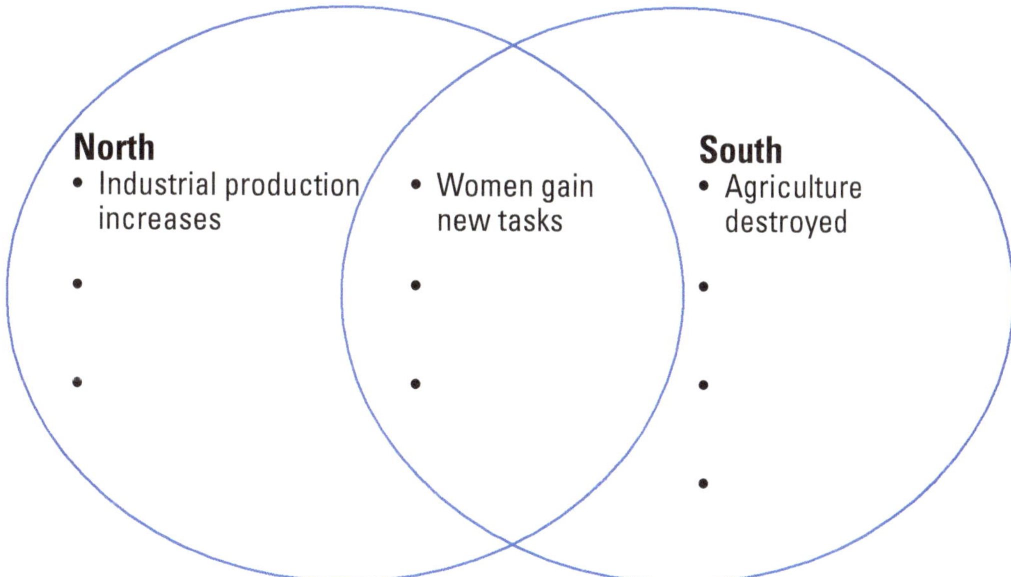

<table><tr><td>**CHAPTER 2**
SECTION 3</td><td>## Section Summary
THE CIVIL WAR</td></tr></table>

In the 1860s, the Union and the Confederacy fought each other in the Civil War. The North had factories to make war supplies. Because of this advantage, northerners anticipated a quick victory. However, the South had a more committed army and strong military leaders, such as General **Robert E. Lee.**

The North tried to starve the South into submission. This strategy was named the **Anaconda Plan** after the snake that slowly squeezes its prey to death. The South hoped the northerners would become tired of fighting and the war would end. Each side won some battles, but neither side took the lead.

In 1863, Lincoln freed slaves in Confederate states with the **Emancipation Proclamation.** Although the proclamation did not actually free any slaves, it did make the war "about slavery."

Some northerners did not agree with the way Lincoln handled the war. To deal with dissent, Lincoln suspended the right of **habeas corpus.** This right guarantees that no one can be held in prison without charges being filed. Meanwhile, severe **inflation,** or price increases, led to food riots in some parts of the South.

In 1863, Union General **Ulysses S. Grant** won several victories and divided Confederate territory. Confederate troops lost a battle at the town of Gettysburg. A few months later, President Lincoln talked about what the Union was fighting for in a speech called the **Gettysburg Address.**

In 1864, General **William T. Sherman** led Union troops on a march through the South. They destroyed many of the resources that the Confederate army needed. This strategy is called **total war.** In April 1865, General Lee surrendered to General Grant. The Civil War was over. The war had helped northern industries to grow, but it had damaged southern agriculture because most of the battles took place in the South.

Review Questions

1. Why was the Emancipation Proclamation important?

____

____

2. How did the Civil War affect northern industries and southern agriculture?

____

____

Note Taking Study Guide

CHAPTER 2 SECTION 4

THE RECONSTRUCTION ERA

Focus Question: What were the immediate and long-term effects of Reconstruction?

As you read, identify the political, social, and economic aspects of Reconstruction.

Political	Social	Economic
• Radical Republicans clash with President. • • • •	• Freedmen's Bureau • • • •	• Sharecropping develops. •

CHAPTER 2

SECTION 4

Section Summary
THE RECONSTRUCTION ERA

During the Civil War, politicians in the North debated how to bring the South back into the Union. President Lincoln had a moderate plan for **Reconstruction.** He helped create the **Freedmen's Bureau** to aid freed slaves and meet the South's immediate needs. On April 14, 1865, Lincoln was assassinated. Vice President **Andrew Johnson** became President.

Johnson wanted southerners to both swear allegiance to the United States and accept the **Thirteenth Amendment,** which ended slavery. **Radical Republicans** wanted full rights for African Americans. Johnson and the Radical Republicans clashed repeatedly. In 1868, Congress began **impeachment** proceedings against Johnson. Although he kept his office, Johnson was not reelected.

Radical Republicans divided the South into five military districts. States had to give African American men the right to vote in order to be readmitted to the Union. In 1868, Congress passed the **Fourteenth Amendment.** This amendment guaranteed full citizenship status and rights to every person born in the United States. In 1870, Congress passed the **Fifteenth Amendment,** which guaranteed male citizens the right to vote.

Many black and white farmers began working under a system called **sharecropping.** Landowners advanced sharecroppers the materials to plant a crop. At harvest, the sharecroppers had to pay back a share of the crop's value. Meanwhile, organized secret societies, such as the **Ku Klux Klan,** used terror and violence to keep African Americans from voting.

Republican Rutherford B. Hayes won the disputed presidential election in 1876. He agreed to withdraw federal troops from the South, ending Reconstruction. The nation was reunited and the South was being rebuilt, but Reconstruction was not completely successful. Voting rights were taken away from African Americans. **Segregation,** or legal separation of the races, became the law in all southern states.

Review Questions

1. Why was the Freedmen's Bureau created?

____

____

2. Why did President Johnson and the Radical Republicans clash repeatedly?

____

____

Note Taking Study Guide
THE TRIUMPH OF INDUSTRY

CHAPTER 3 SECTION 1

Focus Question: What factors led to the industrialization of America, and what impact did industrialization have on society?

A. *Fill in the table below with the causes and effects of industrialization.*

The Industrialization of America	
Causes	**Effects**
• Natural resources • Millions of immigrants from Europe and Asia • •	• Growth of cities • More railroads and industry • • •

Name ______________________ Class ____________________ Date ________

Chapter 3 Section 1

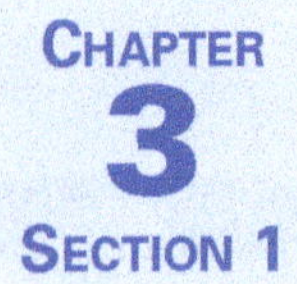

Note Taking Study Guide

THE TRIUMPH OF INDUSTRY

Focus Question: What factors led to the industrialization of America, and what impact did industrialization have on society?

B. *Record the main ideas about the rise of organized labor in the concept web below.*

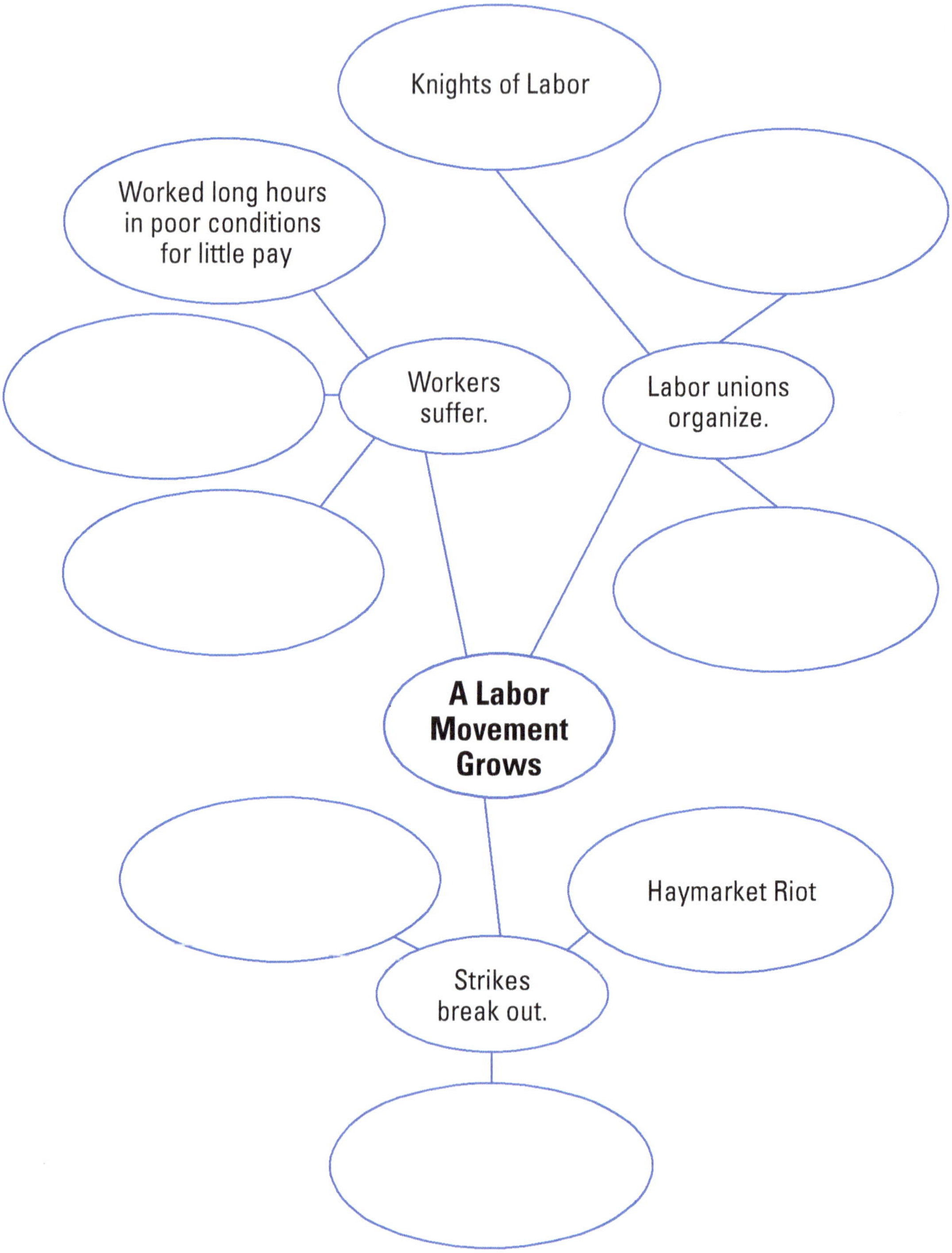

Knights of Labor
Worked long hours in poor conditions for little pay
Workers suffer.
Labor unions organize.
A Labor Movement Grows
Haymarket Riot
Strikes break out.

CHAPTER 3 SECTION 1

Section Summary
THE TRIUMPH OF INDUSTRY

Near the end of the nineteenth century, coal and steel production grew rapidly. Railroads were expanding. Inventions, like the light bulb developed by **Thomas Alva Edison,** helped the economy. There were many reasons for the growth. The nation had lots of coal and oil. Millions of immigrants came from Europe and Asia to fill the labor market. Government policies helped businesses grow. This growth gave many people better living conditions. Cities grew larger. Transportation and communication improved.

At this time, large corporations dominated American business. These corporations and their owners built huge fortunes. **John D. Rockefeller** gained control of the oil industry. **Andrew Carnegie** grew rich from the sale of his steel business. Industrialists established **trusts,** combinations of corporations. Small businesses complained about **monopolies.** Monopolies occur when one corporation controls an entire industry.

Carnegie and others created explanations to defend their business methods and their wealth. **Social Darwinism** stated that life was a struggle in which only the fittest survived. Carnegie developed a doctrine called the **Gospel of Wealth.** He wanted those who had wealth to share their riches to improve society.

In contrast to rich owners, factory workers worked long hours for very low pay. They had no health benefits and no vacation time. To improve their conditions, workers formed unions. The **Knights of Labor** wanted broad social reforms. The **American Federation of Labor (AFL)** focused on improving wages, working hours, and working conditions.

Workers and big business often engaged in violent clashes. The Haymarket Riot in Chicago and a nationwide strike against the railroad companies required government intervention to control the violence.

Review Questions

1. List three reasons that the United States grew as an industrial nation.

   ____

   ____

2. Describe the problems that industrial workers had during this time.

   ____

   ____

READING CHECK

Who developed the Gospel of Wealth?

____

____

____

VOCABULARY STRATEGY

Find the word *doctrine* in the underlined sentence. Look for context clues in the surrounding words, phrases, and sentences. Circle the word below that is a synonym for *doctrine.*

- principle
- exchange

READING SKILL

Identify Causes and Effects Identify one cause and one effect of industrialization.

____

____

____

CHAPTER 3 SECTION 2

Note Taking Study Guide

IMMIGRATION AND URBANIZATION

Focus Question: Why did immigrants come to the United States, and how did they impact society?

As you read the section, use the concept web below to record the various effects of immigrants on American society.

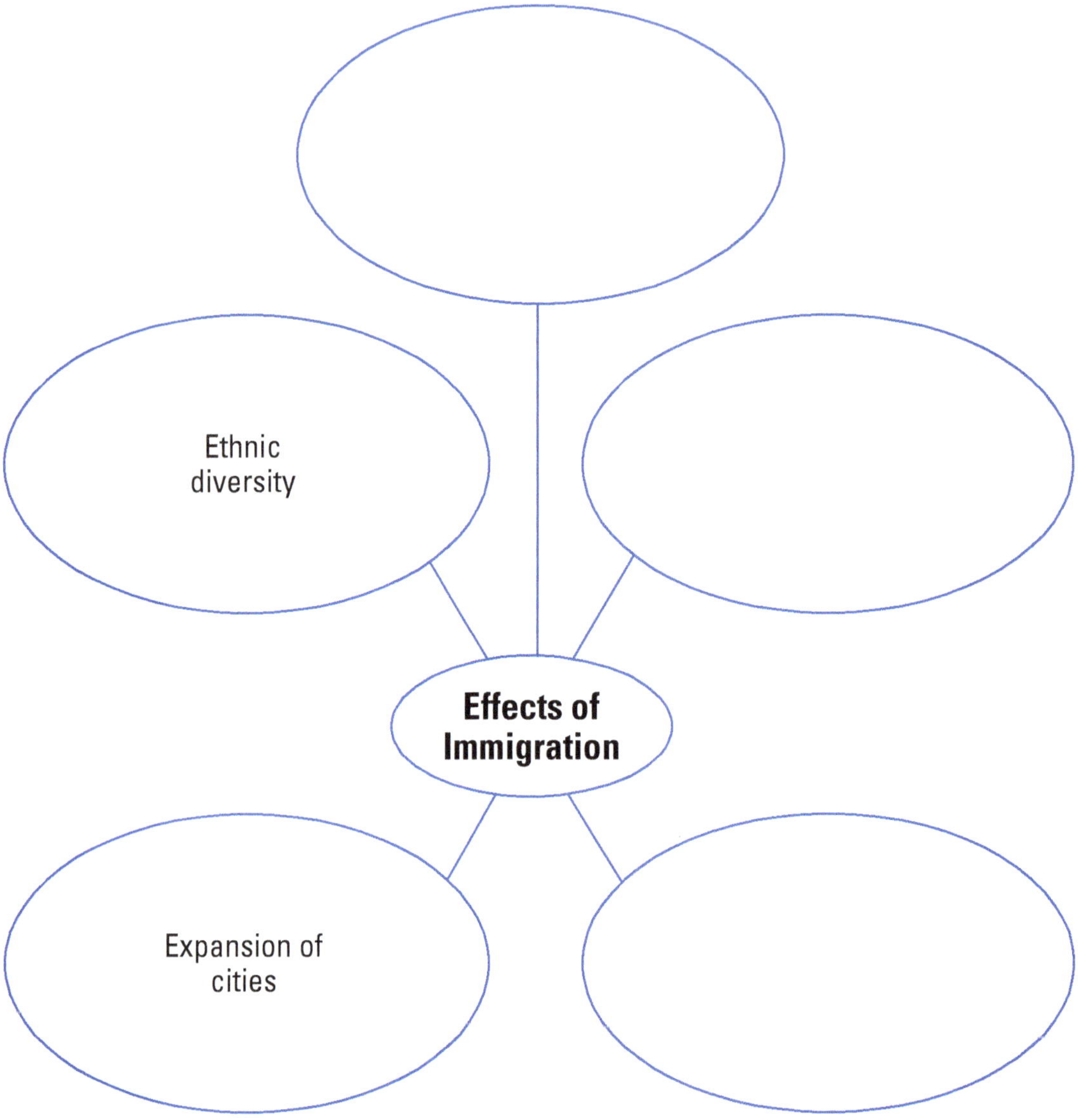

Ethnic diversity

Effects of Immigration

Expansion of cities

CHAPTER 3 SECTION 2

Section Summary

IMMIGRATION AND URBANIZATION

There were two great waves of immigration in the United States. One was during the 1840s and 1850s and another between 1880 and 1920. Immigrants came to the United States to find work and for the promise of political and religious freedom. They contributed to American culture in many ways.

Starting in 1892, most immigrants from Europe first landed at **Ellis Island,** just outside New York City. Government clerks asked the immigrants a series of questions. If authorities believed the newcomers posed a risk to public health, they would demand that the immigrants return to Europe. From the early 1850s to 1882, hundreds of thousands of Chinese immigrants came to the West Coast. From 1910 to 1940, most Asian immigrants arrived at **Angel Island** in San Francisco Bay. They experienced much harsher conditions than those immigrants arriving at Ellis Island. Some waited months or even years before they were allowed into the United States.

Both foreign-born immigrants and American-born farmers moved to the cities. New forms of transportation made possible the first **suburbs.** These were residential areas around the cities. Poorer residents lived in densely populated urban ghettos, or areas where one ethnic or racial group dominates. <u>One of the biggest problems facing urban dwellers was overcrowding.</u> Multistory buildings were subdivided into many homes, often housing twenty families each. These buildings were called **tenements.**

Industrialization and urbanization gave rise to a growing middle class. Industries needed skilled white-collar workers, such as engineers, accountants, and attorneys. Big businesses hired salesclerks to sell their goods. They hired managers to supervise their workers. These workers had enough money to purchase items that in the past only the elite could afford. The growing middle class supported higher education and the arts.

Review Questions

1. Why did immigrants come to the United States?

____

____

2. Name one change that took place in cities in the late nineteenth century.

____

____

READING CHECK

Where did most immigrants from Asia enter the United States?

____

____

____

VOCABULARY STRATEGY

Find the word *urban* in the underlined sentence. What do you think *urban* means? The word *rural* has the opposite meaning of *urban.* Use this antonym to figure out the meaning of *urban.*

____

____

____

READING SKILL

Understand Effects Describe how tenements developed.

____

____

____

CHAPTER 3
SECTION 3

Note Taking Study Guide
THE SOUTH AND WEST TRANSFORMED

Focus Question: What were the most important developments in the South and the West?

Fill in the outline to summarize the main events of the section.

I. The South and West Transformed

  A. The New South

    1. Industries and Cities Grow

      a. Railroad construction

      b. ____

    2. Southern Farmers Face Difficult Times

      a. ____

      b. ____

    3. ____

  B. Cultures Clash in the West

    1. ____

    2. ____

      a. ____

      b. ____

    3. ____

  C. The Transformation of the West

    1. ____

    2. ____

Section Summary
CHAPTER 3 · SECTION 3 — THE SOUTH AND WEST TRANSFORMED

After the Civil War, southerners developed a new mixed economy. It included textile mills, the timber industry, and railway construction. Even with the advances, there were problems. Because businesses needed more money, they borrowed from northern bankers. African Americans lost many political and civil rights. **Sharecropping** made life hard. Landowners gave the sharecropper a place to live, seeds, and tools, in exchange for a share of the crop. Sharecroppers were often cheated.

After the Civil War, many people migrated to the West. Hunters, along with farmers and ranchers, killed large herds of buffalo. The Plains Indians were dependent on hunting the buffalo herds for their livelihood. The Native American way of life was being destroyed.

The federal government forced the Plains Indians to move to reservations, or public land specifically reserved for them. Although some Native Americans moved to reservations without a fight, others decided to defend their land.

The United States enacted the **Dawes Act** in 1887. This law was passed to help Native Americans to **assimilate,** or to be absorbed into the main culture of American society. The act did not achieve its goal.

In the middle decades of the 1800s, the discovery of gold and silver attracted miners to the West in the hope of becoming rich. Farmers and ranchers came in the hope of owning their own land.

At the end of the Civil War, approximately 5 million head of cattle roamed freely in Texas. These cattle, along with the demand for meat back east, led to the great cattle drives. Beginning in the late 1870s, cattlemen raised steers on the northern plains. These herds could feed on **open range**—a vast area of grassland owned by the federal government. Then they were shipped from nearby railroads without the difficulty of the long drive.

Review Questions

1. Describe the economy of the post-Civil War South.

____

____

2. How did the settlers who migrated west affect the Plains Indians?

____

____

READING CHECK

What law did the United States enact to force Native Americans to assimilate?

____

____

____

VOCABULARY STRATEGY

What does the word *decades* mean in the underlined sentence? The Latin root *dec* means "ten." Use this root and context clues to help you figure out the meaning of *decades.*

____

____

____

READING SKILL

Summarize What groups of people moved west? What were their reasons for doing so?

____

____

____

Name ______________________ Class ____________________ Date _______

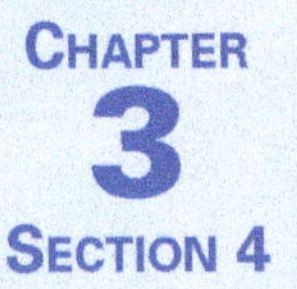

Chapter 3 Section 4

Note Taking Study Guide

ISSUES OF THE GILDED AGE

Focus Question: What challenges arose for the nation during the Gilded Age?

Use the chart below to record key events and developments that led to the Populist movement.

Causes		Event
• Declining crop prices • Accumulating farmer debt • • •	→	Populist movement

<table>
<tr><td>CHAPTER
3
SECTION 4</td><td><h1>Section Summary</h1>ISSUES OF THE GILDED AGE</td></tr>
</table>

The period during the late nineteenth century is often referred to as the **Gilded Age.** One issue that troubled the nation during this period was racial inequality. The southern states passed **Jim Crow laws** that separated blacks and whites. Mexican Americans struggled to keep their lands in the Southwest. Asian immigrants faced discrimination, too. Women experienced both gains and setbacks during the Gilded Age. The fight to gain a women's suffrage amendment stalled, but educational opportunities for women grew.

Corruption plagued government during this period. **Graft,** or bribery and corruption, touched many parts of public life.

After a federal employee assassinated President Garfield, the **Pendleton Act** was passed. This law created a civil service system for the federal government. People who wanted to work for the government were required to take an exam. They were given a job based on their performance on the exam. Both Republicans and Democrats favored a monetary policy called the **gold standard.**

Farmers faced complex problems. The prices paid for crops declined significantly. At the same time, farmers built up debts that they found difficult to repay. <u>Government monetary policies contributed to both of these trends.</u> Farmers from the South and the West formed the People's Party, or the **Populist Party,** to address their problems.

William Jennings Bryan was the Democratic and Populist candidate for the presidency in 1896. He fought for the American farmer and denounced Republican monetary policies, namely the gold standard. Bryan failed to win a state outside of the South and the West. As a result, William McKinley, the Republican candidate, won the presidency. Yet, the Populist movement had an impact on the political system. A number of Populist proposals, such as the graduated income tax and the direct election of senators, later became law.

Review Questions

1. Describe women's lives during the Gilded Age.

____

____

2. What proposals made by the Populists later became law?

____

____

READING CHECK

What law established a civil service system for the federal government?

____

____

____

VOCABULARY STRATEGY

What does the word *trends* mean in the underlined sentence? To what two events in the preceding sentences does the word *both* refer? Use these context clues to help learn what *trends* means.

____

____

____

READING SKILL

Recognize Multiple Causes
What were some of the reasons the Populist Party was created?

____

____

____

Note Taking Study Guide

CHAPTER 4 · SECTION 1

THE DRIVE FOR REFORM

Focus Question: What areas did Progressives think were in need of the greatest reform?

Fill in the chart below with details about Progressivism.

TIP: Look for key words like *muckrakers* and *reform* in headings throughout the section.

Progressivism

Problems	Muckrakers	Reforms
• Industrial hazards • Corrupt governments • • • • • •	• Exposed conditions • • •	• Factory laws • Labor laws • • • • • • • • •

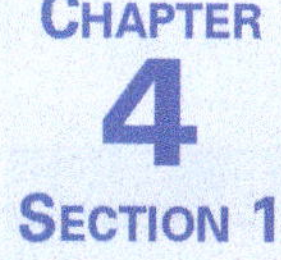

Section Summary
THE DRIVE FOR REFORM

CHAPTER 4 SECTION 1

In the 1890s, a movement called **Progressivism** tried to address social problems. Journalists called **muckrakers** wrote about the need for reform. **Lincoln Steffens,** a magazine editor, was a leading muckraker. He published stories about political corruption. Photographer **Jacob Riis** was also a muckraker. His pictures showed life in urban slums. In his novel *The Jungle,* Upton Sinclair described the despair of immigrants working in Chicago's stockyards.

Many reformers thought that social reform should be based on Christianity. These followers of the **Social Gospel** believed that society would improve if people followed the Bible's teachings about charity and justice. One form of charity was the **settlement house.** Settlement houses offered services such as childcare and classes in English. One famous settlement house was Hull House, opened in Chicago by **Jane Addams.**

Reformers also worked to end child labor and improve education. In 1911, a fire at a garment factory shocked Americans and focused attention on the need to protect workers. Some states passed laws to make workplaces safer.

Finally, Progressives tried to reform the government. Dynamic leaders worked to limit the power of political bosses and business interests. Reformers created the **direct primary.** This let citizens choose for themselves who would run in elections. The **initiative** allowed people to put a proposed new law on the ballot. The **referendum** let citizens approve or reject laws passed by a legislature. The **recall** gave voters the power to remove elected officials from office before their terms ended. The reforms brought about by Progressives still affect society today.

Review Questions

1. Why were muckrakers important to the reform movement?

____

____

2. How did settlement houses help the poor?

____

____

READING CHECK

What were two examples of political reform?

____

____

____

VOCABULARY STRATEGY

What does the word *dynamic* mean in the underlined sentence? Circle the words in the underlined sentence that could help you learn what *dynamic* means. Think about what kind of leader it would take to be a reformer.

____

____

____

READING SKILL

Identify Details List three muckrakers whose work in the 1890s helped increase the public's awareness about social and political problems, and describe their work.

____

____

____

CHAPTER 4 · SECTION 2

Note Taking Study Guide
WOMEN MAKE PROGRESS

Focus Question: How did women of the Progressive Era make progress and win the right to vote?

As you read this section, complete the outline below to capture the main ideas.

TIP: Use headings throughout the section for the letters in your outline.

I. Women Expand Reforms

    A. Hardships for women

        1. Difficult and dangerous jobs outside the home

        2. ____

    B. Reformers pushed for rights

        1. ____

        2. ____

    C. Working for reform at home

        1. ____

        2. ____

        3. ____

II. Women Fight for the Right to Vote

    A. ____

        1. ____

        2. ____

    B. ____

        1. ____

        2. ____

    C. ____

        1. ____

        2. ____

Section Summary

CHAPTER 4 SECTION 2

WOMEN MAKE PROGRESS

In the early 1900s, many women wanted to play a larger role in the community. Reformers sought to help working women by shortening the workday, improving working conditions, and securing fair prices for household goods. **Florence Kelley** helped form the **National Consumers League (NCL).** This group labeled products made under safe working conditions and pushed for workplace reforms.

Many women also wanted to change life at home. Women led the **temperance movement,** which sought a ban on alcohol. They thought that drinking alcohol made men treat their families badly. Women's health was another important issue. Nurse **Margaret Sanger** thought that family life and women's health would improve if mothers had fewer children. She opened the nation's first birth-control clinic. African American women also worked to improve their lives. **Ida B. Wells** helped found the National Association of Colored Women. She worked to provide childcare and education to black families.

One of Progressivism's boldest goals was **suffrage** for women. Suffrage is the right to vote. **Carrie Chapman Catt** led this fight in the 1890s, giving speeches all over the country. She asked women to join the **National American Woman Suffrage Association (NAWSA).** This group asked Congress for the right to vote and used the referendum process to get state suffrage laws passed. <u>This two-pronged strategy helped women get the vote in several states.</u> **Alice Paul** was more forceful. Her National Woman's Party (NWP) staged protest marches and picketed the White House. Some members went on hunger strikes, refusing to eat until they could vote. Those efforts, and the NAWSA's support of World War I, helped win passage of the **Nineteenth Amendment** in 1920. American women had won the right to vote.

Review Questions

1. Why did many women want to end the drinking of alcohol?

____

____

2. What did reformers do to help women get the right to vote?

____

____

READING CHECK

What right did women gain with the Nineteenth Amendment?

____

____

____

VOCABULARY STRATEGY

What does the word *strategy* mean in the underlined sentence? Circle the words in the underlined sentence that could help you learn what *strategy* means. Think about what helped women get the vote.

____

____

____

READING SKILL

Identify Main Ideas What goal did Margaret Sanger, Ida B. Wells, and Florence Kelley share?

____

____

____

Note Taking Study Guide
THE STRUGGLE AGAINST DISCRIMINATION

CHAPTER 4 SECTION 3

Focus Question: What steps did minorities take to combat social problems and discrimination?

Outline the section's main ideas and details.

I. The Struggle Against Discrimination

    A. Progressivism Contradicts Itself

        1. Settlement houses and other civic groups aid in Americanization of immigrants.

        2. ____

        3. ____

        4. ____

    B. Demands for Reform

        1. ____

        2. ____

        3. ____

    C. ____

        1. ____

        2. ____

        3. ____

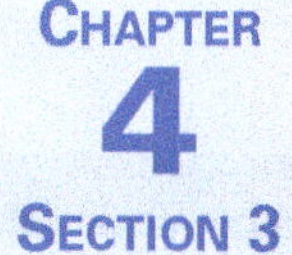

Section Summary
THE STRUGGLE AGAINST DISCRIMINATION

The Progressive Era did not improve the lives of nonwhites and immigrant Americans. Many Progressives looked down on nonwhites and treated them poorly. <u>Some Progressives agreed with so-called scientific theories that said that dark-skinned peoples had less intelligence than whites.</u> Progressives even supported segregation, or separation of the races. They also supported laws to limit minority voting. Progressives favored the policy of **Americanization.** This meant that they tried to make everyone follow white, middle-class ways of life.

African American reformers fought discrimination in different ways. **Booker T. Washington** told blacks to be patient and to earn the respect of white Americans. **W.E.B. Du Bois** said that blacks should be more active in fighting for their rights. W.E.B. Du Bois was a member of the **Niagara Movement.** This group wanted rapid progress and more education for blacks.

After a race riot broke out in Illinois, African Americans joined with whites to form the **National Association for the Advancement of Colored People (NAACP).** The NAACP fought for civil rights in the court system. The NAACP helped middle-class blacks gain civil rights, including the right to vote. The **Urban League** helped poorer workers who lived in cities. It helped families buy clothes and books. The League also helped workers and others find jobs.

Different ethnic groups also wanted more rights and protections. Some of them created self-help agencies. Jews in New York City formed the **Anti-Defamation League.** This group defended Jews against verbal attacks and false statements. Mexican Americans in several states formed **mutualistas.** These groups gave loans and assistance to the poor. While some progress was made, minorities still suffered from discrimination.

Review Questions

1. Why did Progressives not support minorities?

____

____

2. How was the Urban League different from the NAACP?

____

____

READING CHECK

Who organized the Anti-Defamation League?

____

____

____

VOCABULARY STRATEGY

What does the word *so-called* mean in the underlined sentence? Two synonyms for *so-called* are *supposed* and *presumed.* Use the meanings of the synonyms to help you determine the meaning of *so-called.*

____

____

____

READING SKILL

Main Idea and Details How was Booker T. Washington's way of fighting discrimination different from that of W.E.B. Du Bois?

____

____

____

Name ______________________ Class __________________ Date _______

CHAPTER 4 SECTION 4

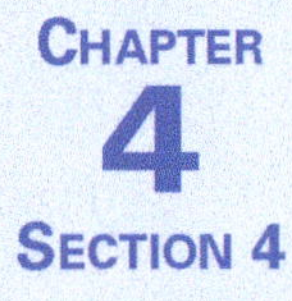

Note Taking Study Guide

ROOSEVELT'S SQUARE DEAL

Focus Question: What did Roosevelt think government should do for citizens?

A. *As you read this section, use the concept web below to record the main ideas.*
TIP: Look for words that are similar to *environmental* and *economic.*

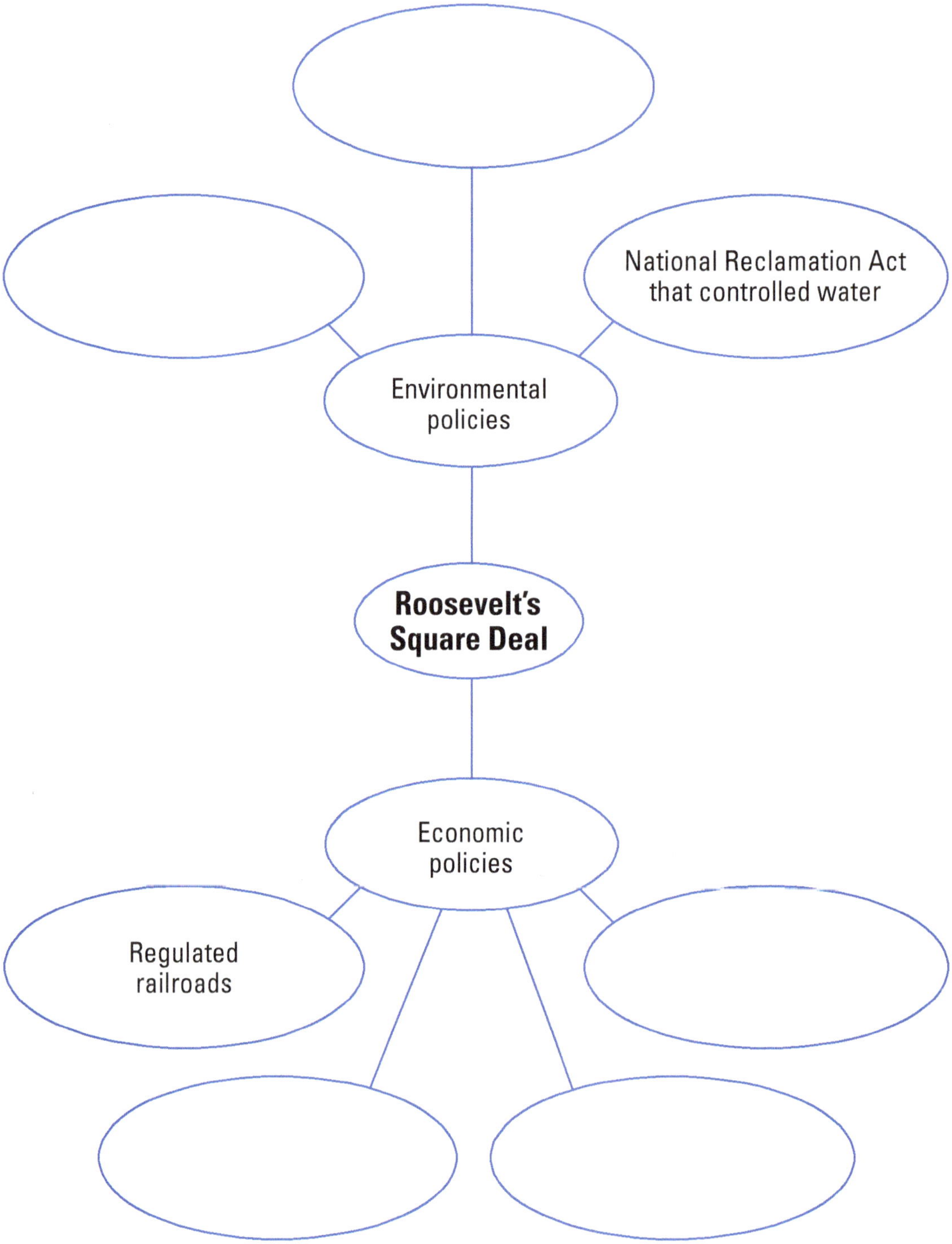

National Reclamation Act that controlled water
Environmental policies
Roosevelt's Square Deal
Economic policies
Regulated railroads

Note Taking Study Guide

ROOSEVELT'S SQUARE DEAL

CHAPTER 4 SECTION 4

Focus Question: What did Roosevelt think government should do for citizens?

B. *As you read, fill in the Venn diagram with similarities and differences between Roosevelt and Taft.*

TIP: When looking for differences, look for key words such as *criticized.*

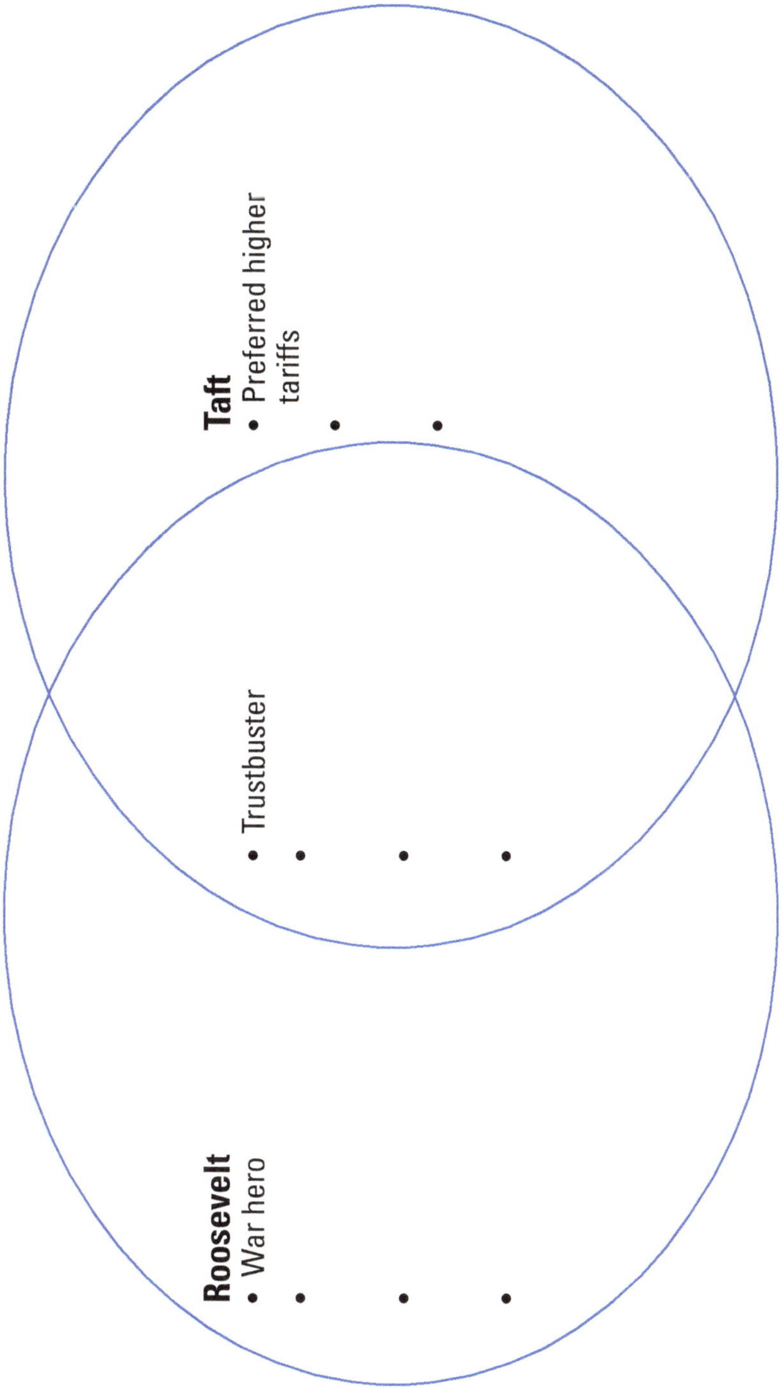

<table>
<tr><td>CHAPTER
4
SECTION 4</td><td><h1>Section Summary</h1>ROOSEVELT'S SQUARE DEAL</td></tr>
</table>

READING CHECK

What was New Nationalism?

____

____

____

VOCABULARY STRATEGY

What does the word *dominating* mean in the underlined sentence? What clues can you find in the surrounding words, phrases, or sentences? Circle the words in the underlined passage that could help you learn what *dominating* means.

____

____

____

READING SKILL

Identify Main Ideas What similarity did the Square Deal and the New Nationalism share?

____

____

____

Theodore Roosevelt was a dedicated reformer when he became President in 1901. <u>He quickly pushed Congress to approve the Square Deal, a program of reform aimed at stopping the wealthy and powerful from dominating small business owners and the poor.</u> Roosevelt took on big business and developed a reputation as a "trustbuster." In 1906, Roosevelt got Congress to pass the **Hepburn Act.** This act ended the railroads' monopoly by limiting how much they could charge for shipping goods.

After reading Upton Sinclair's novel *The Jungle,* Roosevelt pushed Congress to protect Americans' health by passing the **Meat Inspection Act.** This law gave the government power to inspect meat-processing plants to make sure the meat was safe to eat. The **Pure Food and Drug Act** banned interstate shipment of impure food.

Roosevelt loved nature and respected naturalist **John Muir.** Roosevelt put millions of acres of forests under federal control. However, he did not agree with Muir that it should all remain untouched. Like the head of the Division of Forestry, **Gifford Pinchot,** Roosevelt believed in the "rational use" of forests. The forests would be protected as sources of lumber in the future. To help settle fights over sources of water, Roosevelt pushed for passage of the **National Reclamation Act.** That law gave the government power to build dams and control where and how water was used.

William Howard Taft followed Roosevelt as President. They shared a desire to regulate business but had different ideas of how best to do that. Disappointed by Taft's actions, Roosevelt spoke out against Taft. He encouraged a **New Nationalism,** a program to restore the government's trustbusting power. The Republican Party split, and the new **Progressive Party** nominated Roosevelt as its candidate for President in 1912.

Review Questions

1. How did the Meat Inspection Act help the public?

____

____

2. Why did President Roosevelt and Gifford Pinchot want to protect forests?

____

____

Name ____________________ Class ________________ Date ______

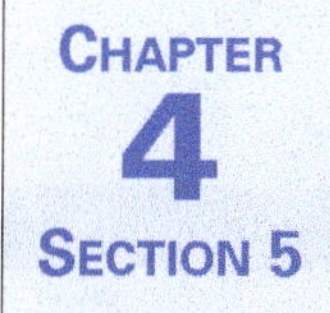

CHAPTER 4
SECTION 5

Note Taking Study Guide

WILSON'S NEW FREEDOM

Focus Question: What steps did Wilson take to increase the government's role in the economy?

As you read this section, fill in the concept web below to record details from the section.

TIP: Look for clues in the section headings.

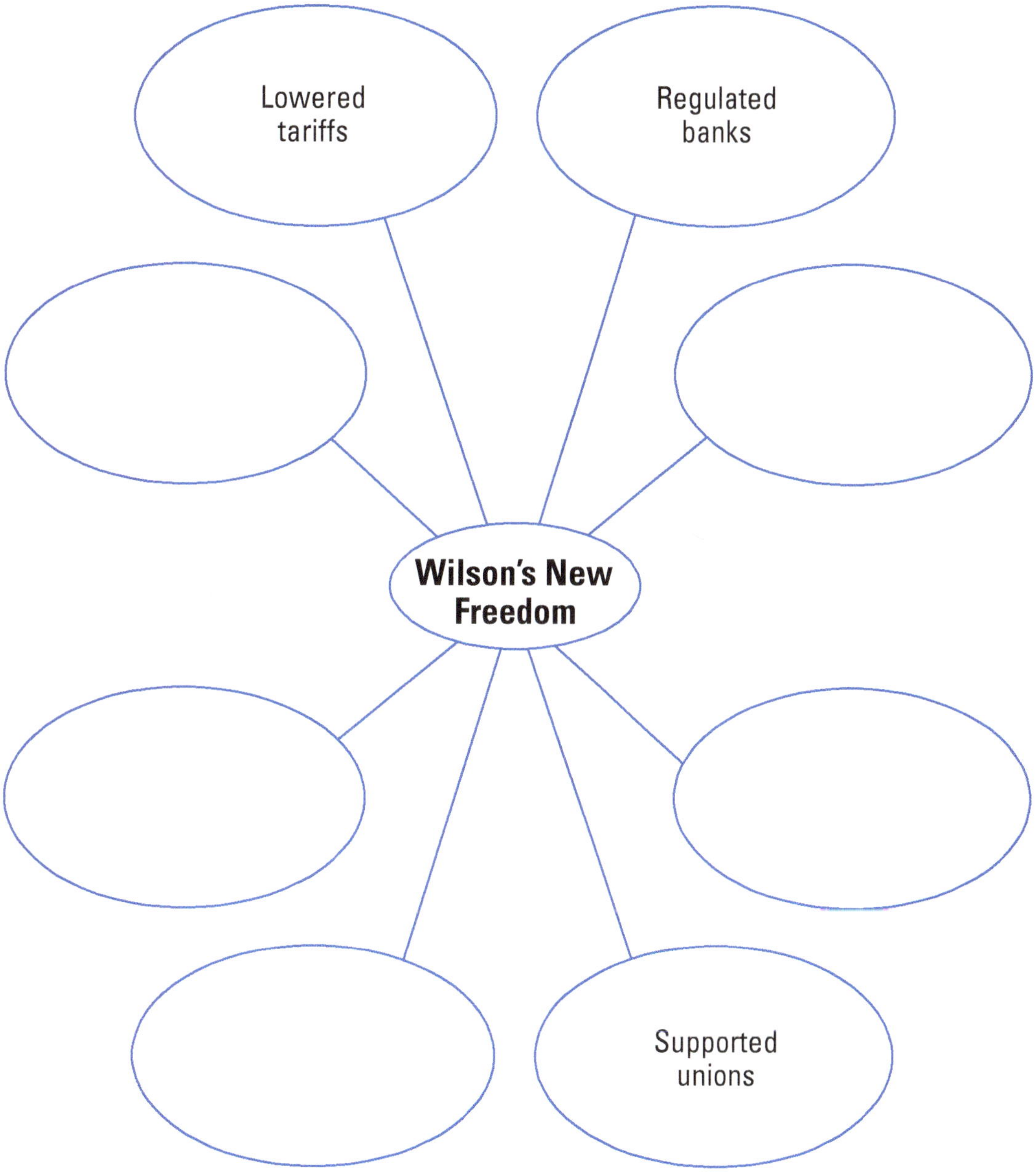

Lowered tariffs
Regulated banks
Wilson's New Freedom
Supported unions

Section Summary
WILSON'S NEW FREEDOM

READING CHECK

What did Wilson call his plan for reform?

____

____

____

VOCABULARY STRATEGY

What does the word *intellectual* mean in the underlined sentence? Circle the words in the underlined sentence that could help you learn what *intellectual* means. Think of the qualities that a professor might have.

____

____

____

READING SKILL

Identify Details Name two laws that Wilson helped pass that reformed banking or business.

____

____

____

Woodrow Wilson became president in 1912. <u>Wilson was an intellectual man from Virginia who had taught college as a professor.</u> Like Roosevelt, Wilson wanted the government to play an active role in the economy and place controls on corporations. Wilson called his plan the **New Freedom.**

Wilson's plan for regulating the economy had three parts. First, he tried to limit the prices that manufacturers could charge for goods. He cut tariffs on imported goods, which made goods cheaper for Americans. He also pushed for an income tax. This would make up for the money the government lost from lower tariffs. The **Sixteenth Amendment** gave Congress the power to create the income tax.

Second, Wilson asked Congress to pass the **Federal Reserve Act,** which placed national banks under the control of a Federal Reserve Board. This system made sure that no one person or bank had too much control over the economy. The Federal Reserve Board, which also sets bank interest rates, became a very important part of the American economy.

Third, Wilson wanted to control big business. He was afraid that huge corporations could crush small businesses. He urged Congress to create the **Federal Trade Commission (FTC).** This office made sure that businesses did not become monopolies. Congress also passed the **Clayton Antitrust Act.** This act strengthened earlier laws that controlled trusts. The act also protected labor unions from being attacked as trusts, which helped workers organize more freely.

Progressivism had a big and lasting impact on the nation. Political reforms gave voters more power over government. Economic reforms gave the government more power to protect the public. New laws made sure that consumer products were safe. The government also began to manage natural resources all over the nation.

Review Questions

1. Why did Wilson support the Federal Reserve Act?

____

____

2. What were three ways Wilson wanted to regulate the economy?

____

____

Name ______________________ Class ____________________ Date ________

CHAPTER 5
SECTION 1

Note Taking Study Guide

THE ROOTS OF IMPERIALISM

Focus Question: How and why did the United States take a more active role in world affairs?

As you read, fill in the concept web below with the key events that marked America's first steps toward world power.

TIP: Look for answers in headings throughout the section.

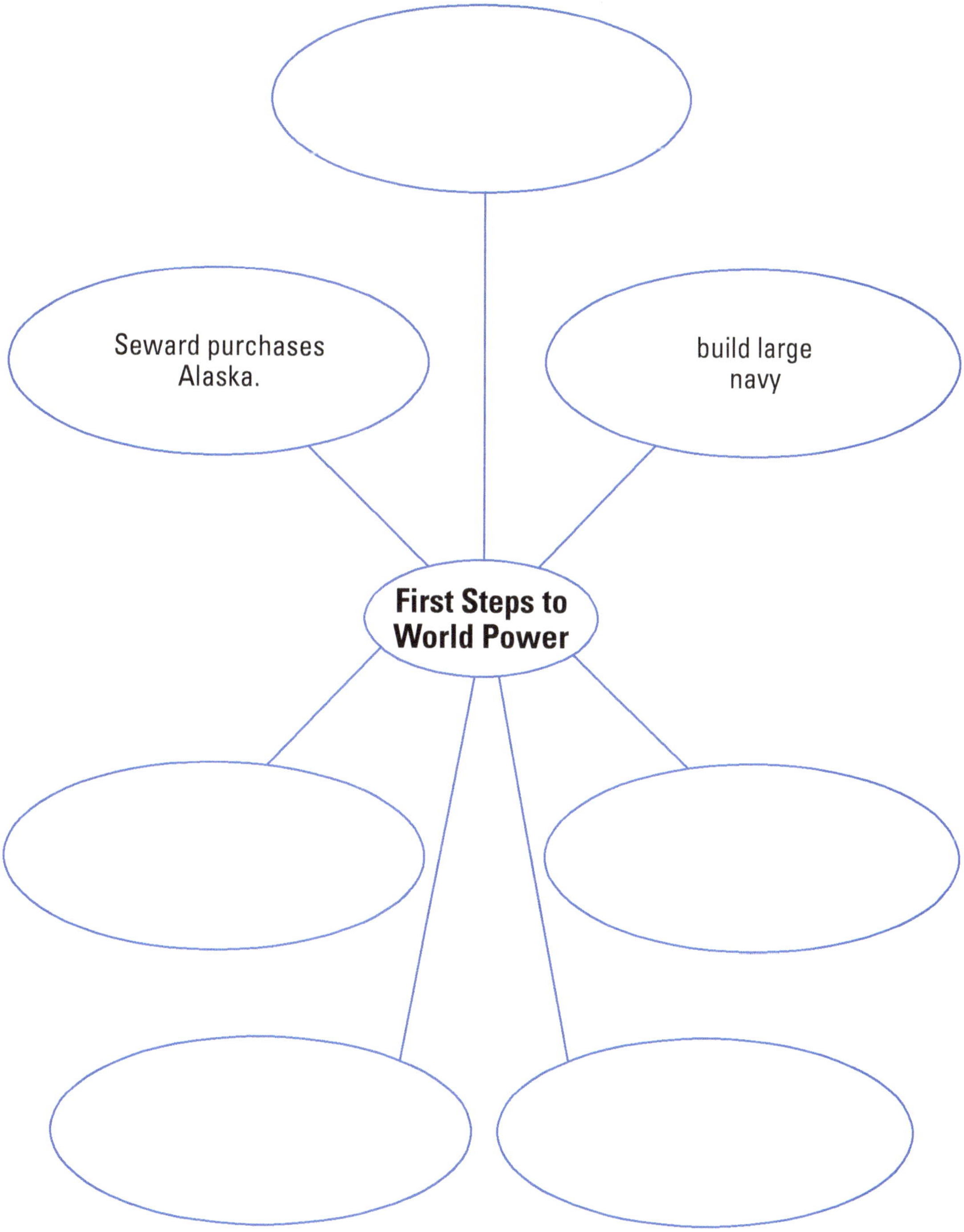

<table>
<tr><td>CHAPTER 5
SECTION 1</td><td><h1>Section Summary</h1>THE ROOTS OF IMPERIALISM</td></tr>
</table>

READING CHECK

How did Frederick J. Turner influence imperialism?

____

____

____

VOCABULARY STRATEGY

What does the word *commodities* mean in the underlined sentence? Circle the words in the underlined passage that could help you learn what *commodities* means. Look for words that relate to business or economics.

____

____

____

READING SKILL

Identify Main Ideas Circle the main idea of this summary.

1. Alfred T. Mahan pushed for a large navy.

2. In the late 1800s, the United States began to expand its influence around the world.

In the mid-1800s, powerful nations followed a policy of **imperialism,** or control over weaker territories. Raw materials would be removed from the colonies and sent to the home country, turning the colonies into **extractive economies.** In the late 1800s, the United States began to expand its influence around the world. Americans did not need raw materials. Instead, American businessmen sought new markets around the world in which to sell their commodities.

Imperialist nations needed military strength to protect their interests. **Alfred T. Mahan,** a historian and officer in the United States Navy, pushed the government to build a large navy. Imperialists around the world used ideas of racial, national, and cultural superiority to justify imperialism. One of these ideas was **Social Darwinism,** the belief that life is a competitive struggle and that some races are superior to others. Historian **Frederick J. Turner** wrote that America needed a large amount of unsettled land to succeed. Because most of the United States was already settled, some Americans felt that the nation should expand into foreign lands.

In 1853, Commodore **Matthew Perry** led a large naval force to Japan. He helped expand trade by getting Japan to agree to trade with the United States. In 1867, Secretary of State William Seward bought Alaska from Russia. Seward's purchase almost doubled the size of the United States and provided timber, oil, and other natural resources.

The Hawaiian Islands had been economically linked to the United States for almost a century. Rich American planters who lived there wanted political power. In 1893, the planters overthrew **Queen Liliuokalani,** the ruler of Hawaii. She had refused to give power to Americans. In 1898, the United States annexed Hawaii.

Review Questions

1. How did Social Darwinism lead to imperialism?

____

____

2. Why did rich American planters overthrow the ruler of Hawaii?

____

____

Note Taking Study Guide

CHAPTER 5 SECTION 2

THE SPANISH-AMERICAN WAR

Focus Question: What were the causes and effects of the Spanish-American War?

As you read, note the causes, key events, and effects of the Spanish-American War.
TIP: Look for answers in the maps and graphics throughout the section.

Cause
- Cubans rebel against Spanish, winning U.S. sympathy
-
-

Spanish-American War
- Dewey destroys Spanish fleet
-
-
-

Effect
- United States acquires Philippines
-
-
-

<table><tr><td>CHAPTER
5
SECTION 2</td><td>**Section Summary**
THE SPANISH-AMERICAN WAR</td></tr></table>

READING CHECK

What was the Yellow Press?

____

____

____

VOCABULARY STRATEGY

What does the word *obsolete* mean in the underlined sentence? Circle the words in the underlined passage that could help you learn what *obsolete* means. Look at the words that describe the weapons and supplies.

____

____

____

READING SKILL

Identify Causes and Effects Identify one cause and one effect of the Spanish-American War.

Cause: ___________________

Effect: ___________________

In April 1898, the United States went to war with Spain. One cause of the war was an independence movement in Cuba. **José Martí,** a Cuban patriot, began fighting for independence from Spain. Many Americans wanted to support him. They thought that his fight was similar to the American struggle for independence from Britain.

Another cause of the war was the **Yellow Press.** These American newspapers pushed for war with Spain by printing exaggerated stories of Spanish atrocities. The Yellow Press also created sympathy for Cuban rebels. Publisher **William Randolph Hearst** sold many newspapers by doing this. His efforts fueled American **jingoism,** or aggressive nationalism.

After the explosion of the U.S. ship *Maine* in a Cuban port, the United States declared war on Spain. Commodore **George Dewey** quickly destroyed a large part of the Spanish fleet in the Philippines. **Emilio Aguinaldo** led Filipino nationalists in defeating the Spanish army.

In Cuba, the United States Army defeated the Spanish despite being poorly supplied and carrying old, obsolete weapons. The most famous soldiers were the **Rough Riders.** Future President Theodore Roosevelt organized this group. The Rough Riders, joined by African American soldiers, won key victories in Cuba.

The **Treaty of Paris** ended the Spanish-American War. Spain gave up control of Cuba, Puerto Rico, and the Pacific island of Guam. Spain also sold the Philippines to the United States. Not every American was happy with the terms of the treaty. Some claimed that not granting independence to the Philippines violated American principles of freedom and democracy. However, the United States had gained colonies and become a world power.

Review Questions

1. How did many Americans feel about José Martí's struggle for independence?

____

____

2. What territory did the United States purchase in the Treaty of Paris?

____

____

Focus Question: How did the United States extend its influence into Asia?

As you read, use the timeline to trace events and developments in East Asia that tested America's new global power.

TIP: Look for dates throughout the section to fill in your timeline.

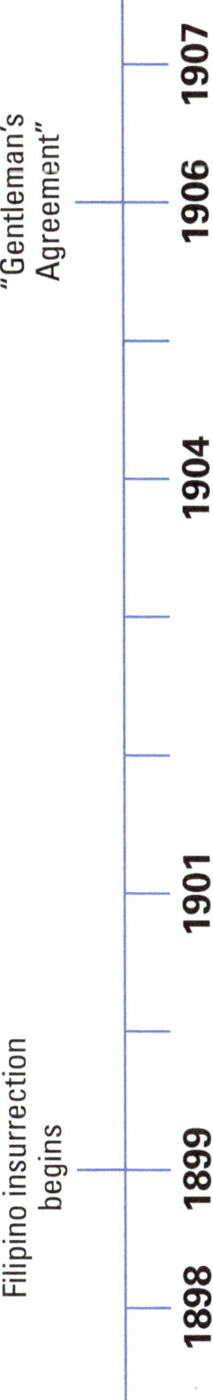

<table>
<tr><td>CHAPTER
5
SECTION 3</td><td><h1>Section Summary</h1>THE UNITED STATES AND EAST ASIA</td></tr>
</table>

What is a sphere of influence?

____

____

____

What does the word *rigors* mean in the underlined sentence? Circle the words in the underlined passage that could help you learn what *rigors* means. Read the sentence several times to figure out exactly what it means.

____

____

____

Recognize Sequence Which happened first, the Boxer Rebellion or the Filipino rebellion?

____

____

____

During the Spanish-American War, Filipinos thought the United States would support their desire for independence. Filipino nationalists became angry when the United States kept control over the islands. They organized an **insurrection,** or rebellion, in 1899. These insurgents relied on **guerrilla warfare** tactics, including surprise raids and hit-and-run attacks.

The conflict highlighted the rigors of fighting against guerrilla insurgents. Eventually, **William Howard Taft,** the U.S. governor of the Philippines, helped to establish peace. His government rebuilt schools and roads on the islands.

Conflict also arose in China. European nations had divided China into **spheres of influence,** or areas where specific nations could conduct trade. U.S. Secretary of State **John Hay** notified foreign nations that America expected equal access to trade in China.

However, nationalist groups in China were angry at the presence of foreigners. They launched the **Boxer Rebellion** in 1900. The uprising was put down by outside troops. The U.S. government once again asked for an **Open Door Policy,** which would allow America to trade freely in China. The United States wanted to trade with, not colonize, China.

The U.S. experience with Japan saw both high and low points. In 1905, President Roosevelt helped to end the **Russo-Japanese War,** a war between Russia and Japan. But later, tensions erupted between Japan and America. Japan was angry at the poor treatment of Japanese children by the San Francisco School Board. The President made a **"Gentlemen's Agreement"** with Japan. According to the agreement, the school board would end the poor treatment of Asians while Japan would limit the number of people moving to the United States.

Roosevelt promoted both diplomacy and military strength. He won congressional support for the **Great White Fleet.** This new force of navy ships was sent around the world to demonstrate America's military power.

Review Questions

1. What problem did U.S. forces face in the Philippines?

____

____

2. What was the Open Door Policy?

____

____

Note Taking Study Guide

THE UNITED STATES AND LATIN AMERICA

CHAPTER 5 SECTION 4

Focus Question: What actions did the United States take to achieve its goals in Latin America?

A. *Complete the table below to note how the United States dealt with Puerto Rico and Cuba.*

TIP: Look for clues in headings throughout the section.

American Policy After Spanish-American War	
Puerto Rico	**Cuba**
• Foraker Act establishes civil government in 1900 • •	• Treaty of Paris grants Cuban independence • •

CHAPTER 5 — SECTION 4

Note Taking Study Guide
THE UNITED STATES AND LATIN AMERICA

Focus Question: What actions did the United States take to achieve its goals in Latin America?

B. *As you read, compare Wilson's moral diplomacy with the foreign policies of Roosevelt and Taft by completing the flow chart below.*

TIP: Search for each president's name and the policies they pursued.

United States Foreign Policy		
Roosevelt	**Taft**	**Wilson**
•	• "Dollar diplomacy" •	• "Moral diplomacy" •
•		•
• Supported rebellion in Panama •		• Sent U.S. troops into Mexico

Section Summary
THE UNITED STATES AND LATIN AMERICA

CHAPTER 5 SECTION 4

After the Spanish-American War, the United States governed Puerto Rico with military rule. In 1900, the U.S. Congress passed the **Foraker Act,** creating a civil government in Puerto Rico. In 1917, Puerto Ricans were given more rights. After the Spanish-American War, Cuba was independent. However, the U.S. Congress forced Cuba to include the **Platt Amendment** in its constitution. This amendment restricted the rights of Cubans. It also gave the United States the right to intervene in Cuba.

President Theodore Roosevelt applied a policy of **"big stick" diplomacy.** This meant the U.S. military would be used to achieve America's goals. Like many Americans, Roosevelt felt that America should be a world leader. Roosevelt used force when he wanted to build the **Panama Canal,** a waterway to connect the Atlantic and Pacific oceans. He used the United States Navy to help Panama gain independence from Colombia. In return, Panama gave the United States control over the "Canal Zone" in Panama.

William Howard Taft followed Roosevelt as President and pursued a similar foreign policy. However, Taft stressed **"dollar diplomacy."** This policy encouraged more American businesses to invest in Latin America. These key investments gave America more influence in Latin America.

President Woodrow Wilson used a new foreign policy called **"moral diplomacy."** Wilson did not base his foreign policy on imperialism, like the presidents before him. Instead, he said he valued human rights and honesty.

<u>Although Wilson tried to practice "moral diplomacy," he nevertheless had trouble dealing with the Mexican Revolution.</u> The most famous figure of the revolution was **Francisco "Pancho" Villa.** After Villa led a raid on New Mexico, Wilson sent U.S. troops into Mexico. Wilson demonstrated that America had emerged as a world power.

Review Questions

1. What did "big stick" diplomacy rely on?

____

____

2. How was Wilson's foreign policy different from Roosevelt's?

____

____

READING CHECK

Why might some Cubans have been upset about the Platt Amendment?

____

____

____

VOCABULARY STRATEGY

What does the word *nevertheless* mean in the underlined sentence? Circle the words in the underlined passage that could help you learn what *nevertheless* means. Notice the phrase at the beginning of the sentence that starts with "Although."

____

____

____

READING SKILL

Identify Supporting Details
What details support the idea that Roosevelt applied "big stick" diplomacy?

____

____

____

CHAPTER 6
SECTION 1

Note Taking Study Guide
FROM NEUTRALITY TO WAR

Focus Question: What caused World War I, and why did the United States enter the war?

As you read, identify the causes of World War I, the conditions facing soldiers, and the reasons for U.S. involvement.

World War I

Reasons for U.S. involvement
- Germany's brutal invasion of Belgium
-
-
-

Nature of warfare
- Each side built trenches.
-
-

Causes of the war
- Nationalism
-
-
-
-

Section Summary
CHAPTER 6 SECTION 1

FROM NEUTRALITY TO WAR

There had been no major wars during the 50 years before World War I, but Europe was not peaceful. Nationalism renewed old grudges between countries. **Militarism,** or the glorification of the military, brought an arms race among Germany, Britain, France, and Russia.

European leaders also prepared for war by forming alliances among their countries. In 1914, a Serbian assassinated **Francis Ferdinand,** the archduke of Austria-Hungary. <u>War spread as European countries entered the fighting to help their allies.</u> Great Britain, France, Russia, and Serbia were allies fighting against Germany and Austria-Hungary. In less than one week, World War I had begun.

Fighting went on in other parts of the world, but the **Western Front** in France was the key battle front. German soldiers settled onto high ground and dug trenches. Then the French and British dug their own trenches. Neither side was able to defeat the other. The war dragged on. Machine guns and artillery led to millions of **casualties,** or soldiers killed, wounded, and missing.

As the war continued in Europe, President Woodrow Wilson asked Americans to be neutral. However, the brutal German invasion of Belgium swayed American opinion against Germany. Americans protested when a German submarine, or **U-boat,** sank the passenger ship *Lusitania.*

In January 1917, German Foreign Minister Arthur Zimmermann sent a telegram to Mexico. He proposed an alliance between Germany and Mexico. The British intercepted the **Zimmermann note** and gave it to American authorities. Americans were shocked by the note. Soon afterward, Germany announced that it would once again use submarines to sink British passenger ships. The United States responded to these events by declaring war on Germany on April 6, 1917.

Review Questions

1. How did alliances help lead to war?

____

____

2. Why did the United States get involved in World War I?

____

____

READING CHECK

Who was Francis Ferdinand?

____

____

____

VOCABULARY BUILDER

What does the word *allies* mean in the underlined sentence? What clues can you find in the surrounding words, phrases, or sentences? Circle the words that could help you learn what *ally* means.

____

____

____

READING SKILL

Identify Causes Identify the causes of World War I.

____

____

____

Name ______________________ Class ________________ Date ______

Chapter 6
Section 2

Note Taking Study Guide

THE HOME FRONT

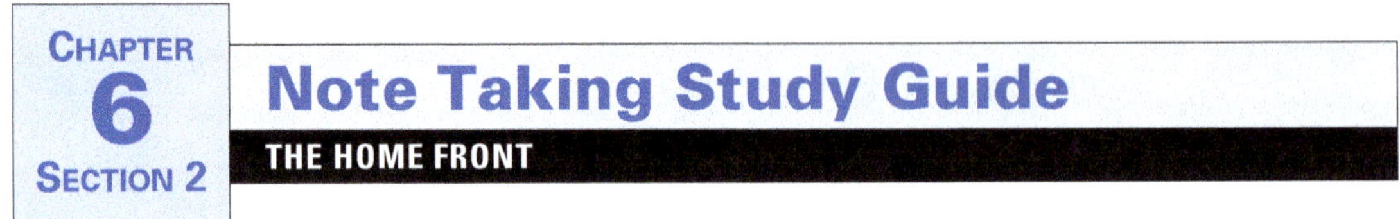

Focus Question: How did the war affect Americans at home?

As you read, summarize the key points in the chart below.

American Home Front

Social change

- The war created new jobs for women.
-
-
-

Opposition

-
- conscientious objectors
-

Mobilization

-
-
-

<table><tr><td>CHAPTER
6
SECTION 2</td><td># Section Summary
THE HOME FRONT</td></tr></table>

When the United States entered World War I, its army was much smaller than the European armies. To build the army, Congress passed the **Selective Service Act.** This act allowed a draft of young men for military service in Europe.

The War Industries Board (WIB), headed by **Bernard Baruch,** controlled all industries involved in the war. The WIB decided what industries would make, where those products went, and how much they would cost. <u>The WIB also urged Americans to conserve food as a patriotic gesture.</u>

In 1914, most Americans did not understand the reasons for the war. The **Committee on Public Information (CPI)** had to convince Americans that the war effort was a just cause. Still, some Americans, including German Americans and Irish Americans, opposed America's entry into the war. Opposition also came from **conscientious objectors,** people whose moral or religious beliefs forbid them to fight in wars.

During the war, Congress limited freedom of speech. In 1917, Congress passed the **Espionage Act,** which punished anyone who interfered with the war effort. In 1918, Congress further limited freedom of speech by passing the Sedition Act. The government used the Sedition Act to prosecute socialists, political radicals, and pacifists.

The war also brought social changes. Women took jobs that were open because men had gone to fight. In 1920, women gained the right to vote. Meanwhile, more than 1.2 million African Americans took part in the **Great Migration.** They moved from the rural South to the industrial North in the hope of escaping racism and finding better jobs.

Many Mexicans also wanted a better life for themselves and their children. They crossed the border into the United States, looking for work on ranches and farms. World War I had opened up new opportunities for women, African Americans, and Mexican Americans.

Review Questions

1. What was the purpose of the Committee on Public Information (CPI)?

____

____

2. Why did conscientious objectors oppose the war?

____

____

READING CHECK

Why did so many African Americans move to the North during the war?

____

____

____

VOCABULARY BUILDER

What does the word *conserve* mean in the underlined sentence? An antonym for *conserve* is *squander.* Use the antonym to help you figure out the meaning of *conserve.*

____

____

____

READING SKILL

Summarize Summarize how the American government won over public support for the war.

____

____

____

CHAPTER 6 SECTION 3

Note Taking Study Guide

WILSON, WAR, AND PEACE

Focus Question: How did Americans affect the end of World War I and its peace settlements?

A. *As you read, sequence the events leading to the end of World War I in the timeline below.*

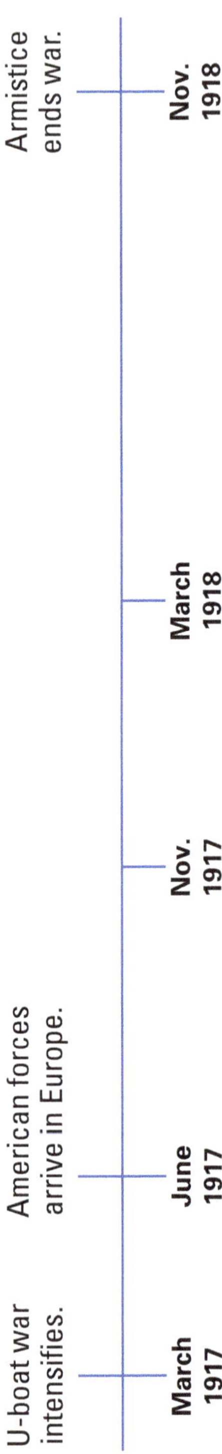

Note Taking Study Guide

CHAPTER 6 SECTION 3

WILSON, WAR, AND PEACE

Focus Question: How did Americans affect the end of World War I and its peace settlements?

B. *As you read, summarize Wilson's goals for peace and whether or not each goal was fulfilled.*

Wilson's Ideas for Peace	Decision Made at Paris Peace Conference
Peace without victory	Great Britain and France make Germany pay reparations.
Open diplomacy	
Freedom of seas and free trade	
Move toward ending colonialism	Iraq is attached to Britain as a mandate.
Self-determination	
League of Nations	

<table><tr><td>**CHAPTER 6**
SECTION 3</td><td>**Section Summary**
WILSON, WAR, AND PEACE</td></tr></table>

When the United States entered World War I, Germany once again began unrestricted submarine warfare. **Convoys** made up of British and American warships protected the merchant ships, providing mutual safety. Shipping losses fell sharply.

When communists led by **Vladimir Lenin** gained control of Russia, fighting stopped between Russia and Germany. Germany then began an all-out offensive on the Western Front. The arrival of American troops under the command of **John J. Pershing** helped counter the German attacks. On November 11, 1918, Germany surrendered. The war was over.

In the **Fourteen Points,** President Wilson outlined America's war aims. The Fourteen Points promoted openness, encouraged independence, and supported freedom. Wilson also emphasized **self-determination,** or the right of people to choose their own form of government. Finally, he asked for a **League of Nations,** a world organization where countries could gather and peacefully resolve their quarrels.

In early 1919, the Allies held a peace conference in France. Although the League of Nations was set up, the peace treaties made at the Paris Peace Conference created almost as many problems as they solved. By forming new states, the Allies established a new map of Europe. This map violated national self-determination many times.

In the United States, many opposed the treaty. A handful of senators known as the **"irreconcilables"** believed the United States should not be a part of world organizations such as the League of Nations. A larger group of senators, led by **Henry Cabot Lodge,** and known as the **"reservationists,"** opposed the treaty as it was written. Wilson and his opponents refused to compromise, and the Senate did not ratify the treaty. Without American support, the League of Nations was unable to maintain peace.

Review Questions

1. Describe the aims of the Fourteen Points.

____

____

2. How did convoys contribute to the success of the Allies?

____

____

Name ______________________ Class __________________ Date ________

CHAPTER 6 SECTION 4

Note Taking Study Guide

EFFECTS OF THE WAR

Focus Question: What political, economic, and social effects did World War I have on the United States?

As you read, identify and record the main ideas of this section in the concept web below.

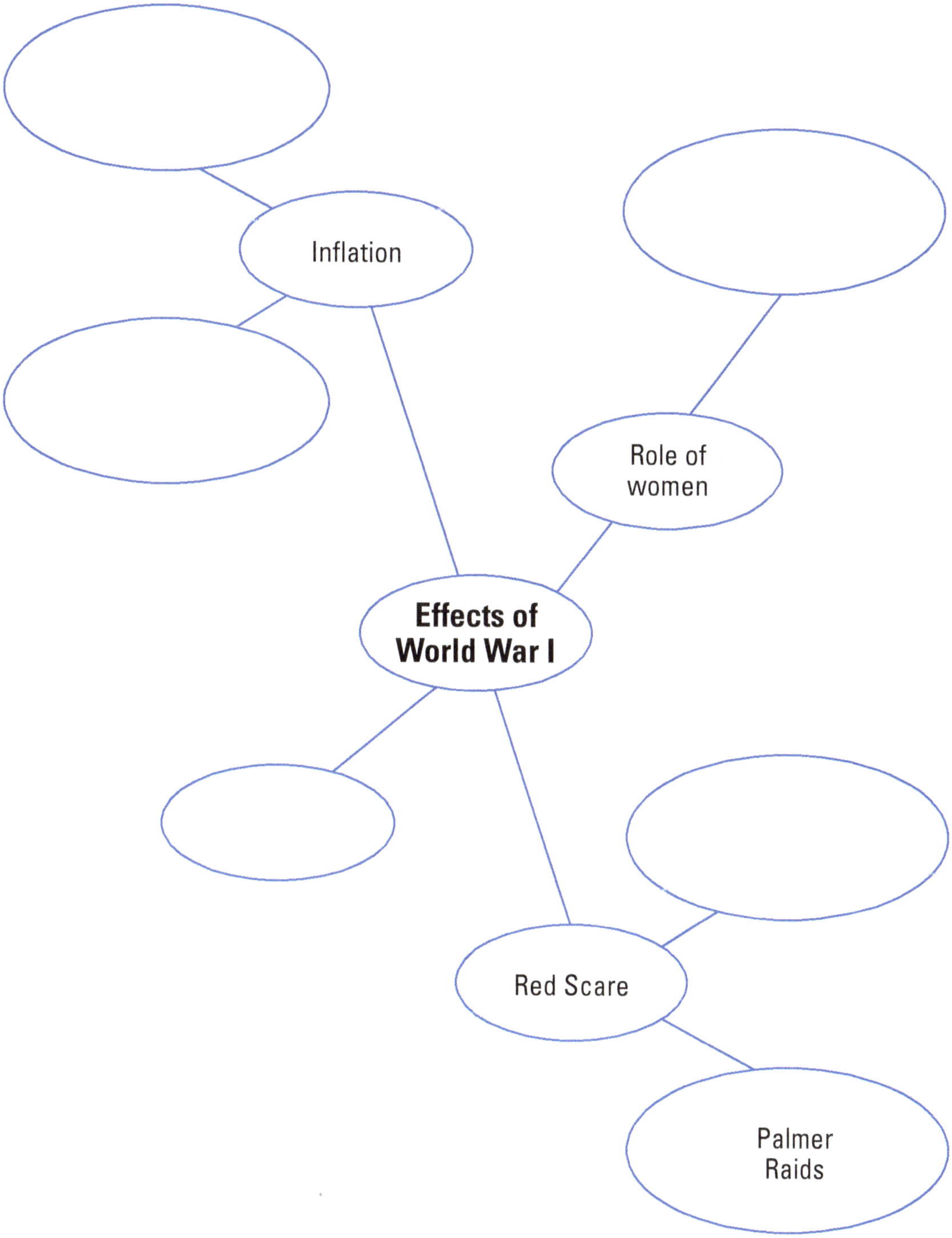
Inflation
Role of women
Effects of World War I
Red Scare
Palmer Raids

<table><tr><td>**CHAPTER**
6
SECTION 4</td><td>**Section Summary**
EFFECTS OF THE WAR</td></tr></table>

World War I significantly changed America. An **influenza** pandemic that killed millions worldwide made the transition to peace even more difficult. The flu pandemic created a sense of doom and dread.

The war produced important economic and social changes. African Americans and women now had to compete with men returning from the war for jobs. Farmers were paid less for their crops, which made it hard for them to pay their bills. **Inflation,** or rising prices, meant industrial workers' wages did not buy as much as they had bought during the war. All around the country, workers went on strike for higher wages.

The violence of some strikes was often attributed to the presence of radicals among the strike leaders. <u>Fear of radicals and communists was made worse by the emergence of the Soviet Union as a communist nation.</u> Communism called for a worldwide workers' revolution, and communist revolts in Europe made it seem like the revolution was starting.

Fear that communists were plotting revolution within the United States set off the first American **Red Scare.** Attorney General A. Mitchell Palmer mounted a series of raids in early 1920 known as the **Palmer Raids.** Police arrested thousands of people, some who were radicals and some who were simply immigrants from southern or Eastern Europe.

Eventually the great fear ended. **Warren G. Harding** was elected President, in part because he talked about America returning to simpler times or to "normalcy."

By 1920, the United States was the richest country in the world. The United States was also the largest **creditor nation** in the world. Other countries owed the United States more money than the United States owed them. World War I had shifted the economic center of the world from London to New York City. America embraced its new role in the world.

Review Questions

1. Describe the problems Americans faced immediately after the war.

____

____

2. How did the war change America's role in world affairs?

____

____

Name ______________________ Class __________________ Date _______

CHAPTER 7
SECTION 1

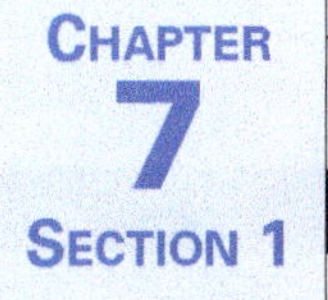

Note Taking Study Guide

A BOOMING ECONOMY

Focus Question: How did the booming economy of the 1920s lead to changes in American life?

As you read, note specific examples that support the idea that the economy changed during the 1920s.

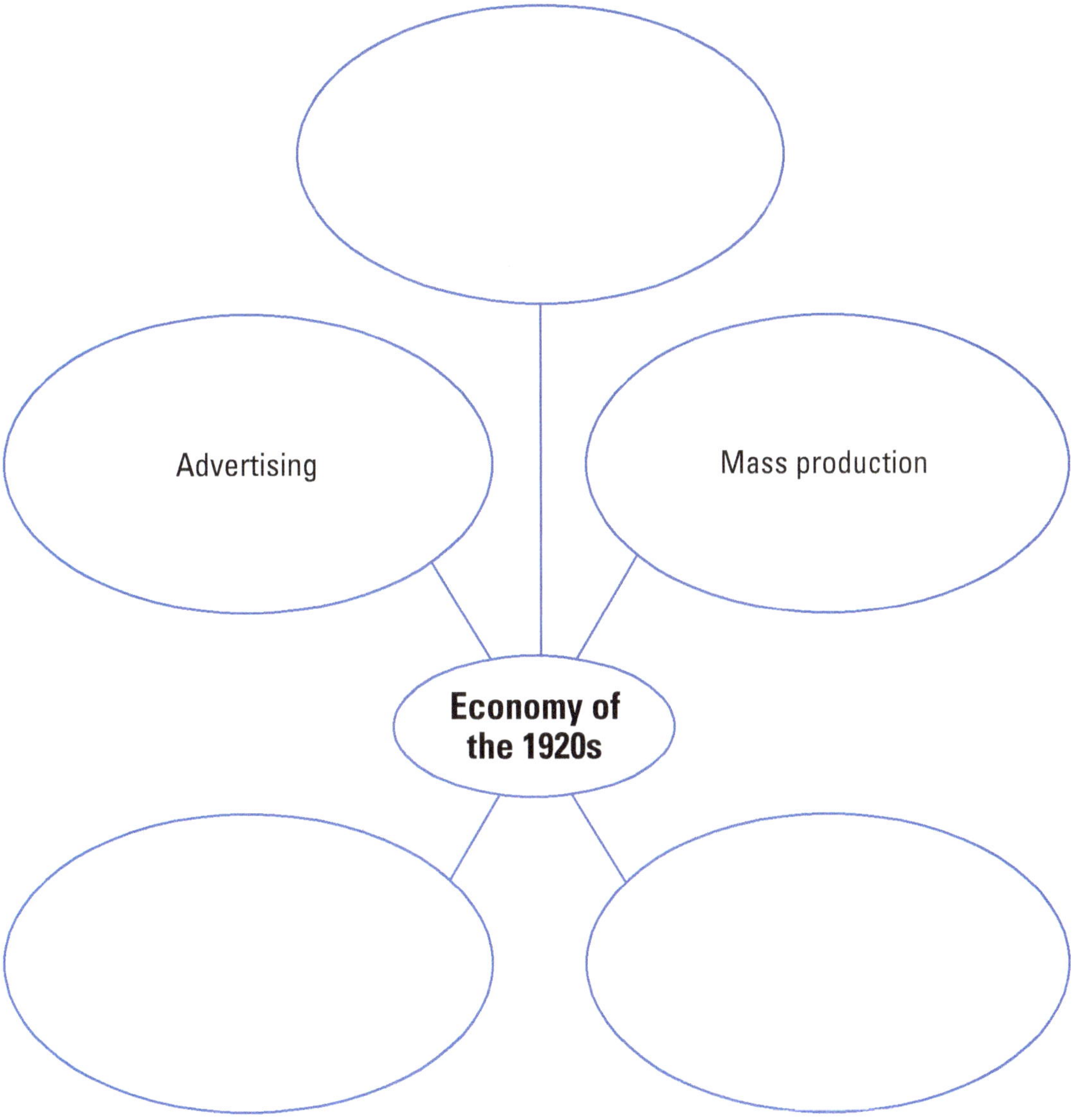
Advertising
Mass production
Economy of the 1920s

<table>
<tr><td>CHAPTER
7
SECTION 1</td><td>## Section Summary
A BOOMING ECONOMY</td></tr>
</table>

In the 1920s, new **mass-production** techniques helped workers make more goods in less time. This led to a booming economy. The automobile industry played a major role in the economic boom. Carmaker **Henry Ford** hired **scientific management** experts to improve his **assembly-line** production of automobiles. He was able to greatly reduce the time it took to build his **Model T** automobile. This made the Model T affordable for most Americans, and automobile ownership skyrocketed.

Ford also used innovation to manage his employees. He more than doubled their wages, shortened their workday, and gave them both Saturday and Sunday off.

The increase in automobile ownership helped other industries, such as steel, glass, rubber, asphalt, wood, gasoline, insurance, and road construction. These industries created new, better-paying jobs. More Americans had more money to spend. A flood of new, affordable goods became available, creating a **consumer revolution.**

Consumers used a new kind of credit called **installment buying** to buy things they otherwise could not have afforded. They paid a small amount at first, then paid the rest of the price in monthly payments. With a **bull market** soaring, Americans also bought stock on credit, which is called **buying on margin.** They paid as little as 10 percent of the stock price upfront to a broker. If the price of the stock rose, buyers made a profit. If it fell, they owed money to the broker.

The economic boom was felt more in cities than in rural areas. Farmers in particular suffered under growing debt, while at the same time crop prices were falling. For farmers, and many others, it was not a decade of prosperity.

Review Questions

1. How did mass production influence the economy?

____

____

2. What was installment buying?

____

____

Note Taking Study Guide

THE BUSINESS OF GOVERNMENT

CHAPTER 7 SECTION 2

Focus Question: How did domestic and foreign policy change direction under Harding and Coolidge?

As you read, note similarities and differences between the characters and policies of Presidents Harding and Coolidge.

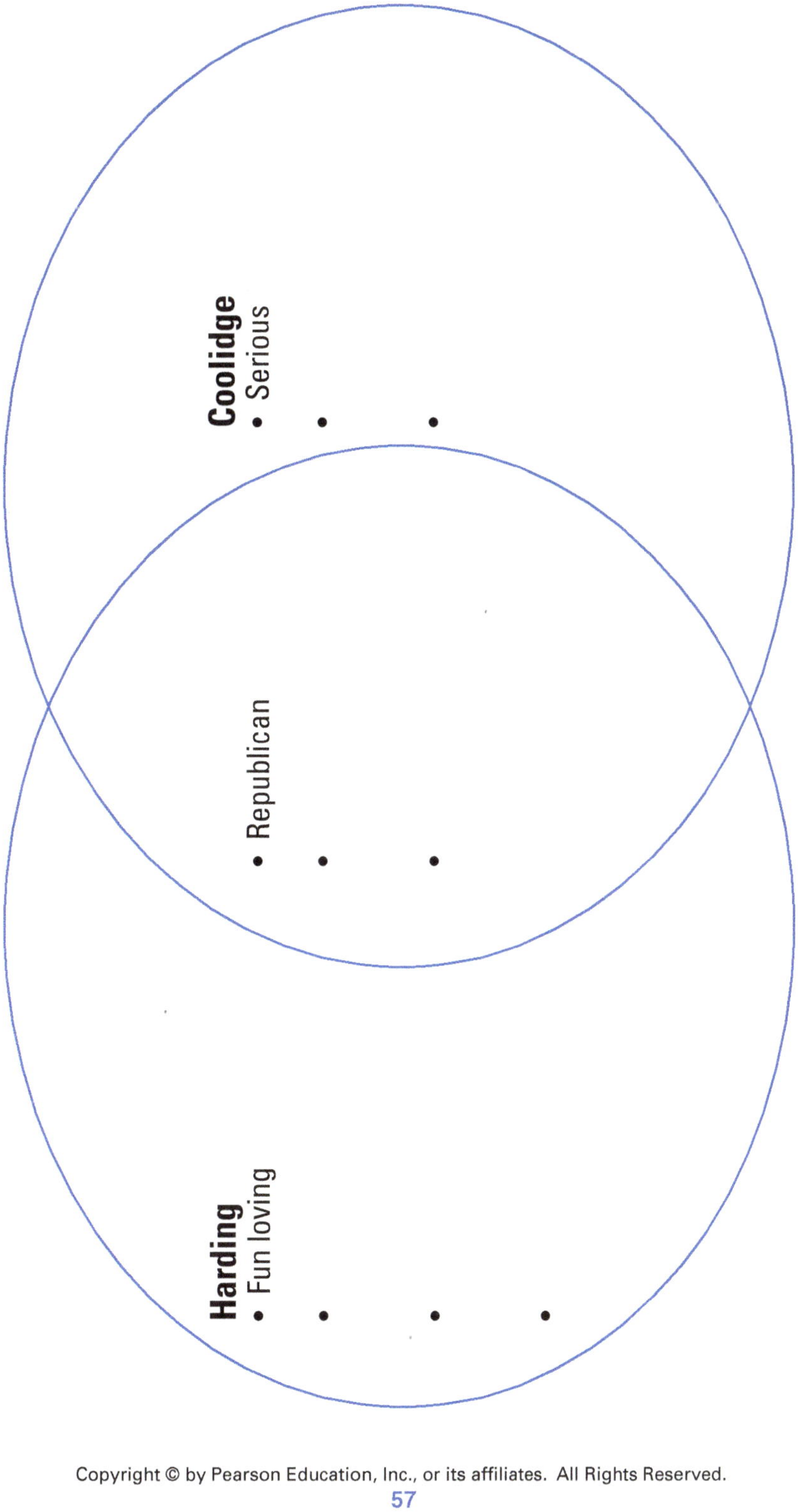

Coolidge
- Serious
-
-

Republican
-
-
-

Harding
- Fun loving
-
-
-

<table>
<tr><td>CHAPTER
7
SECTION 2</td><td>## Section Summary
THE BUSINESS OF GOVERNMENT</td></tr>
</table>

In 1920, fun-loving Warren G. Harding was elected President. Favoring big business, he named banker **Andrew Mellon** as Secretary of the Treasury. Harding raised protective tariff rates, which made it easier for U.S. producers to sell goods at home. In response, Europeans also raised tariffs, weakening the world economy. Harding did not like laws designed to protect workers and reform business. Instead, his Secretary of Commerce, **Herbert Hoover,** asked businesses to make voluntary changes.

Harding was a friendly man but not very intelligent. He named his poker-playing friends to important government positions. One friend, Charles Forbes, wasted millions of dollars while running the Veterans' Bureau. Another, Secretary of the Interior Albert Fall, took bribes to transfer control of oil reserves from the United States Navy to private oilmen. The incident became known as the **Teapot Dome scandal.** Fall was later sentenced to a year in jail. Harding died in 1923, before the full extent of the scandal came to light.

The new President, **Calvin Coolidge,** was quiet and honest. He appointed trustworthy men to jobs in the government. Like Harding, he mistrusted laws that restricted businesses. He reduced the national debt and lowered taxes to give incentives to businesses. Still, he ignored the country's other problems, such as low farm prices, racial discrimination, and low wages for workers.

In foreign policy, Coolidge pushed European governments to repay war debts. The 1924 **Dawes Plan** made it easier for Germany, Britain, and France to repay those loans. In 1928, 62 nations signed the **Kellogg-Briand Pact.** This treaty outlawed war, but it was quickly forgotten because it could not be enforced.

Review Questions

1. What was the Teapot Dome scandal?

____

____

2. How did Presidents Harding and Coolidge feel about laws that restricted businesses?

____

____

Note Taking Study Guide

SOCIAL AND CULTURAL TENSIONS

CHAPTER 7 / SECTION 3

Focus Question: How did Americans differ on major social and cultural issues?

As you read, look for issues that divided Americans in the 1920s.

Differing Viewpoints	
Education	• Viewpoint 1: Urban Americans tended to value education highly. • Viewpoint 2:
Evolution	• Viewpoint 1: Fundamentalists opposed the theory of evolution. Tennessee made it illegal to teach evolution in their public schools. • Viewpoint 2:
Immigration	• Viewpoint 1: • Viewpoint 2:
	• Viewpoint 1: • Viewpoint 2:
	• Viewpoint 1: • Viewpoint 2:

<table><tr><td>**CHAPTER 7**
SECTION 3</td><td>**Section Summary**
SOCIAL AND CULTURAL TENSIONS</td></tr></table>

READING CHECK

What did the Eighteenth Amendment forbid?

____

____

____

VOCABULARY STRATEGY

Find the word *imperial* in the underlined sentence. What does *imperial* mean? Look for clues in the nearby words and phrases. Circle any that help you figure out what *imperial* means.

____

____

____

READING SKILL

Contrast Select an issue that divided Americans. Contrast the ways rural and urban Americans felt about this issue.

____

____

____

As the 1920s began, striking differences arose between urban and rural America. Urban Americans enjoyed a rising standard of living and a modern view of the world. They valued education, and tended to be advocates of science and social change.

By contrast, in rural America times were hard. Formal education was considered less important than working the farm, and people were generally less open to scientific discoveries and social change. Many rural Americans believed in the literal truth of the Bible. This belief was called **fundamentalism.** It opposed modernism, which stressed science.

The two beliefs clashed head-on in the 1925 **Scopes Trial.** That year, Tennessee passed a law making it illegal to teach the theory of evolution in the state's public schools. The attorney **Clarence Darrow** defended John Scopes for teaching this scientific theory to his high school class. Scopes was found guilty.

Many Americans did not appreciate the nation's growing diversity. A wave of immigration inspired nativist politicians to pass laws creating a **quota system** to set limits on the number of new immigrants allowed into the country. In 1915, the **Ku Klux Klan** was reorganized in Georgia. This violent group, whose leaders had titles such as Grand Dragon and Imperial Wizard, promoted hatred of African Americans, Jews, Catholics, and immigrants.

Prohibition was also a controversial issue. In 1919, the states ratified the **Eighteenth Amendment** to the Constitution, which forbade the manufacture, distribution, and sale of alcohol. Congress then passed the **Volstead Act** to enforce the amendment. Organized crime rose as an unexpected result of Prohibition. **Bootleggers** illegally sold alcohol but also involved themselves in prostitution, drugs, robbery, and murder.

Review Questions

1. What were some of the issues and beliefs that rural and urban America clashed over in the 1920s?

____

____

2. What did quota system laws do?

____

____

Name ______________ Class ______________ Date ________

CHAPTER 7
SECTION 4

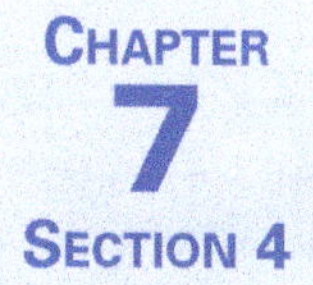

Note Taking Study Guide

A NEW MASS CULTURE

Focus Question: How did the new mass culture reflect technological and social changes?

A. *As you read, look for examples of the ways in which American culture changed during the 1920s.*

TIP: Look for clues in headings throughout the section.

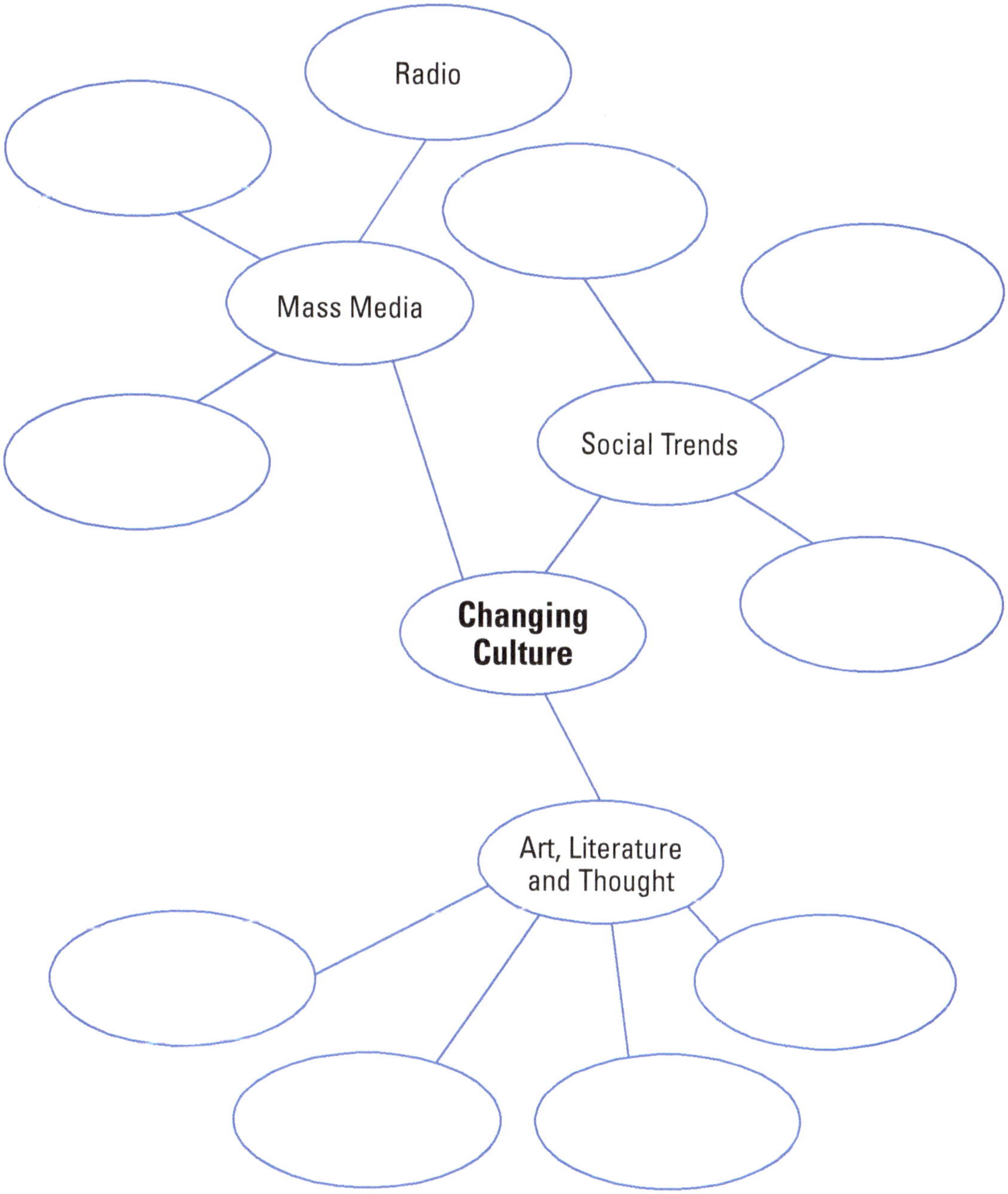

Radio
Mass Media
Social Trends
Changing Culture
Art, Literature and Thought

CHAPTER 7
SECTION 4

Note Taking Study Guide

A NEW MASS CULTURE

Focus Question: How did the new mass culture reflect technological and social changes?

B. *As you read, classify the various types of changes that took place in women's lives in the 1920s.*

Women in the 1920s		
Social Changes	**Political Changes**	**Economic Changes**
• Flappers wore shorter skirts. • • •	• Won the right to vote •	• •

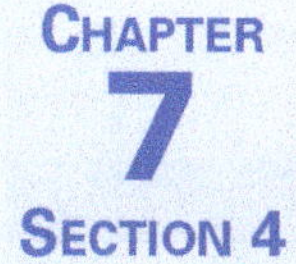

CHAPTER 7 SECTION 4
Section Summary
A NEW MASS CULTURE

As wages rose in the 1920s, American workers also enjoyed shorter workweeks. People had more free time and more money to spend on entertainment. Each week, 60 to 100 million people attended movies. Actors such as comedian **Charlie Chaplin,** heartthrob Rudolf Valentino, and cowboy William S. Hart became stars of these silent films. Then in 1927, the movie *The Jazz Singer* became the first movie to include sound matched to the action. The era of "talkies" began.

For entertainment at home, Americans bought phonographs and radios. Americans all across the continent listened to the same songs, learned the same dances, and shared a popular culture as never before. People admired the same heroes, such as baseball player **Babe Ruth,** the home-run king, and aviator **Charles Lindbergh,** who was the first person to fly alone across the Atlantic Ocean.

American women challenged political, economic, social, and educational boundaries. The Nineteenth Amendment gave women the right to vote, and many ran for political office or joined the workforce. Some women, known as **flappers,** shocked society by wearing short skirts and bobbed hair. At home, new electric appliances made housework easier. Popular magazines, sociological studies, novels, and movies all featured the "New Woman" of the 1920s prominently.

A spirit of modernism grew, especially in cities. Austrian psychologist **Sigmund Freud** contributed to this spirit with his theory that humans behave the way they do because of hidden desires rather than rational thought. Painters experimented with new styles. Writers, including **F. Scott Fitzgerald** and **Ernest Hemingway,** wrote masterpieces that examined subconscious desires and the dark side of the American dream.

Review Questions

1. What were some of the advances in technology in the 1920s?

____

____

2. What changes allowed urban Americans to enjoy more entertainment?

____

____

CHAPTER 7
SECTION 5

Note Taking Study Guide

THE HARLEM RENAISSANCE

Focus Question: How did African Americans express a new sense of hope and pride?

As you read, identify the main ideas.

I. New "Black Consciousness"

    A. New Chances, New Challenges

        1. Migration to North continues

        2. _______________________________________

        3. _______________________________________

    B. Garvey Calls for Racial Pride

        1. _______________________________________

        2. _______________________________________

        3. _______________________________________

II. The Jazz Age

    A. Unique American Music Emerges

        1. _______________________________________

        2. _______________________________________

    B. _______________________________________

        1. _______________________________________

III. The Harlem Renaissance

    A. _______________________________________

        1. _______________________________________

    B. _______________________________________

        1. _______________________________________

<table>
<tr><td>CHAPTER
7
SECTION 5</td><td>## Section Summary
THE HARLEM RENAISSANCE</td></tr>
</table>

After World War I, millions of African Americans left the South to find a better life in the North. In New York, Chicago, and Detroit, they found good-paying jobs, a middle class of African American professionals, and a growing political voice. About 200,000 migrants from the South and immigrants from the Caribbean settled in New York City's Harlem neighborhood. One of these immigrants was a Jamaican named **Marcus Garvey.** Seeing that blacks were treated poorly everywhere, he created a "Back to Africa" movement and urged black unity and separation of the races.

The 1920s saw the birth of a new musical form, **jazz.** Jazz is a truly indigenous American music. It emerged in the South as a combination of African American and European musical styles. Jazz became famous around the world thanks to the talents of musicians such as trumpet player **Louis Armstrong.** Singer **Bessie Smith** was so popular that she became the highest-paid African American entertainer of the 1920s.

The decade also saw the **Harlem Renaissance,** an outpouring of art and literature that explored the African American experience. Among its most famous writers was **Claude McKay,** whose novels and poems were militant calls for action. **Langston Hughes** celebrated African American culture. **Zora Neale Hurston** wrote about women's desire for independence.

The Great Depression ended the Harlem Renaissance. However, the pride and unity it created provided a foundation for the future civil rights movement.

Review Questions

1. Why did many African Americans migrate north?

____

____

2. What was the "Back to Africa" movement?

____

____

Name ______________________ Class ________________ Date ______

CHAPTER 8
SECTION 1

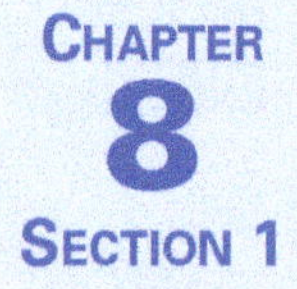

Note Taking Study Guide

CAUSES OF THE DEPRESSION

Focus Question: How did the prosperity of the 1920s give way to the Great Depression?

A. *Identify the causes of the Great Depression.*

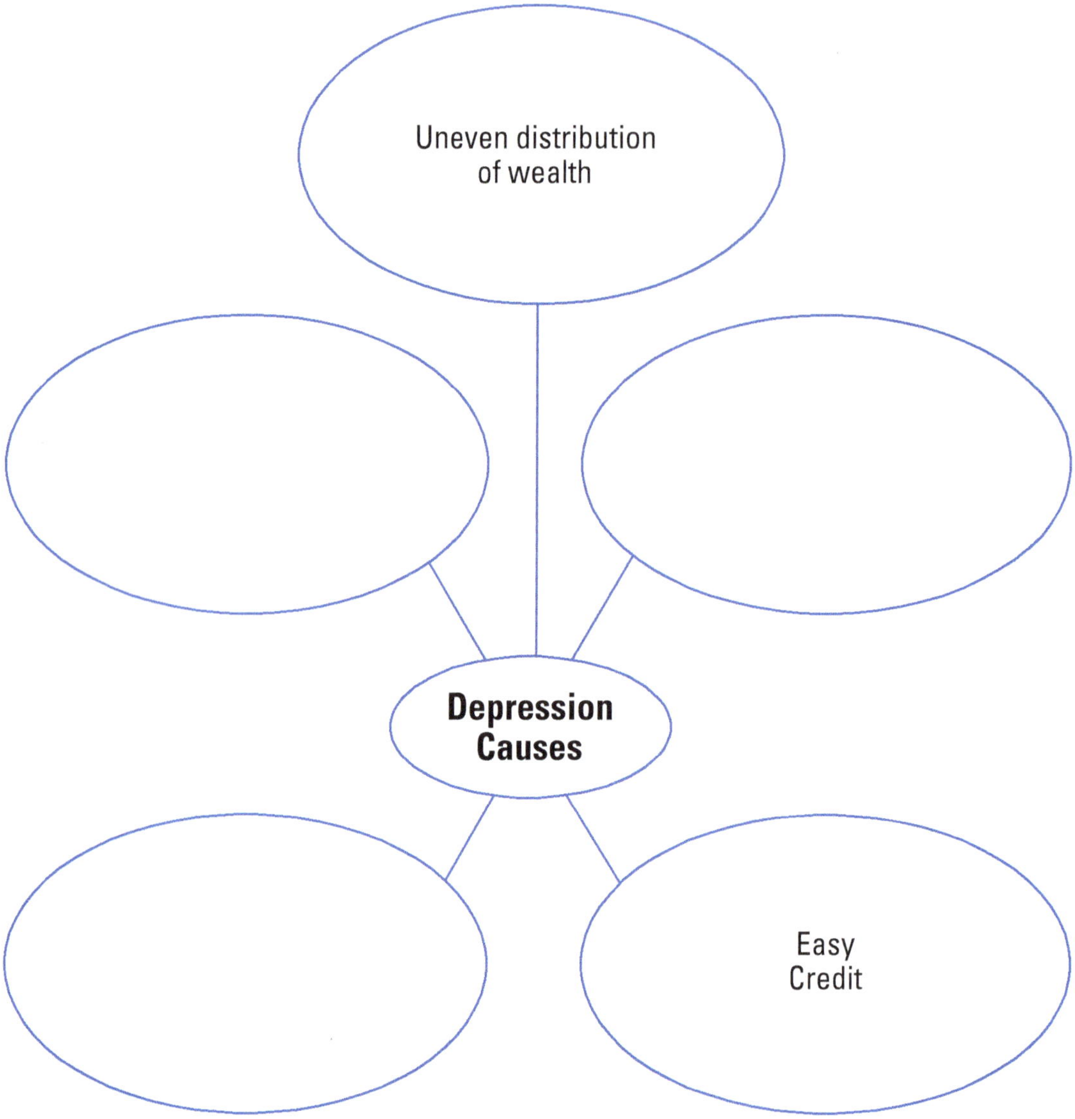

CHAPTER 8 SECTION 1

Note Taking Study Guide

CAUSES OF THE DEPRESSION

Focus Question: How did the prosperity of the 1920s give way to the Great Depression?

B. *Use a flowchart to note what happened in the wake of the stock market crash.*

Stock market crashes.
↓   ↓   ↓
Commercial banks fail.
↓   ↓   ↓
Banking system collapses.
↓   ↓   ↓
↓   ↓   ↓
↓   ↓   ↓
↓   ↓   ↓
↓   ↓   ↓

CHAPTER 8

SECTION 1

Section Summary

CAUSES OF THE DEPRESSION

During the 1920s, times were good. The Republicans in power took credit for the strong economy. In 1928, the country elected Republican **Herbert Hoover** as President. However, hidden economic problems soon caused the Great Depression.

A few people had lots of money in the 1920s. Others had much less. In particular, farmers had money problems. During World War I, they had increased their harvests to raise more food for soldiers. After the war, larger harvests flooded the market with cheap food and brought down profits.

Industrial workers, whose wages rose steadily, did better than farmers. To buy the many new products, workers used easy credit. This hid the problem that not enough people could really afford to buy products. Meanwhile, some Americans enjoyed great wealth. However, rich Americans were only a tiny portion of the population. They would never be able to buy enough goods to keep the economy strong.

Some economists also worried about **speculation** in the stock market. Investors often borrowed money to buy stocks then sell them and turn a quick profit. Rapid buying and selling raised the price of both good and bad stocks, making the economy unstable. Finally, all the problems began to converge. Stock prices bottomed out on **Black Tuesday,** October 29, 1929. Whole fortunes were wiped out in hours.

The stock market crash marked the beginning of the **Great Depression,** a period lasting from 1929 to 1941 in which the U.S. economy faltered, banks closed, and unemployment soared. The government tried to help by passing the **Hawley-Smoot Tariff,** which put high taxes on foreign goods. Other countries then taxed U.S. goods. The result was closed markets and unsold goods worldwide, which destroyed world trade. However, economists still disagree on what was the most important factor leading to the Great Depression.

Review Questions

1. How did World War I affect farmers and help lead to the depression?

____

____

2. Why were some economists worried about stock speculation?

____

____

Name ____________________ Class ____________________ Date ________

Chapter 8
Section 2

Note Taking Study Guide

AMERICANS FACE HARD TIMES

Focus Question: How did the Great Depression affect the lives of urban and rural Americans?

As you read, use the Venn diagram below to note how the depression affected both urban and rural America.

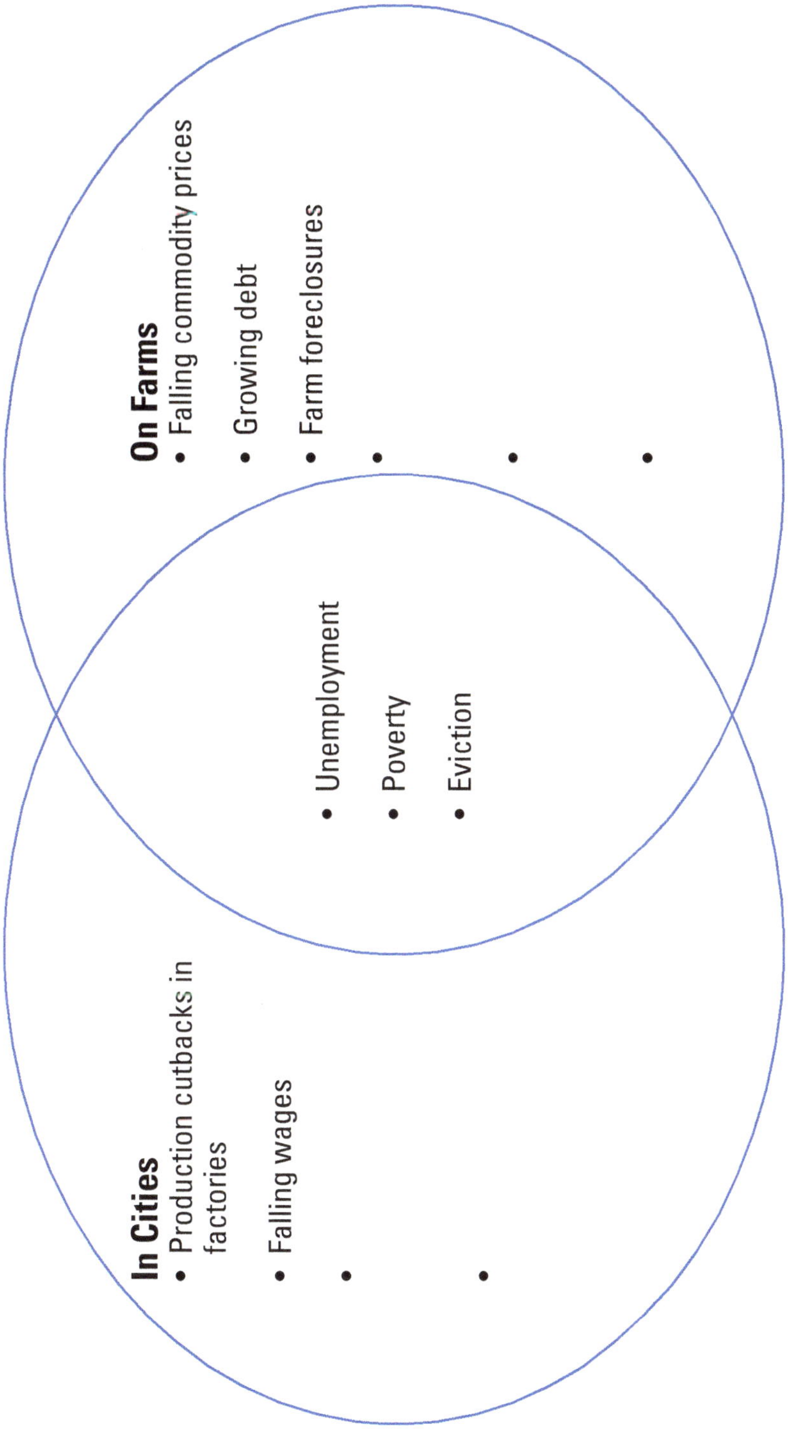
On Farms
• Falling commodity prices
• Growing debt
• Farm foreclosures
•
•
•
• Unemployment
• Poverty
• Eviction
In Cities
• Production cutbacks in factories
• Falling wages
•
•

CHAPTER 8

SECTION 2

Section Summary

AMERICANS FACE HARD TIMES

The Great Depression was felt by all Americans. Some lost everything they had. Others struggled mightily simply to survive. Every American suffered or knew someone who was suffering through the crisis.

In the cities, unemployment was a big problem. Between 1921 and 1929, annual average unemployment rates never rose above 3.7 percent. By 1933, almost 25 percent of workers were without jobs. Soon, unemployed families ran out of money. <u>They took drastic measures and sold their belongings.</u> Sometimes a family's only food came from a **bread line,** where people lined up for handouts from charities or public agencies. Many people were evicted from their homes. With no place else to go, they sometimes grouped together in **Hoovervilles**—makeshift shantytowns of tents and shacks.

In rural America, farmers struggled with low crop prices. A severe drought and overfarming on the Great Plains had turned the soil to dust that made farming impossible, and created huge dust storms. High plains regions in Texas, Oklahoma, Kansas, New Mexico, and Colorado became known as the **Dust Bowl.** Many farmers lost their farms. Some continued as **tenant farmers,** working for large landowners instead of themselves. Others gave up farming altogether and moved to California to look for work. The Dust Bowl migrants became known as **Okies.**

Minorities were hit the hardest by the depression. In 1932, unemployment among African Americans was nearly double the national rate. In the Southwest, Mexican Americans faced a special problem. Many white Americans wanted the government to send them back to Mexico, an act called **repatriation.**

For many Americans, the depression was a time of great hopelessness and despair.

Review Questions

1. What were some of the problems that farmers faced during the depression?

____

____

2. What were Hoovervilles?

____

____

Note Taking Study Guide

HOOVER'S RESPONSE FAILS

Focus Question: Why did Herbert Hoover's policies fail to solve the country's economic crisis?

As you read, fill in the outline with details about President Hoover's response to the depression.

Hoover's Response to the Depression

I. Cautious Response Fails

  A. Hoover Tries Volunteerism

    1. Calls on business leaders to maintain employment, wages, prices

    2. ____

    3. ____

  B. Volunteerism Fails

    1. Businesses cut wages and lay off workers.

    2. ____

II. More Activist Policies

  A. Hoover Uses Federal Resources

    1. Creates the Reconstruction Finance Corporation (RFC)

    2. ____

  B. Trickle-down Economics Plan

    1. Government loans to large businesses will help them hire workers.

    2. Government loans to bankers will help them make loans to businesses.

    3. ____

    4. ____

  C. Activist Policies Fail

    1. Some businesses do not use loans to hire workers.

    2. ____

    3. ____

Section Summary
HOOVER'S RESPONSE FAILS

READING CHECK

Who led the troops against protesters in Washington, D.C., during the summer of 1932?

____

____

____

VOCABULARY STRATEGY

Find the word *simultaneously* in the underlined sentence. What do you think it means? Think about what it means to have many important jobs that have to be done. Which of the following phrases do you think means the same thing as *simultaneously*? Circle the correct answer.

- done at the same time
- done one after the other

READING SKILL

Identify Supporting Details List the details that support the conclusion that Hoover's policy of volunteerism failed.

____

____

____

President Hoover struggled to create a plan to end the depression. One plan he tried was called volunteerism. He asked business leaders to voluntarily keep prices and wages at current levels. <u>He called for the government to simultaneously reduce taxes, lower interest rates, and create public-works programs.</u> The plan would help businesses have more funds to hire workers and create products. Workers would then have money to buy products. Hoover's plan also asked the wealthy to give to charity. Finally, Hoover called for a policy of **localism.** This policy asked local governments to provide more jobs and relief measures. However, businesses cut wages and laid off workers. Local governments did not have enough resources to combat the depression, and charities ran low on money. So, Hoover's economic plan failed.

Next, Hoover urged Congress to create the **Reconstruction Finance Corporation (RFC)** in 1932. The RFC gave loans to banks so they could lend money to businesses. Businesses could then hire workers. However, loans to banks and businesses were not always used as the RFC wished. So this plan also failed.

The **Bonus Army** was a group of World War I veterans. They asked Congress for early payment of their bonus. Congress agreed, but Hoover vetoed the plan. The veterans then protested by setting up camps in Washington, D.C. In July 1932, they rioted and Hoover called in troops. **General Douglas MacArthur** led army troops against the veterans. Many of the veterans were hurt, some badly.

One Hoover success was the building of **Hoover Dam.** Constructed on the Colorado River, it brought jobs to the Southwest in the early 1930s. Still, Americans were appalled at Hoover's treatment of the veterans and handling of the depression. He had little hope of reelection.

Review Questions

1. What was President Hoover's first response to the depression?

____

____

2. What was the Bonus Army?

____

____

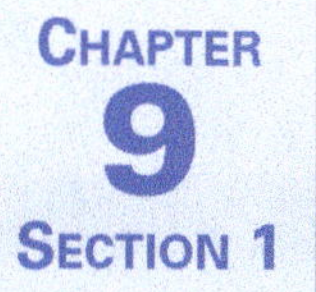

Note Taking Study Guide

FDR OFFERS RELIEF AND RECOVERY

Focus Question: How did the New Deal attempt to address the problems of the depression?

Fill in the chart below with the problems that FDR faced and the steps he took to overcome them.

FDR Tackles Tough Problems	
Problem	**FDR's Policy**
Failing banks	• Federal Deposit Insurance Corporation (FDIC) insures bank deposits.
	•
Desperate plight of farmers	• Tennessee Valley Authority (TVA) builds dams in the Tennessee River valley to control floods and to generate electric power. •
	•
Joblessness	• Civilian Conservation Corps (CCC) provides jobs for more than 2 million young men. • Federal Emergency Relief Act (FERA) grants federal funds to state and local agencies to help the unemployed. •

<table>
<tr><td>CHAPTER
9
SECTION 1</td><td>

Section Summary

FDR OFFERS RELIEF AND RECOVERY
</td></tr>
</table>

Franklin D. Roosevelt was elected President in November 1932. He had lost the use of his legs to polio in 1921. Because of his physical disability, FDR relied heavily on his wife, **Eleanor Roosevelt.** She served as his "eyes and ears."

In his first hundred days in office, FDR acted quickly to help the country recover from the Great Depression. Congress passed 15 bills, which became known as the First New Deal. The **New Deal** had three goals: relief, recovery, and reform. "Relief" meant helping people in great need; "recovery" meant helping businesses; and "reforms" were designed to prevent future depressions.

Relief programs included the **Tennessee Valley Authority (TVA),** which built dams in the Tennessee River valley to control floods and to generate electricity, and the **Civilian Conservation Corps (CCC),** which provided jobs for many young men. They replanted forests, built trails, dug irrigation ditches, and fought fires. <u>The government also began to pay farmers subsidies to reduce the amount of crops they produced.</u>

Recovery efforts included the **National Recovery Administration (NRA)** and the **Public Works Administration (PWA).** The NRA set minimum wages for workers and minimum prices for goods. The PWA created new jobs building bridges, dams, power plants, and government buildings.

Two reform efforts were the **Federal Deposit Insurance Corporation (FDIC),** which insured bank deposits, and the **Securities Exchange Commission (SEC),** which made the stock market safer for investments.

Some Americans thought the New Deal made the government too powerful; others thought the New Deal should help citizens more. Father **Charles Coughlin** was a Roman Catholic priest who expressed his angry views on a weekly radio show. Church officials eventually forced Coughlin to stop his broadcasts. Senator **Huey Long** of Louisiana proposed raising taxes to help the poor.

Review Questions

1. What were the three main goals of the New Deal?

____

____

2. Who disagreed with the New Deal? Why?

____

____

Note Taking Study Guide

THE SECOND NEW DEAL

Focus Question: What major issues did the second New Deal address?

Complete the table below to record problems and the second New Deal's solutions.

The Second New Deal	
Problem	**Solution**
Unemployment	Works Progress Administration (WPA) created new jobs doing public works.
Poverty	

<table>
<tr><td>CHAPTER
9
SECTION 2</td><td>## Section Summary
THE SECOND NEW DEAL</td></tr>
</table>

President Franklin D. Roosevelt used legislation passed by the **second New Deal** to promote the general welfare of the citizens and to protect their rights.

The **Works Progress Administration (WPA)** provided new jobs doing public works. The government paid for WPA programs by spending money it didn't have. According to British economist **John Maynard Keynes,** such deficit spending would help end the depression.

The **Social Security Act** created a pension system for retired people. It also provided unemployment insurance for workers who lost their jobs and aid for the disabled. New programs aided farmers. The Rural Electrification Administration (REA) helped bring electricity to farms.

New laws also helped industrial workers. The **Wagner Act** ensured their right to **collective bargaining.** This meant that employers had to negotiate with unions about hours, wages, and other working conditions. The **Fair Labor Standards Act** of 1938 set a minimum wage, a maximum number of working hours for the week, and outlawed child labor.

<u>During the Great Depression, there was an upsurge in union activity.</u> The **Congress of Industrial Organizations (CIO)** organized workers in major industries. In 1936, CIO members staged a **sit-down strike** against General Motors. Workers refused to leave the workplace until a settlement had been reached. Their success led to other strikes. As a result, union members' wages and working conditions improved.

The Supreme Court struck down a number of the key laws of the New Deal. To change this trend, FDR wanted to add six new Justices to the nine-member court. This was referred to as **court packing.** After 1937, the Supreme Court became more willing to accept the New Deal. FDR stopped trying to force more New Deal reforms through Congress after the economy slumped again in 1938.

Review Questions

1. How did the Social Security Act promote the general welfare of American citizens?

____

____

2. What right did the Wagner Act give to workers?

____

____

READING CHECK

What were the goals of the second New Deal?

____

____

____

VOCABULARY STRATEGY

What does the word *upsurge* in the underlined sentence mean? Look for clues in the surrounding words, phrases, and sentences. Circle the word below that is a synonym for *upsurge.*

• gain

• loss

READING SKILL

Connect Ideas How did second New Deal legislation improve conditions for American workers?

____

____

____

Name ______________________ Class ______________________ Date ________

CHAPTER 9
SECTION 3

Note Taking Study Guide

EFFECTS OF THE NEW DEAL

Focus Question: How did the New Deal change the social, economic, and political landscape of the United States for future generations?

As you read, identify the lasting effects of the New Deal upon American society.

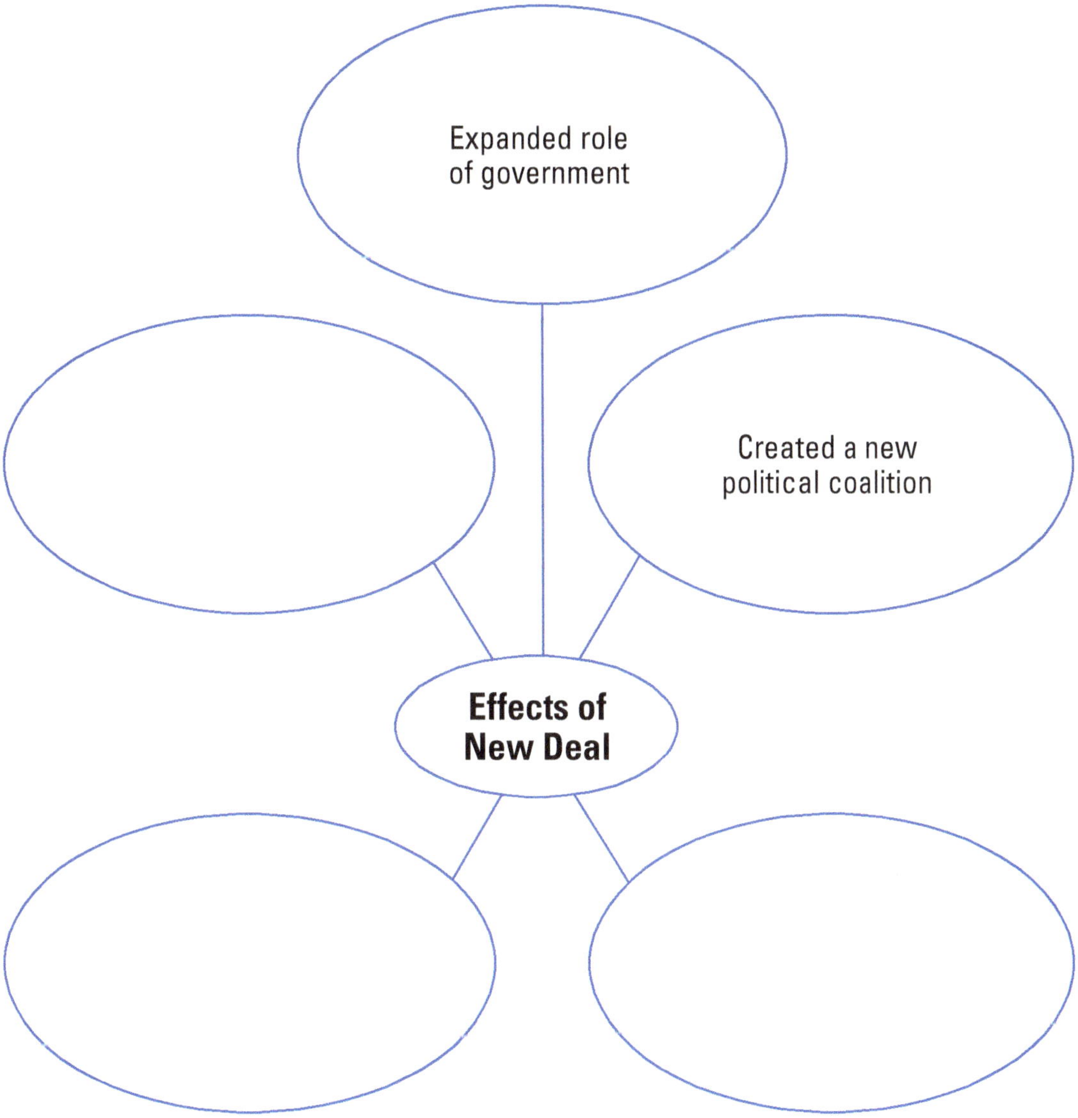
Expanded role of government
Created a new political coalition
Effects of New Deal

CHAPTER 9
SECTION 3

Section Summary
EFFECTS OF THE NEW DEAL

The New Deal brought significant changes to the nation. Some women increased their political influence. Eleanor Roosevelt changed the First Lady's role, becoming active in the political process. She traveled throughout America and called for equal justice for all. Secretary of Labor Frances Perkins was the first female Cabinet member. She played a leading role in establishing Social Security and a minimum wage. Despite the work of these two women, the New Deal did not fight to end gender discrimination in the workplace.

President Roosevelt invited African American leaders to advise him. These unofficial advisers became known as the **Black Cabinet.** One member, **Mary McLeod Bethune,** was a powerful champion of racial equality. However, African Americans continued to be victims of racial discrimination.

The **Indian New Deal** was a program to help American Indians by providing funding for the construction of new schools and hospitals. In 1934, the Indian Reorganization Act gave control of American Indian lands back to tribes. The Bureau of Indian Affairs also stopped discouraging the practice of traditional American Indian customs.

FDR united a culturally diverse group of Americans into a strong political force called the **New Deal coalition.** The coalition helped the Democratic Party gain a large majority in both houses of Congress. New Deal programs allowed people of different backgrounds to get to know one another, breaking down regional and ethnic prejudices.

Under the New Deal, both the size and scope of the federal government grew. The government took responsibility for providing for the welfare of children and the poor, elderly, sick, disabled, and unemployed. This led to the rise of a **welfare state.** This was a major change in government policy.

As the government grew, the executive branch got much more power. Roosevelt was elected President four times. After his death, a President's term of office was limited to two terms.

Review Questions

1. How did the New Deal affect American women?

____

____

2. How did the New Deal create a welfare state?

____

____

Note Taking Study Guide

CHAPTER 9 SECTION 4 · CULTURE OF THE 1930s

Focus Question: How did the men and women of the depression find relief from their hardships in the popular culture?

As you read, complete the table below to record examples of cultural or popular media.

Cultural or Popular Media	Example
Movies	
Radio	
Music	
Art	
Literature	

<table>
<tr><td>CHAPTER
9
SECTION 4</td><td>Section Summary
CULTURE OF THE 1930s</td></tr>
</table>

Entertainment became big business during the 1930s, creating a golden age in American culture. Radio ownership grew during the decade. Nearly two thirds of all Americans attended at least one movie a week.

The movies helped Americans escape the harsh realities of the Great Depression. Movies like *The Wizard of Oz* promised weary audiences that their dreams really could come true. Many films reflected the public's distrust of big business and government. The films of **Frank Capra** focused on American idealism and the triumph of the common man.

National radio networks broadcast dramas, comedies, soap operas, and variety shows. Episodes from *The Lone Ranger* began running in 1933 and lasted for more than 20 years. Sometimes the lines between news and entertainment were blurred. On October 30, 1938, the Mercury Theatre broadcast a drama called *War of the Worlds.* Many people panicked, believing that Martians were actually invading.

Music also provided a diversion from hard times. Americans listened to popular music on the radio or in nightclubs. They enjoyed "swing" music played by "big bands." Blues singers sang of harsh conditions faced by African Americans. Woody Guthrie wrote songs about Okies who fled the Dust Bowl.

For the first time, the federal government provided funding for the arts through programs such as the **Federal Art Project.** Artists were paid to paint huge **murals** on public buildings across the nation. The government also paid photographers such as **Dorothea Lange** to show the plight of America's farmers.

Many writers wrote novels about working-class heroes. **John Steinbeck's** *The Grapes of Wrath* is the story of the fictional Joad family. The novel follows the family from the Oklahoma Dust Bowl to California. **Lillian Hellman** wrote several plays featuring strong roles for women. Americans also enjoyed comic strips and comic books.

Review Questions

1. Why did the movies become popular during the 1930s?

____

____

2. What were some of the major themes of literature in the 1930s?

____

____

Note Taking Study Guide

DICTATORS AND WAR

Focus Question: Why did totalitarian states rise after World War I, and what did they do?

A. *As you read, summarize the actions in the 1930s of each of the countries listed in the table below.*

1930s Actions

Japan	Germany	Italy	Soviet Union
•	• Germany reclaims Saar region from France.	• Mussolini outlaws political parties, takes over the press, creates a secret police.	• Efforts to transform the Soviet Union into industrial power result in deaths of at least 10 million people.
•	•	•	•
	•	•	

Note Taking Study Guide
DICTATORS AND WAR

Focus Question: Why did totalitarian states rise after World War I, and what did they do?

B. *Use the concept web below to record the main ideas about the policies of Great Britain, France, and the United States toward aggressive nations.*

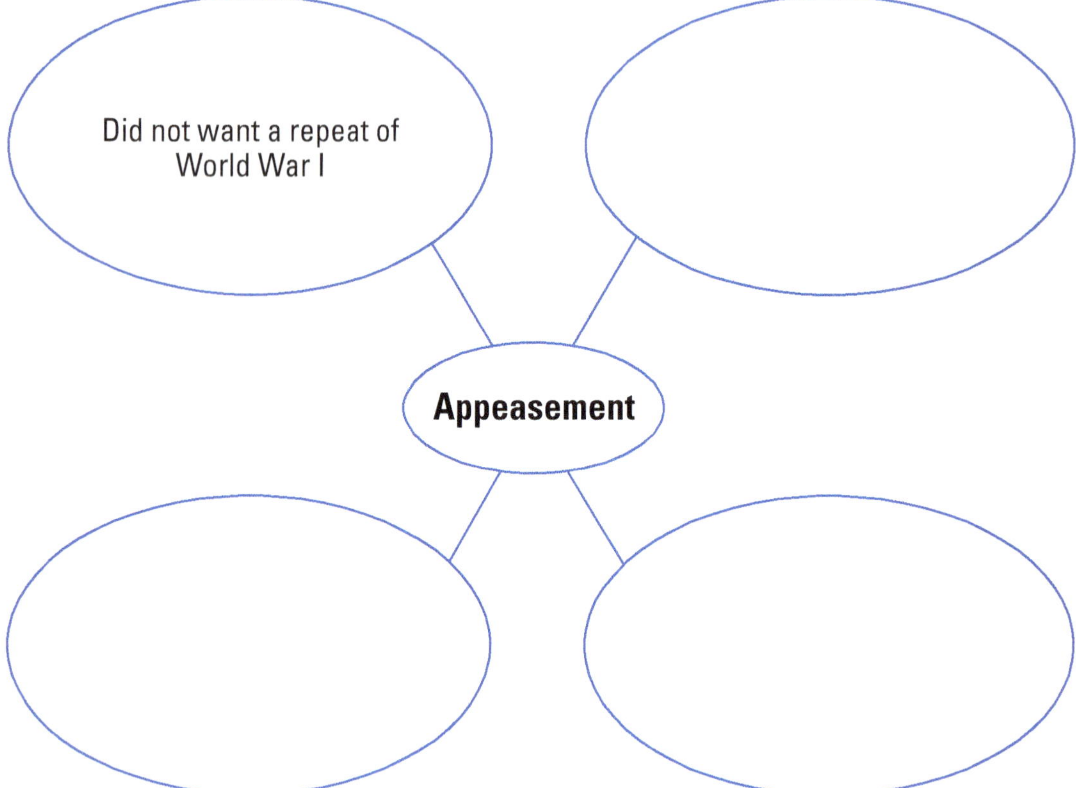

<table>
<tr><td>CHAPTER
10
SECTION 1</td><td><h1>Section Summary</h1>DICTATORS AND WAR</td></tr>
</table>

In the 1920s, some nations moved toward **totalitarianism,** a type of leadership in which a single party or leader completely controls the lives of its people.

The 1917 communist revolution in the Soviet Union produced the first totalitarian country. The leader Vladimir Lenin was replaced by **Joseph Stalin** in 1924.

After World War I, Italy had great money troubles. In 1922, the king asked **Benito Mussolini,** who founded a political party called the Fascists, to lead Italy and form a government. Mussolini controlled the press tightly, created secret police, and outlawed political parties.

Following World War I, Germany became a democracy. However, great money problems occurred in the 1930s. The Nazi Party led by **Adolf Hitler** rose to power. <u>Hitler criticized many people, political programs, and ideologies, but his sharpest assaults were against communists and Jews.</u> Hitler was **antisemitic,** or prejudiced against Jewish people. In 1933, he was appointed chancellor, and became president within two years.

In Japan, the Great Depression ended a period of increased democracy. Military leaders thought that expanding throughout Asia would solve Japan's money problems. Japan attacked Manchuria in 1931. In 1937, Japan raided the capital city of China, Nanjing, with terrible brutality.

In the 1930s, Italy and Germany acted aggressively like Japan did in Asia. Hitler took over the Saar region from French control and sent troops into the Rhineland, while Mussolini led an invasion into Ethiopia.

France, Britain, and the United States responded to the aggression of Italy, Germany, and Japan with the policy of **appeasement.** Appeasement means compromising with a potential enemy to maintain peace. However, this approach failed. Italy, Germany, and Japan grew more aggressive.

Review Questions

1. After World War I, what kind of government was set up in Germany? Who became the country's leader?

____

____

2. How did the military leaders of Japan want to solve the country's problems?

____

____

READING CHECK

How did Benito Mussolini come to rule Italy?

____

____

____

VOCABULARY STRATEGY

What does the word *ideologies* mean in the underlined sentence? What context clues can you find in the surrounding words or phrases? Circle any words or phrases in the paragraph that help you figure out what *ideologies* means.

____

____

____

READING SKILL

Summarize Name the countries and leaders discussed in this section.

____

____

____

CHAPTER 10
SECTION 2

Note Taking Study Guide

FROM ISOLATION TO INVOLVEMENT

Focus Question: How did Americans react to events in Europe and Asia in the early years of World War II?

Sequence the major events described in the section using the timeline below.

TIP: Search for dates throughout the section.

CHAPTER 10 SECTION 2

Section Summary

FROM ISOLATION TO INVOLVEMENT

In September 1939, Germany invaded Poland. Britain and France declared war on Germany. World War II had begun. Germany used a new kind of warfare called **blitzkrieg,** or "lightning war." <u>Tanks and planes attacked in a coordinated effort.</u> In this way, Germany quickly conquered Poland. In the spring of 1940, Germany conquered Denmark, Norway, the Netherlands, Belgium, and Luxembourg. Germany then invaded France. In July, Germany attacked Britain from the air.

Most Americans still did not want to get involved in the war. Isolationists in America believed that fighting in Europe would be wasteful and dangerous. It took two years before the United States joined the **Allies.** The Allies included Britain, France, and later, the Soviet Union and China. The Allies fought the **Axis Powers,** which included Germany, Italy, Japan, and several other nations.

Winston Churchill, the prime minister of Britain, often mentioned the United States in his speeches, hoping to convince America to join the Allies. Despite America's isolationism, Congress passed the **Neutrality Act of 1939.** This law was designed to help the Allies buy goods and war supplies from the United States.

President Roosevelt often talked about helping Britain. In early 1941, Congress approved the **Lend-Lease Act.** This act gave the President the power to sell, give, or lease weapons to protect the United States. All the aid went to the Allies.

Later in 1941, Roosevelt met with Churchill to discuss the war and their hopes for a peaceful world. They also signed the **Atlantic Charter,** a document that supported national self-determination and a worldwide plan for peace after the war.

Hitler knew the United States was helping the Allies. Therefore, in the fall of 1941 he ordered German U-boats to attack American ships. U.S. involvement in the war seemed unavoidable.

Review Questions

1. What nations made up the Axis Powers?

____

____

2. What was President Roosevelt's position on the war in Europe?

____

____

READING CHECK

What is a blitzkrieg?

____

____

____

VOCABULARY STRATEGY

What does the word *coordinated* mean in the underlined sentence? Circle the words in the underlined sentence that could help you learn what *coordinated* means. The word describes an important part of fighting a battle.

____

____

____

READING SKILL

Sequence List the countries Germany invaded by order of date.

____

____

____

CHAPTER 10 SECTION 3 — Note Taking Study Guide

AMERICA ENTERS THE WAR

Focus Question: How did the United States react to the Japanese attack on Pearl Harbor?

A. *As you read, record the causes and effects of the attack on Pearl Harbor, as well as details about the attack itself, in the chart below.*

TIP: Look for key words such as *attack* in the section.

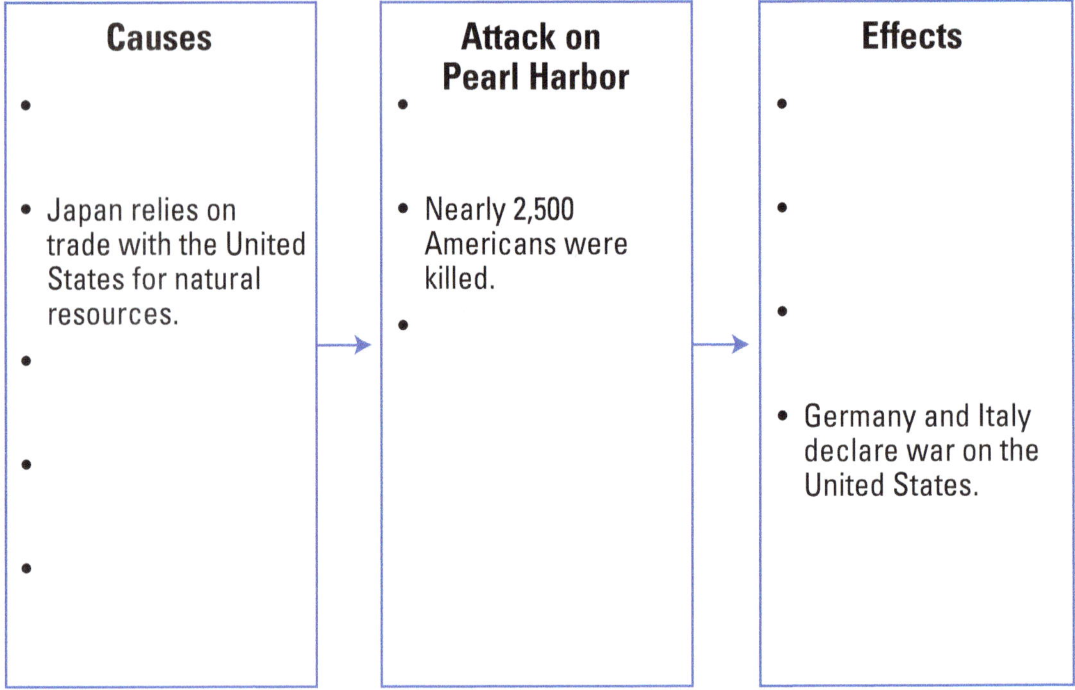

B. *Sequence the fighting that followed Pearl Harbor in the timetable below.*

TIP: Search for dates throughout the section.

Early War in the Pacific	
May 1942	The Philippines fall to the Japanese.
May 1942	Bataan Death March

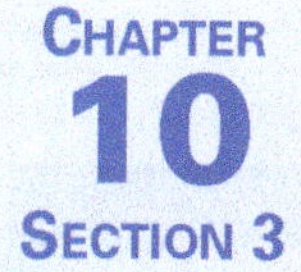

CHAPTER 10 SECTION 3

Section Summary

AMERICA ENTERS THE WAR

As Japan expanded its empire throughout Asia, its relationship with the United States worsened. Japan needed resources such as oil, steel, and rubber to maintain its military. The United States began to withhold these goods as a way to limit Japan's expansion. The United States also instituted a trade embargo against Japan.

Hideki Tojo, the Japanese prime minister, tried to reach a trade agreement with the United States. When he failed, Tojo decided to attack the United States. Hundreds of airplanes were launched from Japanese aircraft carriers. These planes bombed **Pearl Harbor,** Hawaii, the site of the United States Navy's main base in the Pacific. The surprise attack killed nearly 2,500 Americans and sunk many ships.

After the attack, Congress declared war on Japan. Because of their alliance with Japan, Germany and Italy declared war on the United States.

America prepared for war immediately. Men joined the military by the millions. Thousands of women joined the **Women's Army Corps (WAC)** as clerical workers, truck drivers, instructors, and lab technicians. The government created agencies to help produce military equipment. <u>These agencies allocated scarce materials to the proper industries.</u>

In Asia, United States Army General **Douglas MacArthur** struggled unsuccessfully to hold the Philippines against the Japanese forces. In May 1942, Japan defeated U.S. forces in the Philippines. Thousands of U.S. troops surrendered. Japanese troops forced these sick and malnourished men to march many miles. More than 7,000 of them died on the march known as the **Bataan Death March.**

In May 1942, the United States Navy finally stopped Japan's progress. At the **Battle of Coral Sea,** the navy prevented Japan from taking a key spot in New Guinea. This kept the Japanese from expanding further.

Review Questions

1. Why did the United States want to limit how much oil, steel, and rubber it sent to Japan?

____

____

2. What happened to U.S. forces in the Philippines?

____

____

Note Taking Study Guide

CHAPTER 11 SECTION 1

THE ALLIES TURN THE TIDE

Focus Question: How did the Allies turn the tide against the Axis?

List the ways in which the Allies turned back the Axis advance.

Turning Back the Axis	
In Europe	**In the Pacific**
• Battle against U-boats in Atlantic • Battle of Stalingrad • • • • British and American bombers batter Germany.	• Battle of Coral Sea • •

CHAPTER 11
SECTION 1

Section Summary
THE ALLIES TURN THE TIDE

The attack on Pearl Harbor brought the United States into World War II. <u>The Allies' ultimate goal was to fight and win a two-front war.</u> However, their first concern was to defeat Hitler. To do that, it was necessary to get American supplies to Europe. German U-boats sank thousands of supply ships. By mid-1943, the Allies were sinking U-boats faster than Germany could build them.

To prepare for an invasion of Italy, the Allies wanted to push the Germans out of North Africa. American General **Dwight Eisenhower** led the Allied invasion in February 1942. He put **George S. Patton, Jr.,** in charge of American forces. In May 1943, German and Italian forces in North Africa surrendered. FDR announced that only the **unconditional surrender** of the Axis Powers would end the war. This meant that they had to give up completely. In July 1943, British and American armies invaded Sicily, off the mainland of Italy. From there, they invaded Italy. In September, Italy surrendered.

In January 1943, the Russians turned back a German invasion at Stalingrad. Stalin demanded that Roosevelt and Churchill open a second front in France. In early 1942, British planes dropped large numbers of bombs on German cities. This was called **saturation bombing.** American bombers targeted key political and industrial centers. This was known as **strategic bombing.** An **African American** squadron known as the Tuskegee Airmen played a key role in the campaign.

The United States did not ignore the Pacific. Japanese forces continued to advance. In June 1942, the Japanese attacked Midway. Midway was an important American naval base in the central Pacific. Losing Midway would drive American defenses back to California. The American naval commander, Admiral **Chester Nimitz,** was prepared. The United States dealt Japan a decisive defeat. The **Battle of Midway** ended Japanese expansion.

Review Questions

1. What did the Allies do to weaken Germany?

____

____

2. Why was the Battle of Midway an important turning point in the war?

____

____

READING CHECK

Who were the Tuskegee Airmen?

____

____

____

VOCABULARY STRATEGY

Find the word *ultimate* in the underlined sentence. What do you think it means? Think about what the word *goal* means. The next sentence tells you that the Allies wanted to defeat Hitler first. That would be their first goal. Circle the word that you think means the same thing as *ultimate.*

- first
- final

READING SKILL

Summarize What steps did the Allies take to get ready to invade Italy?

____

____

Note Taking Study Guide

CHAPTER 11 SECTION 2

THE HOME FRONT

Focus Question: How did the war change America at home?

As you read, identify the major effects of World War II on the home front.

The Home Front, World War II

Economy

- War bonds
- Wage controls
-
-
-

Effects on Women

-
- New relationships
-
-

Effects on Minorities

-
-
- African Americans worked toward equal rights.
-
-

Section Summary

THE HOME FRONT

World War II provided new opportunities for women and minorities. Many women found jobs, especially in heavy industry where they had not worked before. In addition to a paycheck, they gained confidence, knowledge, and organizational skills.

At the same time, few African Americans could get jobs with defense employers. In response, they planned a massive protest march on Washington, D.C. To prevent this, FDR issued **Executive Order 8802.** It assured fair hiring practices in any job paid for by government money.

People began to move to the South and Southwest to get jobs in wartime industries. <u>To make up for the rural population drain, the United States initiated the **bracero program.**</u> It brought Mexican laborers to work on American farms. The braceros contributed greatly to the war effort.

After Pearl Harbor, the federal government moved 100,000 Japanese Americans away from the West Coast. They were placed in camps under an **internment** policy. There they were held in jail-like conditions for the rest of the war. Some Japanese Americans went to court to protest. In the 1944 case of *Korematsu* v. *United States,* the Supreme Court said the government had the right to intern people in wartime. In spite of this, the Japanese American **442nd Regimental Combat Team** fought in Italy. This team became the most decorated military unit in American history.

The war cost Americans $330 billion. To help pay for it, Congress placed a tax on all working Americans. To make sure that there would be enough raw materials for war production, a system of **rationing** was used. It limited the amount of certain goods people could buy. The federal **Office of War Information (OWI)** worked with the media to encourage support of the war effort. Americans bought war bonds. They also voluntarily contributed to the war effort in many other ways.

Review Questions

1. What benefits did women gain from work during World War II?

____

____

2. What happened to Japanese Americans during World War II?

____

____

CHAPTER 11
SECTION 3

Note Taking Study Guide
VICTORY IN EUROPE AND THE PACIFIC

Focus Question: How did the Allies defeat the Axis Powers?

Identify the steps that led to the Allied victory.

Europe	The Pacific
• Allies land at Normandy on D-Day.	•
•	
	• American forces capture Iwo Jima and Okinawa near Japan.
•	•
• Allies advance northward in Italy.	• Soviet Union declares war on Japan.
•	•

Allies Win World War II

CHAPTER 11 · SECTION 3

Section Summary

VICTORY IN EUROPE AND THE PACIFIC

June 6, 1944, is known as **D-Day.** It is the day that British and American forces invaded France from the west. More than 11,000 planes prepared the way. They were followed by more than 4,400 ships and landing crafts. By the end of D-Day, the Allies had gained a toehold in France. By July, more than one million Allied troops had landed.

Germany now faced a hopeless war on two fronts. In December 1944, Hitler ordered a major counterattack, known as the **Battle of the Bulge.** Hitler's scenario called for German forces to capture communication and transportation centers. The attack almost succeeded. However, Allied bombers came to help, and they successfully attacked German positions. The Allies then continued to push the Germans out of France. By April, the Soviet and United States armies were close to Berlin. On May 7, 1945, Germany surrendered.

American forces in the Pacific followed an **island-hopping** strategy. They took a steady path toward Japan. U.S. pilots finally made their way to the island of Okinawa in April 1945. From Okinawa, U.S. pilots bombed the Japanese home islands. They destroyed factories and military bases.

Advances in technology also helped the Allies win the war. **Albert Einstein** was a famous scientist. He had warned FDR of the need for atomic development. The program to develop the atomic bomb is known as the **Manhattan Project.** Physicist **J. Robert Oppenheimer** was in charge of the work. The first atomic bomb was tested on July 16, 1945. To save American lives and to end the war, President **Harry S. Truman** decided to use the atomic bomb against Japan. On August 6, 1945, U.S. pilots dropped an atomic bomb on Hiroshima. Three days later, the United States dropped another atomic bomb on Nagasaki. On August 15, Japan surrendered. World War II was over. It had been the most costly war in history. As many as 60 million people had died in the conflict.

Review Questions

1. Why was D-Day important?

____

____

2. Why did Truman use the atomic bomb against Japan?

____

____

READING CHECK

What was the Manhattan Project?

____

____

____

VOCABULARY STRATEGY

Find the word *scenario* in the underlined sentence. What does *scenario* mean? Circle any that help you figure out what *scenario* means.

____

____

____

READING SKILL

Recognize Sequence Which country surrendered first, Japan or Germany?

____

____

Name ______________________ Class ________________ Date ______

CHAPTER 11 SECTION 4

Note Taking Study Guide

THE HOLOCAUST

Focus Question: How did the Holocaust develop and what were its results?

A. *As you read, identify the steps that led to Hitler's attempt to exterminate European Jews.*

1933: Hitler becomes dictator of Germany; begins persecution of Jews.

↓

1933:

↓

1935:

↓

1938: Kristallnacht—Nazi officials order attacks on Jews in Germany.

↓

1933–1945:

↓

1945: Awareness of the Holocaust increases demand and support for an independent Jewish homeland.

Name ______________________ Class ____________________ Date _______

CHAPTER 11
SECTION 4

Note Taking Study Guide

THE HOLOCAUST

Focus Question: How did the Holocaust develop and what were its results?

B. *As you read, identify different ways in which the United States and other nations responded to the treatment of Jews in Nazi Germany before, during, and after the war.*

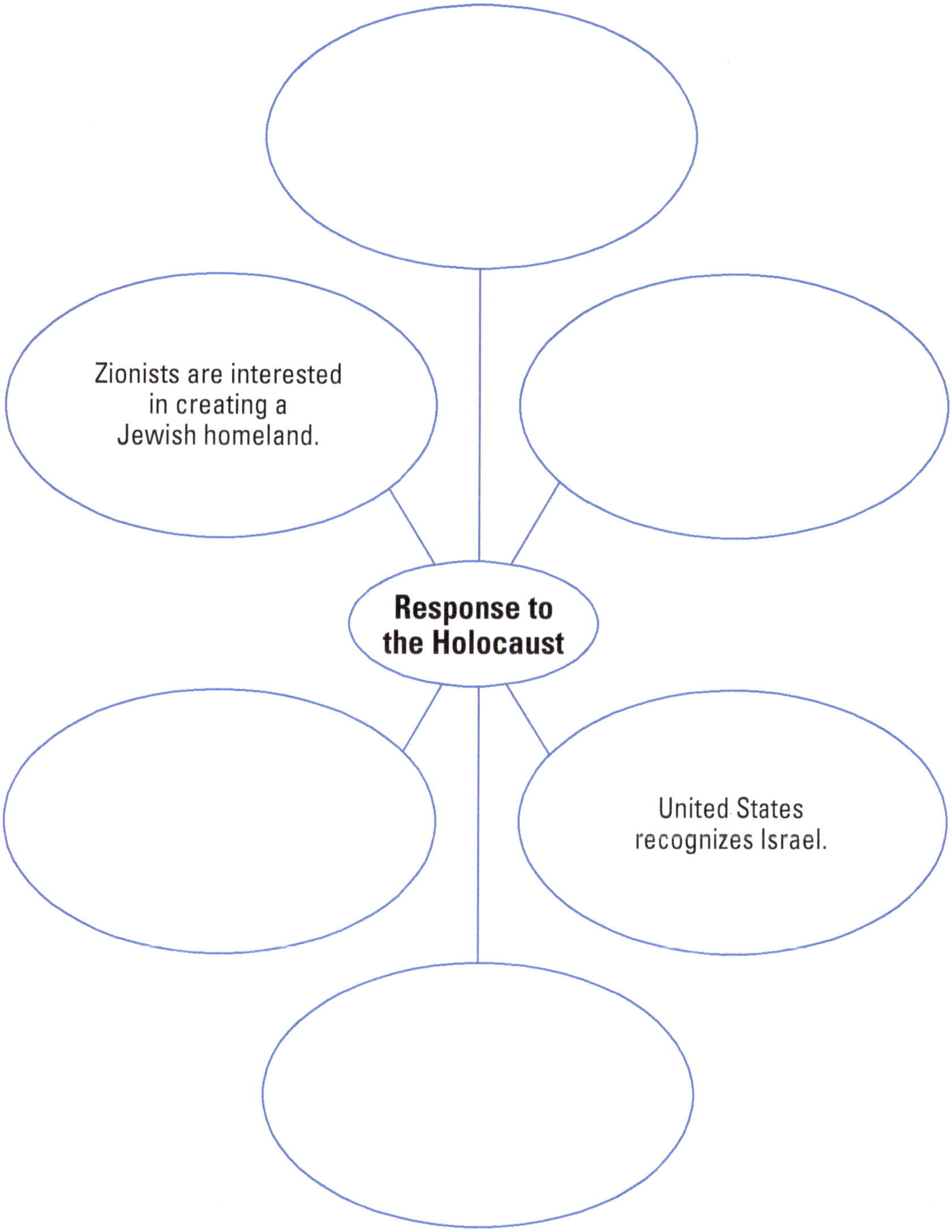

CHAPTER 11 SECTION 4

Section Summary

THE HOLOCAUST

The **Holocaust** was the Nazi attempt to kill all Jews, as well as other "undesirables," under their control. It was part of the Nazis' racist ideology. The Nazis considered white Northern European gentiles to be superior to other people. Hitler began to persecute the Jews as soon as he came to power. In 1935, the **Nuremberg Laws** denied Jews their German citizenship. The laws also segregated Jews at every level of society. Violence against Jews was common. The worst took place on November 9, 1938, which is known as **Kristallnacht,** the "Night of Broken Glass." Secret police and military units destroyed synagogues and Jewish businesses. They also killed more than 200 Jews and injured more than 600 others.

Hitler's "Final Solution to the Jewish question" was **genocide.** He wanted to kill all the Jews living in regions under his control. In 1933, Hitler opened the first Nazi **concentration camp.** Jews and other "undesirables" were placed in these camps. The camps were supposedly designed to turn prisoners into "useful members" of society. <u>There were no restraints on guards, who tortured and killed prisoners without fear of reprisals.</u> Doctors conducted cruel experiments that killed prisoners or left them deformed. Many concentration camps were **death camps.** There, prisoners were systematically killed.

Before the war, the United States and other countries could have done more. They could have relaxed immigration policies to let in more Jewish refugees. After war started, news of the mass killings began to reach the West. In early 1944, FDR formed the **War Refugee Board.** It worked with the Red Cross to save thousands of Eastern European Jews. However, most Americans did not realize the extent of the Nazi crime until Allied soldiers liberated the concentration camps. The revelation of the Holocaust increased American support for a Jewish state in Israel.

Review Questions

1. What was the purpose of Hitler's concentration camps?

____

____

2. How did the Americans respond to news about the Holocaust?

____

____

Name ______________________ Class ______________________ Date ________

CHAPTER 11 SECTION 5

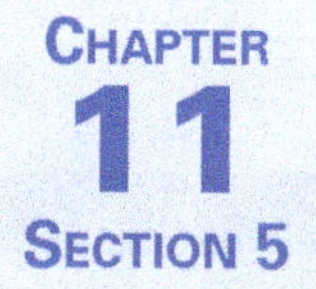

Note Taking Study Guide

EFFECTS OF THE WAR

Focus Question: What were the major immediate and long-term effects of World War II?

As you read, look for various developments in the postwar world that resulted from World War II.

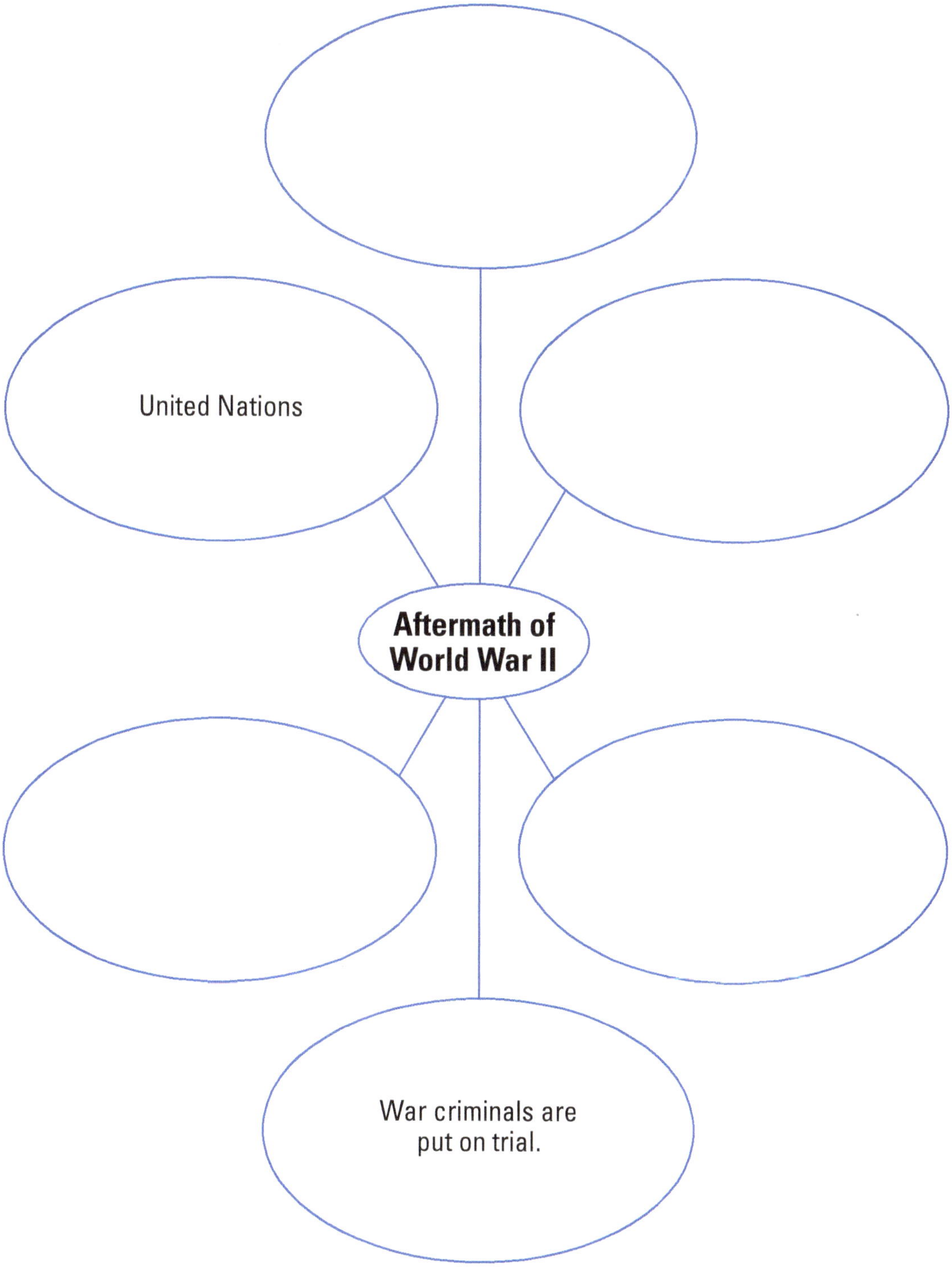

United Nations
Aftermath of World War II
War criminals are put on trial.

<table><tr><td>CHAPTER
11
SECTION 5</td><td>**Section Summary**
EFFECTS OF THE WAR</td></tr></table>

Japan and Germany kept fighting long after their defeat in the war was certain. This prolonged fighting gave the Allies time to make plans for a postwar world. In February 1945, Roosevelt, Churchill, and Stalin met at Yalta on the Black Sea. They discussed final strategy and the future of Germany, Eastern Europe, and Asia after the war. This meeting was called the **Yalta Conference.** A few months later, the Big Three, now composed of Stalin, Truman, and Atlee, met at Potsdam. There they agreed to divide Germany into four zones of occupation. Western domination of the world had ended. <u>Two superpowers—the United States and the Soviet Union—became the predominant nations of the postwar world.</u>

The postwar world did not turn out quite as the Allies had planned. Communists and noncommunists clashed in Eastern Europe. In China, civil war began once again. Japan gained a new constitution that abolished the armed forces and enacted democratic reforms. The United States had boomed economically during the war and helped to shape the postwar world economy. The United States also led the charge to establish the **United Nations (UN).** In 1948, the UN issued the **Universal Declaration of Human Rights.** This document condemns slavery and torture, upholds freedom of speech and religion, and affirms the right to an adequate standard of living.

During the war, the Axis Powers had repeatedly violated the **Geneva Convention.** This international agreement calls for the humane treatment of wounded soldiers and prisoners of war. At the end of the war, more than a thousand Japanese were tried for war crimes. At the **Nuremberg Trials** in Germany, key Nazi leaders were brought to justice for their crimes.

At the end of the war, Americans saw themselves as democratic, tolerant, and peaceful. The war renewed energy in the fight for civil rights at home. It also ushered in a long period of economic growth and prosperity.

Review Questions

1. What happened at the Yalta Conference?

____

____

2. How did Japan change as a result of World War II?

____

____

Note Taking Study Guide

THE COLD WAR BEGINS

Focus Question: How did U.S. leaders respond to the threat of Soviet expansion in Europe?

A. *As you read, contrast the conflicting goals of the United States and the Soviet Union.*

American Goals	Soviet Goals
Stop spread of communism	Spread communism beyond Eastern Europe

Name ______________________ Class __________________ Date _______

CHAPTER 12 SECTION 1

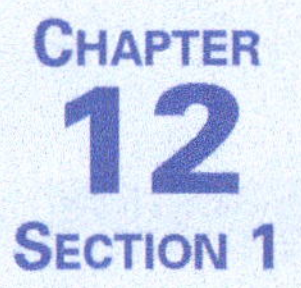

Note Taking Study Guide

THE COLD WAR BEGINS

Focus Question: How did U.S. leaders respond to the threat of Soviet expansion in Europe?

B. *As you read, trace events and developments in Europe that contributed to the growth of Cold War tensions.*

Yalta and Potsdam: Allies have conflicting goals for Eastern Europe.
↓
Stalin increases his control over Eastern European nations, making some of them Soviet satellites.
↓
↓
↓
↓
↓

<table>
<tr><td>

CHAPTER

12

SECTION 1

</td><td>

Section Summary
THE COLD WAR BEGINS

</td></tr>
</table>

In February 1945, Roosevelt, Stalin, and Churchill met at Yalta. The postwar goal of the United States and Great Britain was to create a united Germany and independent nations in Eastern Europe. The Soviet dictator Stalin wanted a weak, divided Germany and an Eastern Europe under communist control. He also took steps to make Poland, Czechoslovakia, Hungary, Romania, and Bulgaria **satellite states** of the Soviet Union. He did the same with the eastern part of Germany. The Allies met again at Potsdam. <u>It was then that President Harry S. Truman became certain that Stalin aspired to dominate the world. Thus began the 46-year-long **Cold War.**</u>

Churchill agreed with President Truman. Churchill spoke about an **iron curtain** that had divided Europe. East of the curtain, Stalin was increasing his control of some countries and trying to spread communism to others. Truman asked Congress for money to help Turkey and Greece fight communism. His promise of aid became known as the **Truman Doctrine**. It set a new course for American foreign policy.

Another American policy, called **containment,** also used financial aid to help nations fight communism. The **Marshall Plan** sent about $13 billion to Western European nations.

In 1948, Stalin tried to fold West Berlin into communist East Germany by blockading supplies to the city. The United States and Britain saved West Berlin by airlifting supplies to the city.

The **Berlin airlift** showed that communism could be contained. In 1949, the **North Atlantic Treaty Organization, NATO,** was formed. Twelve Western European and North American nations joined and agreed to act together to defend Western Europe. In 1955, West Germany joined NATO. The Soviet Union formed the **Warsaw Pact** as a response to NATO. All communist states of Eastern Europe except Yugoslavia promised to defend one another if attacked.

Review Questions

1. What was Truman's promise of aid to countries fighting communism called?

____

____

2. Which event proved that the policy of containment worked?

____

____

READING CHECK

President Truman asked Congress for aid for which two countries?

____

____

____

VOCABULARY STRATEGY

What does the word *aspired* mean in the underlined sentence? Circle the words in the underlined sentence that could help you learn what *aspired* means.

____

____

____

READING SKILL

Contrast What were the differences in goals between Stalin and the Soviets and Truman and the United States after World War II?

____

____

____

CHAPTER 12 SECTION 2

Note Taking Study Guide

THE KOREAN WAR

Focus Question: How did President Truman use the power of the presidency to limit the spread of communism in East Asia?

As you read, note problems and the steps that President Truman took to solve them. Use the problem-solution table below.

Problem	Solution
Communists threaten takeover of China.	United States sends aid to Chinese Nationalists fighting the communists.
Communist North Korea invades South Korea.	
	President Truman fires MacArthur.

Section Summary

THE KOREAN WAR

The Soviets had tried to export communism around the world for many years. They were sure that they would be successful. Events in China in 1949 seemed to prove them right.

Chinese Nationalist leader **Jiang Jieshi** (known as Chiang Kai-shek in the United States) and communist leader **Mao Zedong** teamed up to fight Japan during World War II. After the war, the two Chinese leaders became enemies again. The United States supported Jiang. The Soviet Union aided Mao. In 1949, Mao's communists took over the Chinese mainland.

The conflict over communism then moved to Korea. The United States and the Soviet Union had split Korea into two nations divided by the **38th parallel** of latitude after World War II. On June 25, 1950, North Korean troops, armed with Soviet weapons, attacked South Korea.

President Truman sent American troops to join South Korean and United Nations forces. General **Douglas MacArthur** organized a surprise attack on the port city of Inchon. The attack pushed the North Koreans back north into their own country.

Truman worried about what China might do if he continued the war. MacArthur told him China would not intervene and continued to push northward. Soon, however, 300,000 Chinese soldiers attacked. Truman did not want to expand the war. When MacArthur publicly criticized Truman's policy of a **"limited war,"** Truman fired him.

By the spring of 1951, the war had settled into a stalemate, or deadlock. President Eisenhower hinted that he might use nuclear weapons to end the war. A cease-fire was declared in 1953.

No side really won the Korean War. Korea is still divided. Some changes did result, however. Firstly, Truman's use of American forces expanded the power of the presidency. Secondly, a new alliance was formed to prevent communist aggression. It was called the **Southeast Asia Treaty Organization (SEATO).** SEATO is the Asian version of NATO.

Review Questions

1. What is the significance of the 38th parallel?

____

____

2. How did President Eisenhower cause the cease-fire that ended the Korean War?

____

____

READING CHECK

What did China do that MacArthur said would not happen?

____

____

____

VOCABULARY STRATEGY

What does the word *intervene* mean in the underlined sentence? Look at the context clues in the sentence to help you figure out what the word means. Circle the words that could help you learn what *intervene* means.

____

____

____

READING SKILL

Categorize What idea and event led Truman to fire MacArthur?

____

____

____

CHAPTER 12
SECTION 3

Note Taking Study Guide
THE COLD WAR EXPANDS

Focus Question: What methods did the United States use in its global struggle against the Soviet Union?

Identify the tactics used to wage the Cold War.

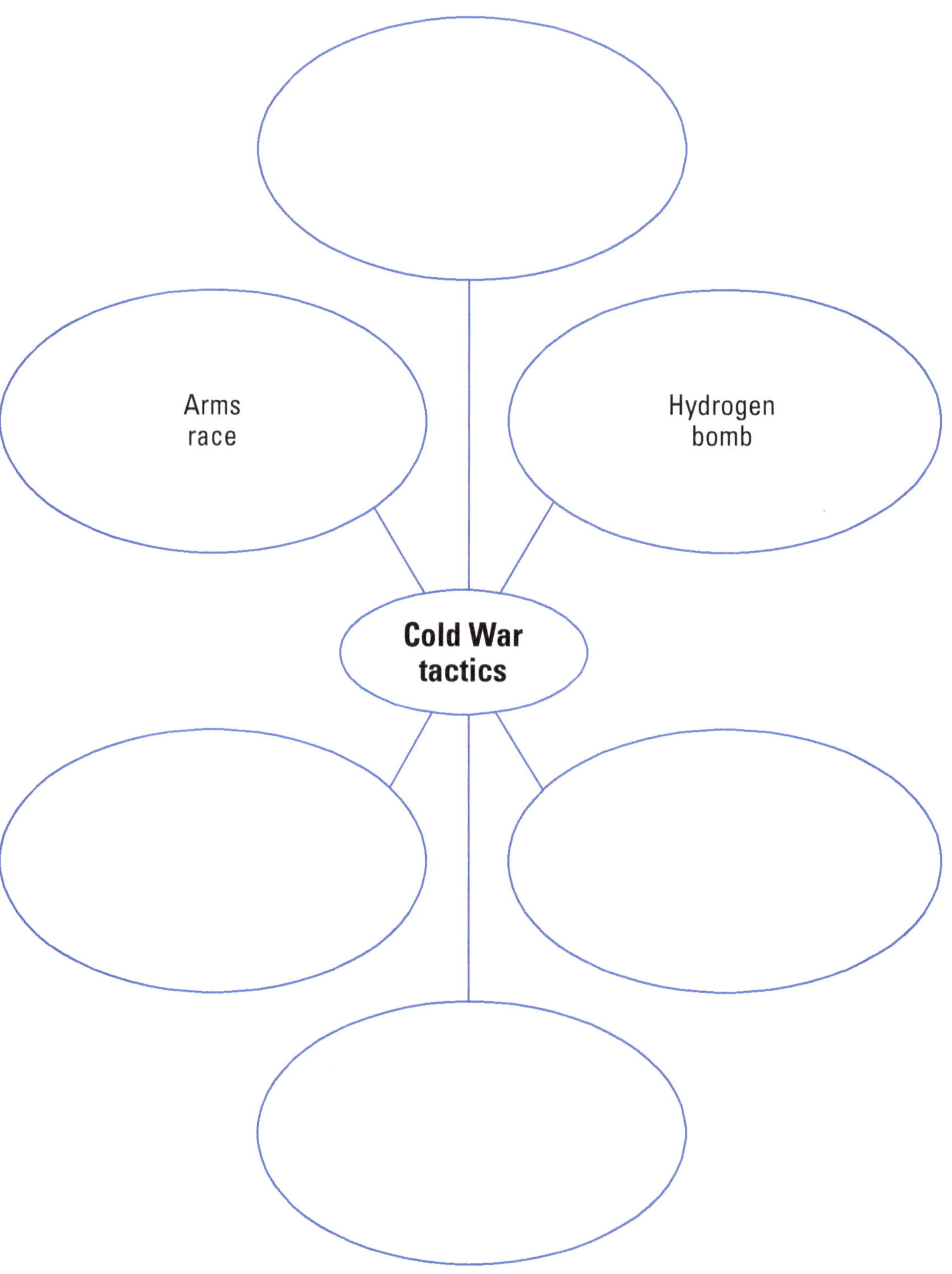

Section Summary
THE COLD WAR EXPANDS

On September 2, 1949, America learned that the Soviets had an atomic bomb. The next month, communists took over China.

Truman soon ordered the development of a hydrogen bomb. <u>Some scientists warned that this development would lead to a perpetual **arms race.**</u> For the next four decades, the United States and the Soviet Union built and stockpiled nuclear weapons. Each country had more then enough weapons to destroy the other. They hoped that this threat of **mutually assured destruction** would keep the weapons from being used.

President Eisenhower continued to build nuclear weapons and emphasized **massive retaliation.** Secretary of State John Foster Dulles believed in brinkmanship. This meant going to the brink of war to discourage the spread of communism.

Nikita Khrushchev became the leader of the Soviet Union in 1953. He continued to try to spread communism. In 1956, workers in Poland rioted against Soviet rule, and won greater control of their government. When students and workers in Hungary tried the same thing, Khrushchev crushed the revolt.

In 1956 Egypt's president, Gamal Abdel Nasser, wanted to build a dam on the Nile River. When Egypt recognized communist China and began talks with the Soviet Union, the United States cut off aid. Nasser responded by **nationalizing** the Suez Canal. This led to the **Suez crisis,** and British and French forces attacked Egypt. When the United States criticized the invasion, Britain and France withdrew.

Eisenhower then announced that the United States would use force to help any nation threatened by communism. This **Eisenhower Doctrine** was used to ensure pro-American governments in Lebanon, Iran, and Guatemala.

In 1957, the Soviets launched the satellite *Sputnik 1.* Congress, alarmed, passed an act to produce more scientists and created the **National Aeronautics and Space Administration (NASA).**

Review Questions

1. How was the policy of massive retaliation supposed to stop communist aggression?

____

____

2. What three countries were the focus of the Eisenhower Doctrine?

____

____

CHAPTER 12
SECTION 4

Note Taking Study Guide
THE COLD WAR AT HOME

Focus Question: How did fear of domestic communism affect American society during the Cold War?

A. *List efforts taken to protect Americans from communism and how these policies affected rights.*

Anticommunist Policy	Effect on Rights
Federal Employee Loyalty Program	About 3,000 federal employees lose their jobs.

B. *As you read, identify similarities and differences between the Hiss case and the Rosenberg case. Consider both the facts and the impact of the two spy cases.*

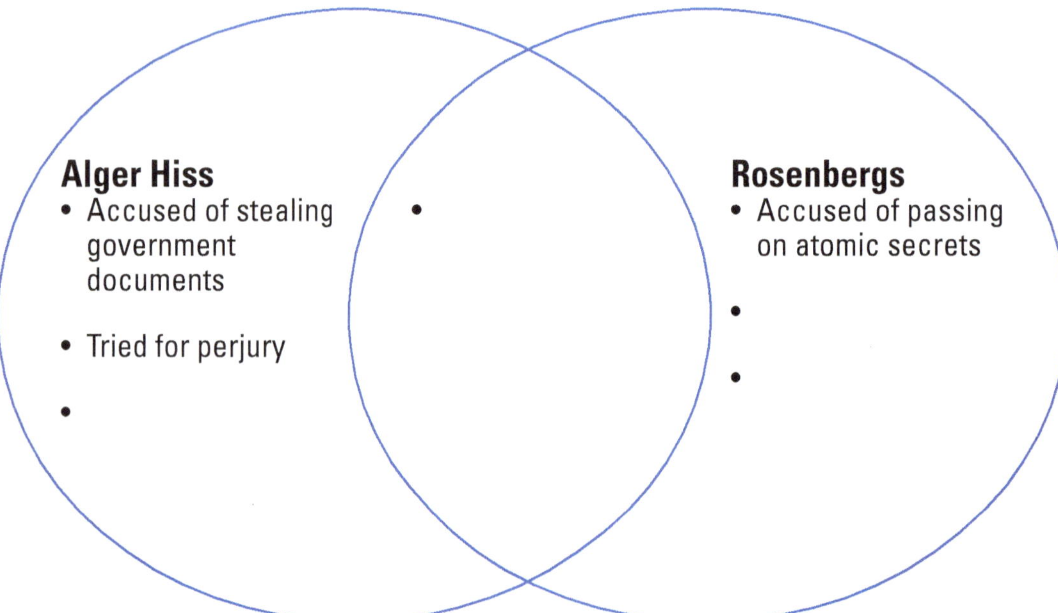

<table><tr><td>**CHAPTER 12**
SECTION 4</td><td>## Section Summary
THE COLD WAR AT HOME</td></tr></table>

The **Red Scare** was the public's fear that communists were working at home and in other countries to destroy the United States. This fear caused President Truman to screen federal employees for disloyalty. The Truman administration also used the **Smith Act** to cripple the Communist Party in the United States. This act made it illegal to promote or teach the violent overthrow of the government.

The **House Committee on Un-American Activities (HUAC)** also used its power to investigate communist activities. In 1947, HUAC went after a group of left-wing writers, directors, and producers. The **Hollywood Ten** refused to testify against themselves. They were sent to prison anyway. A **blacklist** named entertainment figures who were thought to have communist ties. Communists working in academic institutions, labor unions, and city halls were also blacklisted.

Two sensational spy trials increased the country's suspicion of communists. **Alger Hiss,** a government employee who had helped organize the United Nations, was accused of being a spy. Hiss denied the charges but was still sentenced to prison. The second trial involved **Julius and Ethel Rosenberg.** They were accused of passing secret information about nuclear science to Soviet agents. Although the trial was controversial, the couple was executed in 1953.

Joseph R. McCarthy, a senator from Wisconsin, claimed he had a long list of communists who were working in the State Department. He never produced the list. With the outbreak of the Korean War in 1950, however, McCarthy's popularity soared. **McCarthyism** became a catchword for making vicious and reckless charges. In 1954, McCarthy went after the United States Army. He lost his strongest supporters after he badgered witnesses and twisted the truth during hearings that were shown on television. The end of the Korean War in 1953 and McCarthy's downfall in 1954 brought the end of the Red Scare.

Review Questions

1. How were the Smith Act and the HUAC meant to discourage communism in the United States?

____

____

2. What events led to the end of the Red Scare?

____

____

READING CHECK

What happened to the Hollywood Ten?

____

____

____

VOCABULARY STRATEGY

What does the word *academic* mean in the underlined sentence? Use your prior knowledge to help you figure out what *academic* means.

____

____

____

READING SKILL

Identify Causes and Effects
Discuss the events that led to McCarthyism.

____

____

____

Name ______________________ Class ____________________ Date _______

CHAPTER 13 SECTION 1

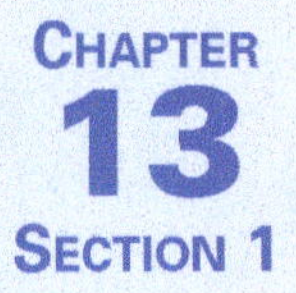

Note Taking Study Guide

AN ECONOMIC BOOM

Focus Question: How did the nation experience recovery and economic prosperity after World War II?

List the problems raised by the shift to a peacetime economy and the steps taken to solve them.

United States After WWII

Problem	Solution
• Returning soldiers need jobs.	• GI Bill
•	•
• Striking union workers	•

Section Summary
AN ECONOMIC BOOM

When World War II ended, the production of military supplies stopped. Millions of American workers lost their jobs. Many feared the return of economic problems. Instead, America experienced the longest period of economic growth in its history.

President Harry Truman **demobilized,** or sent members of the army home. To calm fears about the economy, the government passed the **GI Bill of Rights.** The bill gave veterans unemployment benefits and financial aid for college. Veterans also received home loans, leading to an upsurge in home construction. Many veterans started families, creating a **baby boom.** Between 1940 and 1955, the U.S. population grew by 27 percent.

At the same time, demand for consumer products increased. Businesses employed more people to produce these goods. The United States soon dominated the world economy, producing nearly 50 percent of the world's total output.

Prices and inflation rose. Trade unionists demanded pay increases to keep up with inflation. Employers refused and millions of workers went on strike. Congress then enacted the **Taft-Hartley Act** to outlaw closed shops, workplaces that hired only union members.

Truman supported civil rights by desegregating the military. However, his support for civil rights angered Southern Democrats. During the 1948 presidential election, unhappy Democrats established two new political parties. Many thought that the Republican candidate, Thomas Dewey, would win. However, Truman won by a narrow margin.

Truman introduced the **Fair Deal** to strengthen existing New Deal reforms and establish new ones. However, Congress did not pass many of the proposals. In 1952, Republican Dwight Eisenhower won the presidency. Eisenhower's presidency was one of the most prosperous, peaceful, and politically tranquil in the twentieth century.

Review Questions

1. Why did many people worry about economic problems after World War II?

____

____

2. Why did Congress enact the Taft-Hartley Act?

____

____

READING CHECK

By what percentage did the U.S. population grow between 1940 and 1955?

____

____

____

VOCABULARY STRATEGY

What does the word *upsurge* mean in the underlined sentence? The word *decrease* is an antonym of *upsurge.* Use the meaning of the antonym and context clues to help you figure out the meaning of *upsurge.*

____

____

____

READING SKILL

Understand Effects How did the GI Bill benefit the American economy?

____

____

____

CHAPTER 13 SECTION 2

Note Taking Study Guide

A SOCIETY ON THE MOVE

Focus Question: What social and economic factors changed American life during the 1950s?

A. *Complete the chart below to capture the main ideas.*

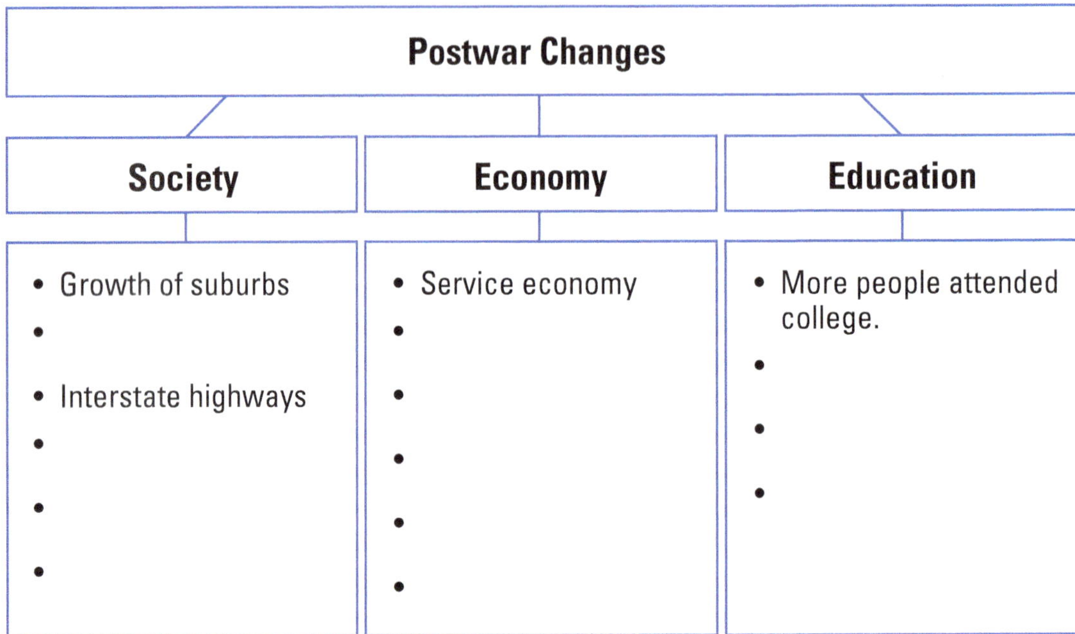

B. *As you read, identify the effects of the population shift to the Sunbelt.*

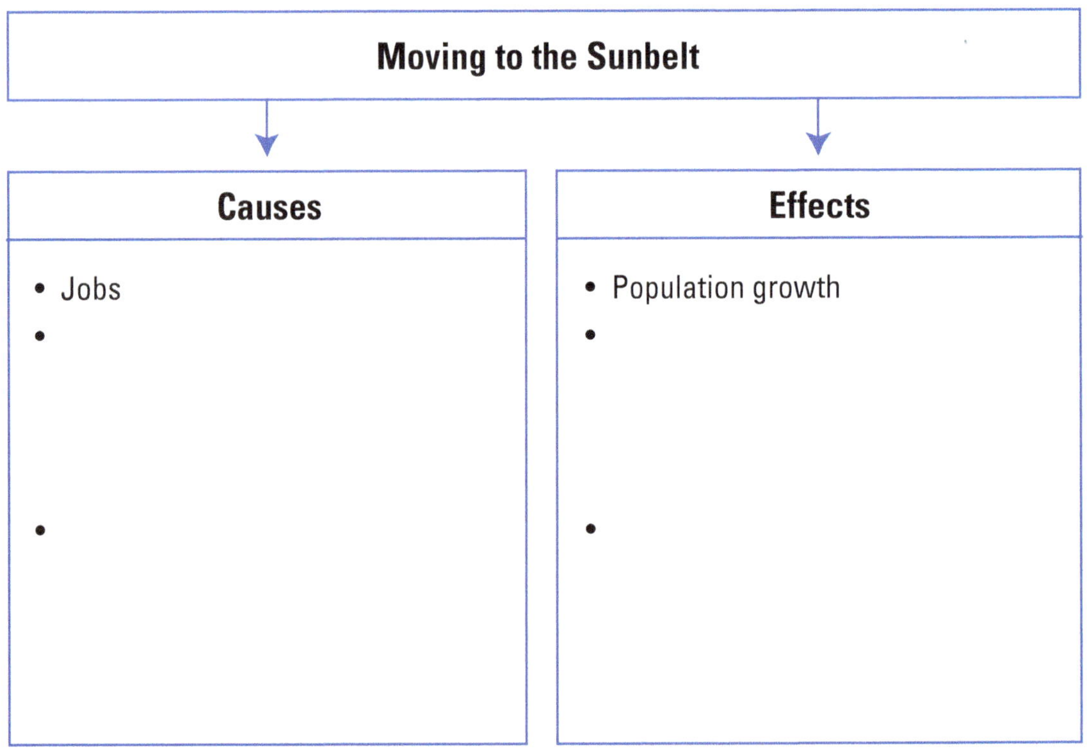

Section Summary
A SOCIETY ON THE MOVE

In the years following World War II, many Americans moved to the suburbs. Developers built affordable housing in a hurry. The government provided low-interest loans so that more people could purchase homes.

The growth of suburbs caused Americans to become even more dependent on their cars. In 1956, Congress passed the **Interstate Highway Act.** This act approved the building of new highways to connect the nation's major cities. These highways eased the commute from suburbs to cities.

Southern and western states, known as the **Sunbelt,** also experienced rapid growth. The climate in the Sunbelt appealed to many Americans. In addition, the Sunbelt held a large number of jobs in the defense industry. As people moved, their political power moved with them.

At the same time, the American economy was changing dramatically. Many people took jobs in the **service sector,** where they provided services such as healthcare, law, retail, banking, or insurance. Others worked in **information industries,** including those related to computers. **Franchise businesses** allowed companies to sell their products and services through retail outlets owned by independent operators. **Multinational corporations** also expanded. These companies produced and sold their goods and services all over the world.

Unions experienced change as well. In 1955, the AFL and the CIO joined to form the **AFL-CIO.** The new organization had more political power.

As the economy grew, so did educational opportunities. By the early 1960s, more Americans were going to college. The federal government and many states increased funding to public universities. California undertook a **California Master Plan.** This plan created three levels of higher education: research universities, state colleges, and community colleges.

Review Questions

1. Name the three things that fostered suburban growth.

____

____

2. What industries and types of businesses saw job growth in the postwar period?

____

____

CHAPTER 13 SECTION 3

Note Taking Study Guide

MASS CULTURE AND FAMILY LIFE

Focus Question: How did popular culture and family life change during the 1950s?

Identify postwar changes in daily life and popular culture.

I. The Culture of Consumerism
- **A.** Americans spend more
  - **1.** Increased family income
  - **2.** ____
- **B.** New conveniences
  - **1.** Supermarkets
  - **2.** ____

II. Family life in the Fifties
- **A.** ____
  - **1.** Nuclear family
  - **2.** ____
- **B.** ____
  - **1.** ____
  - **2.** ____
- **C.** ____
  - **1.** ____
  - **2.** ____
- **D.** ____
  - **1.** ____
  - **2.** ____

III. Television Takes Center Stage
- **A.** ____
- **B.** ____

IV. Rock-and-Roll Shakes the Nation
- **A.** ____
- **B.** ____
  - **1.** ____
  - **2.** ____

CHAPTER 13 SECTION 3 — Section Summary

MASS CULTURE AND FAMILY LIFE

After World War II, the U.S. economy began to prosper. Americans bought as much as they could in a wave of **consumerism. Median family income** is average family income. It rose dramatically during this period. Shopping became a national pastime.

During the 1950s, a more traditional image of the family took hold. According to this image, men worked and women stayed home. A **nuclear family** is a household made up of a mother and father and their children. The nuclear family was seen as the backbone of American society. For the nuclear family to function smoothly, experts claimed, women had to accept their role as homemakers. <u>Nevertheless, as the 1950s progressed, more women challenged this view.</u>

More so than in the past, family life revolved around children. Dr. **Benjamin Spock's** *Common Sense Book of Baby and Child Care* was the best-selling book of the era. Spock emphasized the importance of nurturing children. He suggested that children could not get too much comfort and love. Parents were also spending more money on their children. Some parents defended their spending. They thought it would stop a recurrence of economic depression.

During this period, regular church attendance rose. At the same time, several advances in medicine were made. Antibiotics were widely used to help control infectious diseases.

Television changed American society, particularly family life. Children watched cartoons. Sitcoms about families strengthened the ideal of the 1950s family. Television also helped to create a national culture because Americans in every region of the country watched the same shows.

Like television, **rock-and-roll** appealed to Americans. Rock-and-roll borrowed from the rhythm and blues music of African Americans. Singer **Elvis Presley** set off this new craze. His first hit, "Heartbreak Hotel" sold in the millions. Rock music symbolized the growing influence of youths on American culture.

Review Questions

1. Why did shopping become a new national pastime?

____

____

2. Who was Dr. Benjamin Spock?

____

____

READING CHECK

What medical advancement helped control infectious diseases?

____

____

____

VOCABULARY STRATEGY

Find the word *nevertheless* in the underlined sentence. What does *nevertheless* mean? Look for clues in nearby words and phrases. Circle any that help you figure out what *nevertheless* means.

____

____

____

READING SKILL

Identify Main Ideas How did television and rock-and-roll impact postwar American society?

____

____

____

Name ______________________ Class ____________________ Date _______

CHAPTER 13 SECTION 4

Note Taking Study Guide

DISSENT AND DISCONTENT

Focus Question: Why were some groups of Americans dissatisfied with conditions in postwar America?

Record the main ideas and supporting details.

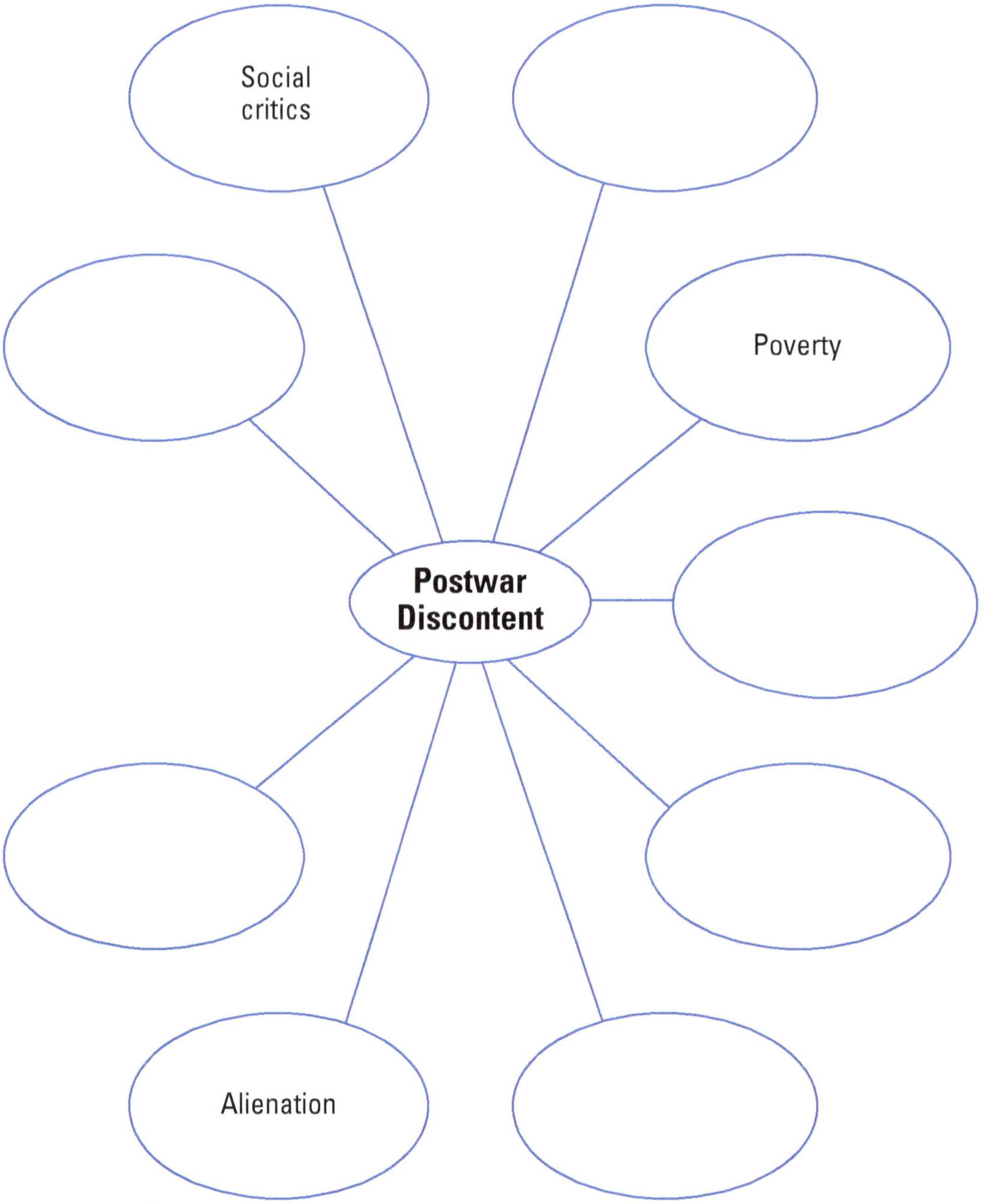
Social critics
Poverty
Postwar Discontent
Alienation

Section Summary

DISSENT AND DISCONTENT

Not everyone benefited from the economic prosperity of the 1950s. <u>Some Americans were unhappy with the changes brought by affluence.</u> A small group of writers and artists known as **beatniks** criticized the middle class for encouraging materialism and conformity. Popular authors wrote about alienation, or the feeling of being cut off.

At the same time, many Americans faced urban slums, rural poverty, and discrimination. In his book *The Other America*, Michael Harrington argued that poverty was widespread in the United States. According to Harrington, poverty afflicted inner-city African Americans, rural whites, and Hispanics in migrant farm camps and urban barrios. Harrington's statements shocked many Americans.

As the middle class moved from the cities to the suburbs, cities lost revenue and political power. Minorities in search of better economic opportunities moved to these **inner cities.** Strained city services such as garbage removal deteriorated, and crime increased. The government funded **urban renewal** projects to try to restore downtowns by creating developments. These projects often pushed people from their homes into areas that were already overcrowded. The federal government also tried to ease the shortage of affordable housing by constructing public housing. However, the housing was often built in poor neighborhoods. This, in turn, further concentrated poverty and problems such as crime.

Rural poor also relocated to cities. Small farmers slipped into poverty. They could not compete with the corporations that dominated farm production.

Latinos and Native Americans struggled with many of the same problems as African Americans. In 1953, the federal government enacted the **termination policy.** This law sought to end tribal government and to relocate Native Americans to the nation's cities. Supporters thought it would help Native Americans assimilate, or merge, into American society.

Review Questions

1. List three problems many minorities faced in the 1950s.

____

____

2. How did cities change in this period?

____

____

CHAPTER 14

SECTION 1

Note Taking Study Guide

EARLY DEMANDS FOR EQUALITY

Focus Question: How did African Americans challenge segregation after World War II?

Fill in the timeline below with events of the early civil rights movement. When you finish, write two sentences that summarize the information in your timeline.

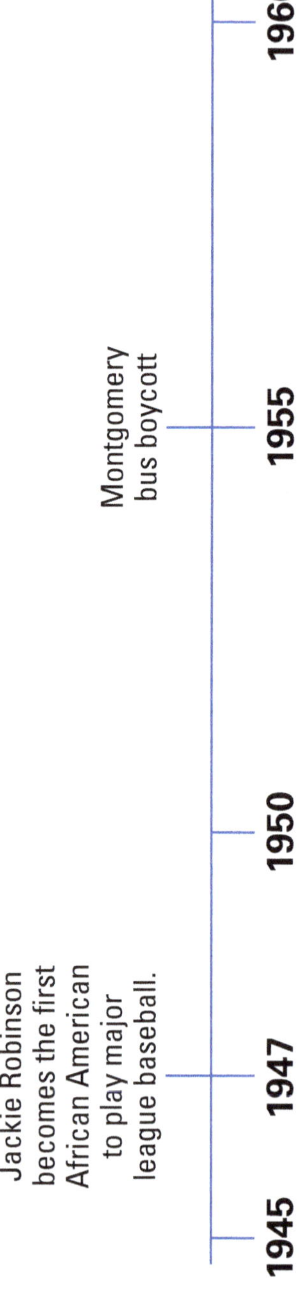

____

____

Section Summary
EARLY DEMANDS FOR EQUALITY

In the South, African Americans were separated from white Americans. Jim Crow laws made this separation legal. Segregation that is enforced by law is called **de jure segregation.** African Americans in the North also faced segregation, even where there were no explicit laws. Segregation by tradition is known as **de facto segregation.**

In the 1950s, the NAACP turned to the federal courts to end segregation. In *Brown v. Board of Education,* the NAACP challenged segregation in public schools. **Thurgood Marshall,** an African American lawyer, was part of the legal team. The Supreme Court agreed that segregation in public schools was illegal. Chief Justice **Earl Warren** wrote the *Brown* decision. He declared that the idea of "separate but equal" was wrong.

However, southern states found ways to resist compliance with the law. In Little Rock, Arkansas, nine African American students volunteered to desegregate the high school. The governor ordered the National Guard to stop the students from entering the school. President Eisenhower then sent federal troops to protect the students.

In 1955, **Rosa Parks,** an African American woman who lived in Montgomery, Alabama, refused to give up her bus seat to a white passenger. She was arrested. Civil rights activists organized a bus boycott to protest her arrest. On the evening following the boycott, a Baptist minister named **Martin Luther King, Jr.,** spoke to a group of African Americans. He asked them to protest segregation in a nonviolent way. The **Montgomery bus boycott** continued for over a year.

In 1956, the Supreme Court ruled that the Montgomery law that segregated buses was illegal. The boycott showed that African Americans could be powerful if they worked together. The protest also made King very important within the civil rights movement.

Review Questions

1. Why was *Brown* v. *Board of Education* important?

____

____

2. How did the Montgomery bus boycott help the civil rights movement?

____

____

READING CHECK

What action did the governor of Arkansas take to prevent the desegregation of schools in Little Rock?

____

____

____

VOCABULARY BUILDER

Find the word *compliance* in the underlined sentence. What do you think it means? Here is a clue. An antonym for *compliance* is *disobedience.* Use this clue to figure out what *compliance* means.

____

____

____

READING SKILL

Summarize List three key events of the 1950s that helped to end segregation.

____

____

Name ____________________ Class ____________________ Date ________

CHAPTER 14 SECTION 2

Note Taking Study Guide

THE MOVEMENT GAINS GROUND

Focus Question: How did the civil rights movement gain ground in the 1960s?

Use the concept web below to record information about the civil rights protests of the 1960s.

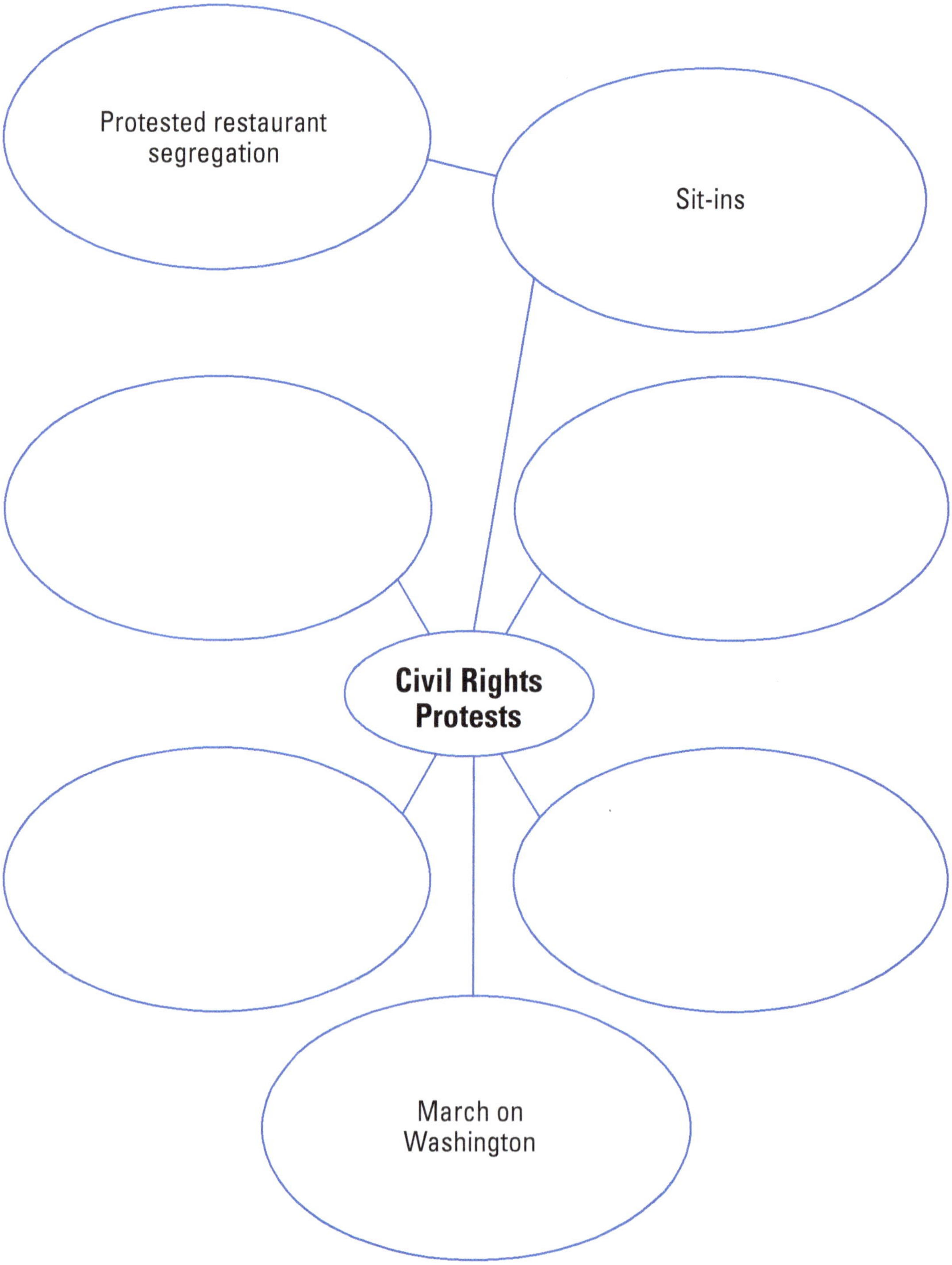
Protested restaurant segregation
Sit-ins
Civil Rights Protests
March on Washington

<table>
<tr><td>

CHAPTER

14

SECTION 2

</td><td>

Section Summary
THE MOVEMENT GAINS GROUND

</td></tr>
</table>

Despite some victories, activists continued to struggle for civil rights for African Americans. In North Carolina, four college students started a sit-in at a restaurant to protest discrimination. This **sit-in** led to sit-ins across the nation. A new civil rights organization, the **Student Nonviolent Coordinating Committee,** or **SNCC,** began a grass-roots movement.

The next battleground was interstate transportation. The Supreme Court had ruled that segregation on interstate buses was illegal. In 1961, riders set off on two buses on a **"freedom ride."** After the freedom riders met with violence, President John F. Kennedy intervened. The riders were successful.

In 1962, **James Meredith** enrolled at the all-white University of Mississippi. Civil rights activist **Medgar Evers** helped win the federal court case that ordered the university to desegregate. A riot broke out the night before Meredith's arrival. Still, Meredith went on to graduate.

In 1963, Martin Luther King, Jr., began a civil rights campaign in Birmingham, Alabama. It began with nonviolent marches and sit-ins. However, Birmingham's Public Safety Commissioner would not tolerate the demonstrations. He used police dogs and fire hoses on the peaceful protesters. Many Americans were shocked by images of violence on the news.

To put pressure on Congress to pass a new civil rights bill, supporters planned a **March on Washington.** On August 28, 1963, more than 200,000 Americans gathered in Washington, D.C. The highlight was King's "I Have a Dream" speech.

On November 22, 1963, President Kennedy was assassinated. Vice President Lyndon B. Johnson became President. Johnson used his political skills to gain the passage of the **Civil Rights Act of 1964.** This act banned segregation in public places. The civil rights movement had changed the relationships between races. It also set the stage for future reforms.

Review Questions

1. What was the purpose of the March on Washington?

____

____

2. Describe the Civil Rights Act of 1964.

____

____

Note Taking Study Guide

NEW SUCCESSES AND CHALLENGES

Focus Question: What successes and challenges faced the civil rights movement after 1964?

Complete the outline below to summarize the contents of this section.

I. **Push for Voting Rights**

   A. Freedom Summer

   B. ____

II. **Frustration Explodes into Violence**

   A. ____

   B. ____

III. **New Voices for African Americans**

   A. ____

   B. ____

IV. ____

   A. King continues to seek nonviolent methods.

   B. ____

V. ____

   A. ____

   B. ____

<table>
<tr><td>CHAPTER
14
SECTION 3</td><td>**Section Summary**
NEW SUCCESSES AND CHALLENGES</td></tr>
</table>

The civil rights movement had made some progress. However, many African Americans were still unable to vote. In 1964, the SNCC organized a project known as **Freedom Summer.** Volunteers registered African Americans to vote in Mississippi.

In 1965, Martin Luther King, Jr., organized a march in Selma, Alabama. He wanted the government to pass laws to protect voting rights. <u>The march met with a series of violent confrontations.</u> Television coverage of the violence outraged the nation. In response, Congress passed the **Voting Rights Act** of 1965. This law banned literacy tests. In 1964, the **Twenty-fourth Amendment** banned the poll tax. It had been used to keep poor African Americans from voting.

Some African Americans were angry that discrimination and poverty continued. In many cities, this anger led to violent riots. The **Kerner Commission** was established to figure out the cause of the riots. The commission blamed discrimination against African Americans over a long period of time.

At the same time, many young African Americans were becoming more radical. **Malcolm X** was the most well-known African American radical. He was a minister of the **Nation of Islam.** This religious group demanded that the races be separated. However, Malcolm X was shot and killed in 1965.

Many young African Americans wanted to continue the policies of Malcolm X. They no longer supported the idea of nonviolence. SNCC leader Stokely Carmichael thought African Americans needed **"black power."** He wanted African Americans to use their economic and political power to gain equality. Not long after, the Black Panther Party was formed. The **Black Panthers** became the symbol of young militant African Americans.

In 1968, Martin Luther King, Jr., was assassinated. The civil rights movement had made segregation illegal. However, the radical methods that had been used left some people bitter.

Review Questions

1. Why was the march in Selma important?

____

____

2. Why did violence occur in many American cities during the 1960s?

____

____

READING CHECK

Which group became the symbol for young militant African Americans?

____

____

____

VOCABULARY BUILDER

Find the word *confrontations* in the underlined sentence. What does *confrontations* mean? Look for clues in nearby words or phrases. Circle any that help you figure out what *confrontations* means.

____

____

____

READING SKILL

Summarize Summarize the effect Malcolm X had on the civil rights movement.

____

____

____

CHAPTER 15 SECTION 1

Note Taking Study Guide

KENNEDY AND THE COLD WAR

Focus Question: How did Kennedy respond to the continuing challenges of the Cold War?

As you read, list the Cold War crises Kennedy faced and the effects of each event.

TIP: Look for the part of the section that is organized into three events.

Cold War Crisis	Result
Bay of Pigs Invasion	• Invasion plan failed. • •
Cuban Missile Crisis	• • • •
Berlin Wall	• • • • •

<table><tr><td>**CHAPTER**
15
SECTION 1</td><td>## Section Summary
KENNEDY AND THE COLD WAR</td></tr></table>

Democrat **John F. Kennedy** and Republican **Richard M. Nixon** ran against each other for the office of President in 1960. Kennedy won the election narrowly. He succeeded partly because of his good performance in a television debate.

As President, Kennedy expanded the military. He wanted a **"flexible response"** policy, which meant that the military would be able to fight many different kinds of battles. He also wanted to prevent the spread of communism in poor nations. He created the **Peace Corps,** a group that sent American volunteers to help poor countries.

Kennedy's first major challenge came in Cuba. **Fidel Castro** took over Cuba in 1959. <u>Castro aligned Cuba closely with the Soviet Union.</u> In 1961, Kennedy approved a plan to invade Cuba and overthrow Castro. A CIA-led force of Cuban exiles invaded Cuba with the **Bay of Pigs invasion.** Most of the invaders were killed or captured, creating a huge failure.

Kennedy's next challenge was in Berlin. The Soviet premier **Nikita Khrushchev** demanded that America remove its troops from West Berlin. When Kennedy refused, Khrushchev ordered the construction of a wall between East and West Berlin. The **Berlin Wall** became a symbol of the divide between communism and democracy.

Kennedy's third challenge was the **Cuban missile crisis.** The Soviets began building nuclear missile sites in Cuba in range of East Coast cities. Kennedy demanded that the Soviets remove the missiles. Nuclear war seemed possible. After several tense days, Khrushchev agreed to remove the missiles. The event inspired the leaders to install a **"hot line"** between Moscow and Washington, D.C., to improve communication. A year later in 1963, the United States, Great Britain, and the Soviet Union signed the first nuclear-weapons agreement.

Review Questions

1. Why did the United States want to overthrow Fidel Castro?

____

____

2. Why did the Soviets build nuclear missile sites in Cuba?

____

____

READING CHECK

Who was the leader of the Soviet Union during the Cuban missile crisis?

____

____

____

VOCABULARY STRATEGY

What does the word *aligned* mean in the underlined sentence? What context clues can you find in the surrounding words or phrases? Circle any words or phrases in the paragraph that help you figure out what *aligned* means.

____

____

____

READING SKILL

Understand Effects What effects did the Cuban missile crisis have on the Soviet Union and the United States?

____

____

____

Focus Question: What were the goals of Kennedy's New Frontier?

A. *List the characteristics of John F. Kennedy that appealed to the American people.*

The Kennedy Image
• Youthful
•
•
•
•
• Sense of humor

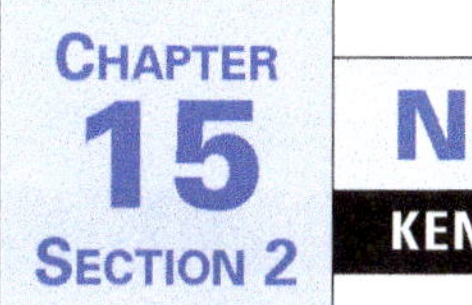

Note Taking Study Guide
KENNEDY'S NEW FRONTIER

CHAPTER 15 · SECTION 2

Focus Question: What were the goals of Kennedy's New Frontier?

B. *As you read, identify details of Kennedy's New Frontier program.*

TIP: Read the topic sentences of paragraphs for clues.

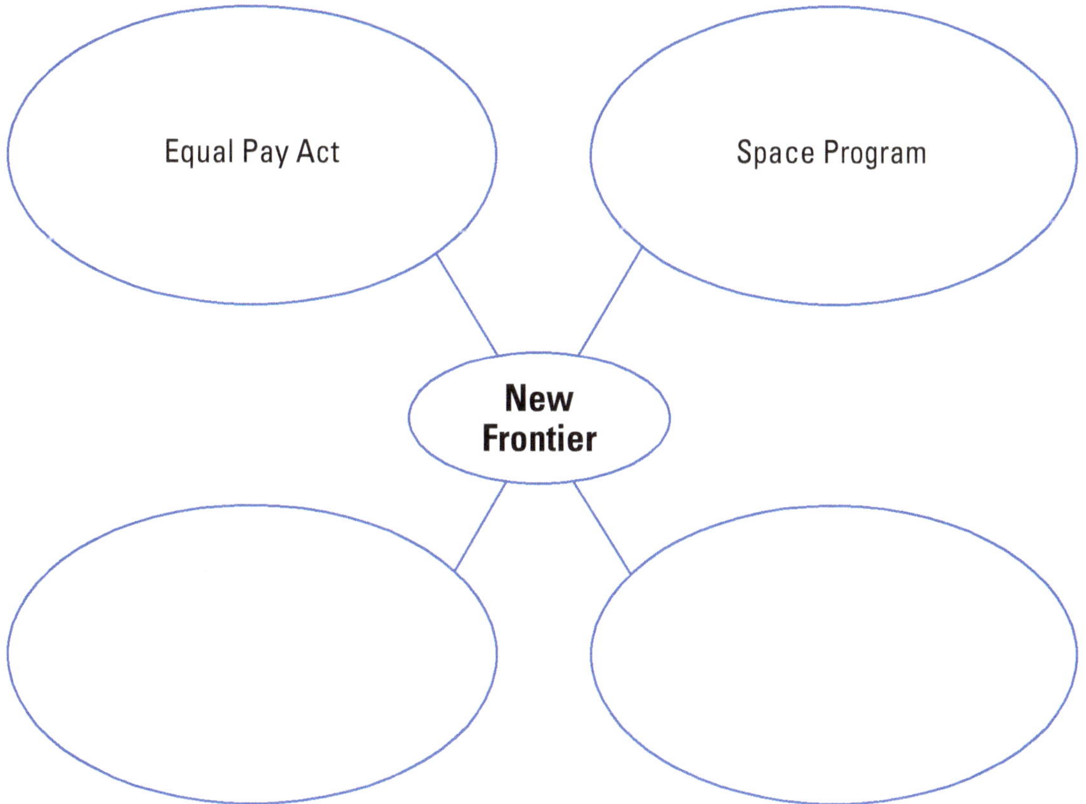

<table><tr><td>CHAPTER
15
SECTION 2</td><td>**Section Summary**
KENNEDY'S NEW FRONTIER</td></tr></table>

Early in his presidency, Kennedy was mostly concerned with foreign affairs. Later, he was more concerned about problems at home. Kennedy promised to tackle these problems in a program called the **"New Frontier."**

Kennedy was troubled by the high levels of poverty in America. He achieved an increase in the minimum wage and improvements in the welfare system. He also tried to make sure that women were paid equal wages for "equal work." The **Equal Pay Act** required this.

The economy was weak and unemployment was high when Kennedy took office. Kennedy accepted the "new economics" theory of John Maynard Keynes that advocated **deficit spending** to stimulate the economy. Deficit spending is the government practice of borrowing money in order to spend more than it receives from taxes.

At first, Kennedy moved slowly on civil rights. Over time, however, Kennedy realized that African Americans needed the federal government to protect their rights. He introduced a bill that would protect civil rights and aid school desegregation.

Perhaps the most famous part of the New Frontier was the active space program. Americans were afraid of falling behind the Soviets in the **"space race."** Kennedy called for the government to land a man on the moon in less than 10 years. The goal was met in 1969.

Kennedy's term as president was ended by his assassination. Lee Harvey Oswald shot Kennedy while he was riding in a car in Dallas, Texas. Not everyone thought that Oswald acted alone. However, the **Warren Commission** investigated the shooting. It declared that Oswald acted alone. The assassination deeply saddened Americans across the nation. It seemed as if part of America's innocence had died with Kennedy.

Review Questions

1. Why did Kennedy want a change in the minimum wage?

____

____

2. What was Kennedy's goal for the space program?

____

____

CHAPTER 15 SECTION 3

Note Taking Study Guide

JOHNSON'S GREAT SOCIETY

Focus Question: How did Johnson's Great Society programs change life for most Americans?

Identify details about the Great Society programs.

TIP: Read the topic sentences of paragraphs for clues.

The Great Society			
Education	**Healthcare**	**Immigration**	**Poverty**
•	• Medicare	•	• 1964 Economic Opportunity Act
	•		•
•			•
			•

<table><tr><td>**CHAPTER 15**
SECTION 3</td><td>## Section Summary
JOHNSON'S GREAT SOCIETY</td></tr></table>

Lyndon Johnson became President after Kennedy's assassination. Johnson was born in a small town in Texas. He attended a state college and taught for several years in a poor, segregated school. After being elected to Congress, he slowly began to work his way up.

Johnson became an excellent politician. After becoming President, he had a quick success. He ensured that Congress passed the **Civil Rights Act.** The outcome of this important bill was an end to discrimination in voting, in education, and in public services.

The **War on Poverty** was a big part of Johnson's plans. He wanted to give more training, education, and healthcare to those who needed it. The **Economic Opportunity Act** began this process. It created programs such as the Job Corps and Head Start for underprivileged children.

Johnson called his vision for America the **Great Society.** He said the Great Society demanded "an end to poverty and racial injustice." In 1965, Congress began to pass Johnson's legislation. This legislation addressed the need for healthcare insurance. Johnson created **Medicare,** a program to provide basic hospital insurance for older Americans. He also created **Medicaid** to provide basic medical services to poor and disabled Americans.

Education and immigration policy were also reformed. The Elementary and Secondary Education Act aided schools in poorer communities. The **Immigration and Nationality Act of 1965** allowed more immigrants to move to the United States. Over the next two decades, millions of immigrants came.

During the 1960s, the Supreme Court was also interested in reform. The court decided cases on controversial social, religious, and political issues. The court was led by Chief Justice Earl Warren, and was often called the **Warren Court.** The court supported civil rights, civil liberties, voting rights, and personal privacy.

Review Questions

1. What did Johnson call his vision for America?

____

____

2. What is Medicaid?

____

____

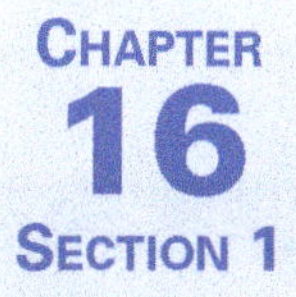

Note Taking Study Guide
ORIGINS OF THE VIETNAM WAR

CHAPTER 16 SECTION 1

Focus Question: Why did the United States become involved in Vietnam?

As you read, describe the Vietnam policies of Presidents Truman, Eisenhower, Kennedy, and Johnson.

TIP: Look for the names of the Presidents throughout the section.

U.S. Policy in Vietnam		
Truman/Eisenhower	**Kennedy**	**Johnson**
•	•	• Responds to the *Maddox* incident
		•
• Believe in domino theory	•	
•		• Gulf of Tonkin Resolution

CHAPTER 16 SECTION 1

Section Summary
ORIGINS OF THE VIETNAM WAR

READING CHECK

Who were the Vietcong?

____

____

____

VOCABULARY STRATEGY

What does the word *ensure* mean in the underlined sentence? Circle the words in the surrounding sentences that could help you learn what *ensure* means. Think about what the United States needed from France.

____

____

____

READING SKILL

Summarize Why did the United States help France in Vietnam?

____

____

____

France had controlled Vietnam since the 1800s. After World War II, many Vietnamese wanted independence. This independence movement was led by **Ho Chi Minh.** Ho Chi Minh traveled around the world and had formed ties with the Soviet Union. He wanted independence and believed in communism.

The United States became involved in Vietnam for several reasons. First, it wanted to keep France as an ally. <u>The United States needed to ensure French support in the Cold War.</u> As a result, President Truman agreed to help France regain control over Vietnam. Second, both Truman and Eisenhower wanted to stop the spread of communism. They believed in the **domino theory.** This idea said that if communists took over in Vietnam, Vietnam's neighbors would fall to communism. Communism would then spread throughout the entire region.

Despite billions of American dollars in support, France lost in Vietnam. In 1954, the French surrendered at a military base at **Dien Bien Phu.** The peace agreement between France and the communists gave Vietnam its independence. It also divided the country. Ho Chi Minh and the communists ruled North Vietnam. An anticommunist government ruled South Vietnam.

The United States provided aid to South Vietnam through the **Southeast Asia Treaty Organization (SEATO).** However, a communist rebel group began attacking the South. The communist guerrilla fighters were called **Vietcong.** The Vietcong attacked government officials and destroyed roads and bridges.

In 1961, President Kennedy began sending U.S. troops to help South Vietnam. President Johnson increased U.S. involvement there. In 1964, North Vietnamese forces attacked a U.S. destroyer in the Gulf of Tonkin. Johnson asked Congress for the right to fight back. Congress passed the **Gulf of Tonkin Resolution.** It gave the President the power to send U.S. troops to fight in Vietnam without asking Congress to declare war.

Review Questions

1. What was the domino theory?

____

____

2. How did the Gulf of Tonkin Resolution expand the powers of the presidency?

____

____

Note Taking Study Guide

CHAPTER 16 SECTION 2

U.S. INVOLVEMENT GROWS

Focus Question: What were the causes and effects of America's growing involvement in the Vietnam War?

As you read, fill in the outline with details about the escalation of the American war effort.

TIP: Read all headings closely for clues about the topics in each section.

I. "Americanizing" the War

   A. ____

     1. ____

     2. ____

   B. ____

     1. ____

     2. ____

   C. Costly and Frustrating War

     1. ____

     2. ____

II. Patriotism, Heroism, and Sinking Morale

   A. ____

     1. ____

     2. ____

   B. ____

     1. ____

     2. ____

   C. ____

     1. ____

     2. ____

III. Doubt Grows on the Homefront

   A. ____

     1. ____

     2. ____

   B. ____

     1. ____

     2. ____

Section Summary

U.S. INVOLVEMENT GROWS

READING CHECK

Which group in Congress opposed the war in Vietnam?

In February 1965, the war in Vietnam became more intense. After the Vietcong attacked American troops, President Johnson ordered a large bombing campaign called Operation Rolling Thunder. However, communist forces continued to fight. President Johnson then ordered more troops to fight on the ground. One of the President's most important advisers was the American commander in South Vietnam, General **William Westmoreland,** who believed in more active fighting.

The American military dropped millions of tons of bombs on Vietnam. They also dropped **napalm,** a jellied gasoline. Napalm covered large areas in flames.

American troops fought mostly in small battles. The enemy fought with guerrilla tactics in the jungle. They followed Ho Chi Minh's doctrine, which stated that fighting should never be on the opponents' terms. The communists knew that they could not win a traditional war against the United States. Instead, they used hit-and-run attacks, nighttime ambushes, and booby traps, hoping to wear down the United States.

VOCABULARY STRATEGY

What does the word *doctrine* mean in the underlined sentence? Circle the words in the underlined sentence that could help you learn what *doctrine* means.

By 1967, neither side was winning. Johnson asserted again and again that victory was near. However, there was little progress. By 1968, more than 30,000 U.S. troops had been killed. Troop morale began to fall.

The costs of the war were growing. President Johnson was forced to raise taxes to pay for the war and for his Great Society domestic programs. Social programs had to be cut.

Members of Congress had questions about the war. In 1967, Congress was divided into two camps: hawks and doves. **Hawks** supported the war. **Doves** questioned whether it was right to fight the war. They also were not convinced that Vietnam was a vital Cold War battleground.

READING SKILL

Identify Supporting Details Why did President Johnson raise taxes?

Review Questions

1. Why did Johnson send more American troops to fight on the ground in Vietnam?

____

____

2. What tactics did the Communist forces use against U.S. troops in Vietnam?

____

____

Name ______________________ Class ____________________ Date _______

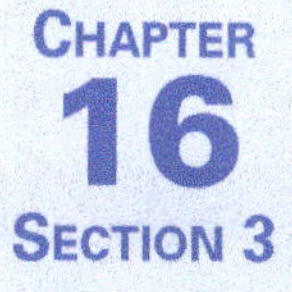

CHAPTER 16 SECTION 3

Note Taking Study Guide

THE WAR DIVIDES AMERICA

Focus Question: How did the American war effort in Vietnam lead to rising protests and social divisions back home?

Note the events leading up to the 1968 election.

TIP: Look for dates and key events throughout the section.

Antiwar demonstrations
↓ ↓ ↓
↓ ↓ ↓
↓ ↓ ↓
↓ ↓ ↓
↓ ↓ ↓
Richard Nixon becomes President.

<table><tr><td>**CHAPTER**
16
SECTION 3</td><td>## Section Summary
THE WAR DIVIDES AMERICA</td></tr></table>

Although many Americans supported the war in Vietnam, many others opposed it. Because the government lacked enough volunteer soldiers, the military drafted young men to serve in the armed forces. Some **draftees** thought that the method of selecting men was unfair. <u>Draft boards gave deferments to college students and men who worked in certain occupations.</u> As a result, African Americans, the poor, and working-class men served in disproportionately high numbers.

Many college students opposed the war. One organization, called the **Students for a Democratic Society (SDS),** organized antiwar demonstrations. Opposition to the war grew as Americans watched bad news about it on television every night. Still, government reports about the war continued to be positive. This difference created a **"credibility gap."**

In early 1968, the North Vietnamese conducted a major attack, the **Tet Offensive.** Because the U.S. government often gave positive reports about the war, the offensive surprised the country. The United States repelled the attack, but it showed that the enemy was still strong.

Antiwar Democrats began to campaign for President in 1968. Senator **Eugene McCarthy** was successful in an early primary election. Senator **Robert Kennedy** also entered the race. In March, President Johnson announced that he would not run for a second term as President.

In the spring and summer of 1968, both Martin Luther King, Jr., and Robert Kennedy were assassinated. Police clashed with antiwar protesters at the Democratic National Convention in Chicago. The chaos helped Republican candidate Richard Nixon to win the presidency. Nixon promised to achieve "peace with honor" in Vietnam.

Review Questions

1. Why did some people think that the draft system was unfair?

____

____

2. How did television play a role in the Vietnam War?

____

____

Note Taking Study Guide
THE WAR'S END AND IMPACT

Focus Question: How did the Vietnam War end, and what were its lasting effects?

A. *Note the similarities and differences between Nixon's Vietnam policy and that of Lyndon Johnson.*

TIP: Look for clues in headings throughout the section.

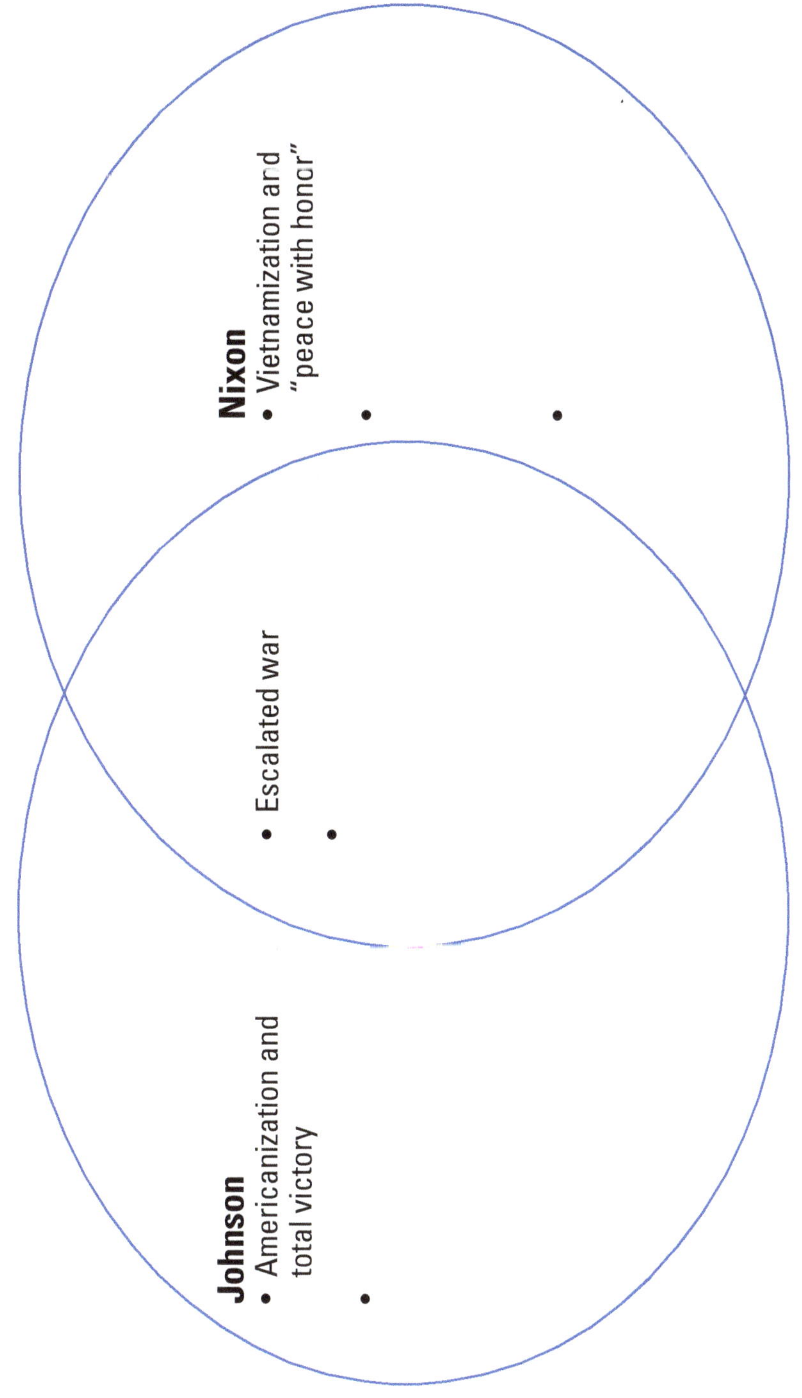

Name ______________________ Class ________________ Date ______

CHAPTER 16 SECTION 4

Note Taking Study Guide

THE WAR'S END AND IMPACT

Focus Question: How did the Vietnam War end, and what were its lasting effects?

B. *As you read, use the concept web below to identify the effects of the Vietnam War.* TIP: Think about effects that happened in the United States and in Vietnam.

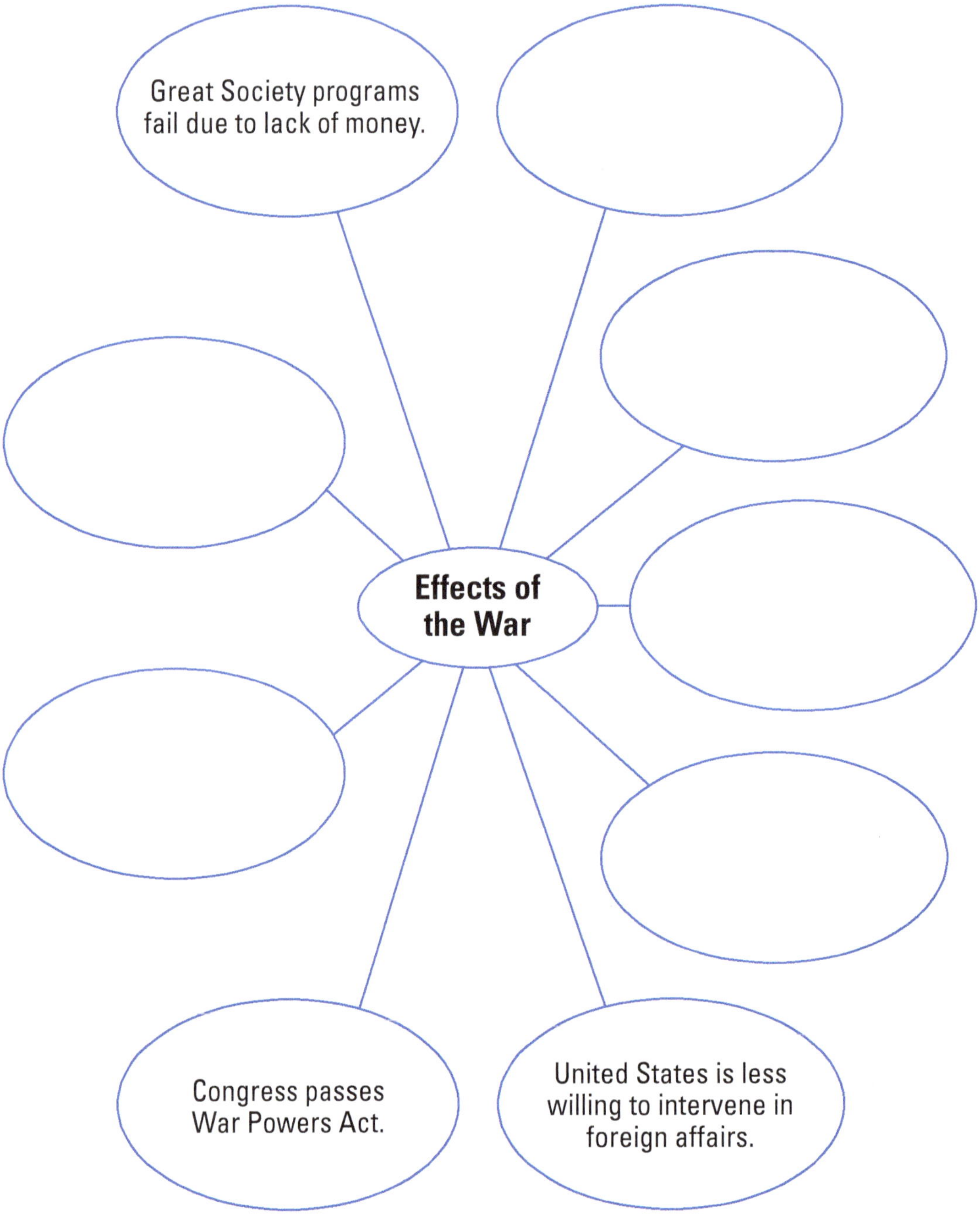
Great Society programs fail due to lack of money.
Effects of the War
Congress passes War Powers Act.
United States is less willing to intervene in foreign affairs.

Section Summary

THE WAR'S END AND IMPACT

President Nixon believed that he could make a peace deal with North Vietnam. At first, he did not succeed, and he began to pull U.S. troops out of Vietnam. The South Vietnamese Army, he said, should fight the war on its own. The United States would continue to send supplies to the South Vietnamese Army to help them—a plan called **Vietnamization.**

In 1970, Nixon ordered an American ground attack on communists in Cambodia, angering antiwar activists at home. They claimed that Nixon was not ending the war, but widening it. Protests erupted on many college campuses. At **Kent State University,** members of the National Guard fired into a group of protesters, killing four youths. This led to protests on other campuses across the country.

Other events also outraged the public. American troops killed over four hundred unarmed Vietnamese in the village of **My Lai.** The **Pentagon Papers** showed that the government had been dishonest with the public and with Congress about the Vietnam War.

American bombing finally induced the North Vietnamese to resume negotiations. In January 1973, the warring parties signed the **Paris Peace Accords.** American troops left Vietnam. The war was over for the United States. North Vietnamese troops, however, remained in South Vietnam, and fighting continued. The communists, supplied by the Soviet Union, defeated the South Vietnamese Army. Vietnam was then united under a communist regime.

More than 58,000 American troops and over 2 million Vietnamese had been killed in the Vietnam War. Southeast Asia suffered turmoil for many years afterward. Americans became less willing to intervene in the affairs of other countries. Americans had less trust in their leaders, as well. In 1973, Congress passed the **War Powers Act,** which restricted the President's authority to commit American troops to foreign conflicts. The effects of the war lasted for many years.

Review Questions

1. What was Vietnamization?

____

____

2. Why did the Pentagon Papers outrage Americans?

____

____

Note Taking Study Guide

NIXON AND THE COLD WAR

Focus Question: How did Richard Nixon change Cold War diplomacy during his presidency?

As you read, describe Nixon's Cold War foreign policies in dealing with China and the Soviet Union.

Nixon's Cold War Strategies	
China	**Soviet Union**
• Normalization of relations will drive wedge between China and Soviet Union. • China would make a good trading partner. •	• Diplomacy with China will create Soviet fear of isolation. • •

<table>
<tr><td>CHAPTER
16
SECTION 5</td><td>## Section Summary
NIXON AND THE COLD WAR</td></tr>
</table>

President Richard Nixon changed the way the United States approached the world. **Henry Kissinger,** his top adviser on international affairs, helped him.

Nixon and Kissinger shared the idea of **realpolitik,** which said that a government should make decisions based on what is good for the nation, not just on ideologies. Nixon and Kissinger insisted on a flexible, pragmatic foreign policy. They believed that this approach would have many benefits for the United States.

Nixon had always been a strong opponent of communism. When he decided to create better relations with communist China, many people were surprised. The United States had no official relationship with communist China in the 1960s. Nixon wanted to reach out to China for several reasons. He hoped to drive a wedge between China and the Soviet Union. Nixon thought that China could be a good trading partner. He also hoped that China might help persuade North Vietnam to end the Vietnam War. In 1972, Nixon traveled to China to meet with Premier **Zhou Enlai** and Chairman Mao Zedong. The trip greatly improved the relations between the two countries.

Nixon's trip to China also led the Soviet Union to invite him to visit Moscow. There, the United States and the Soviet Union signed the first **Strategic Arms Limitation Treaty.** This agreement limited each nation's missiles. It was a first step toward limiting the arms race.

The United States and Soviet Union now tried a new policy called **détente** to reduce tensions between them. Détente replaced diplomatic policies based on suspicion and distrust.

Nixon's foreign policy changed the nation's views about communism. The new relationships he made helped to end the Vietnam War. Nixon's policies also moved the world closer to the end of the Cold War.

Review Questions

1. Why did Nixon want to reach out to communist China?

____

____

2. What was the effect of the Strategic Arms Limitation Treaty?

____

____

READING CHECK

What is realpolitik?

____

____

____

VOCABULARY STRATEGY

What does the word *pragmatic* mean in the underlined sentence? Circle the words in the underlined sentence that could help you learn what *pragmatic* means. The word describes Nixon's foreign policy.

____

____

____

READING SKILL

Categorize Circle the statement that most accurately reflects President Nixon's attitudes toward communism.

- If Vietnam fell to communism, its closest neighbors would follow, spreading communism throughout the region.

- A flexible, pragmatic foreign policy would benefit the United States in many ways.

- The United States should support all independence movements, no matter what their political beliefs.

Name ______________________ Class ________________ Date ______

CHAPTER 17 SECTION 1

Note Taking Study Guide

THE COUNTERCULTURE

Focus Question: What was the counterculture, and what impact did it have on American society?

As you read, use the concept web below to record main ideas about the counterculture.

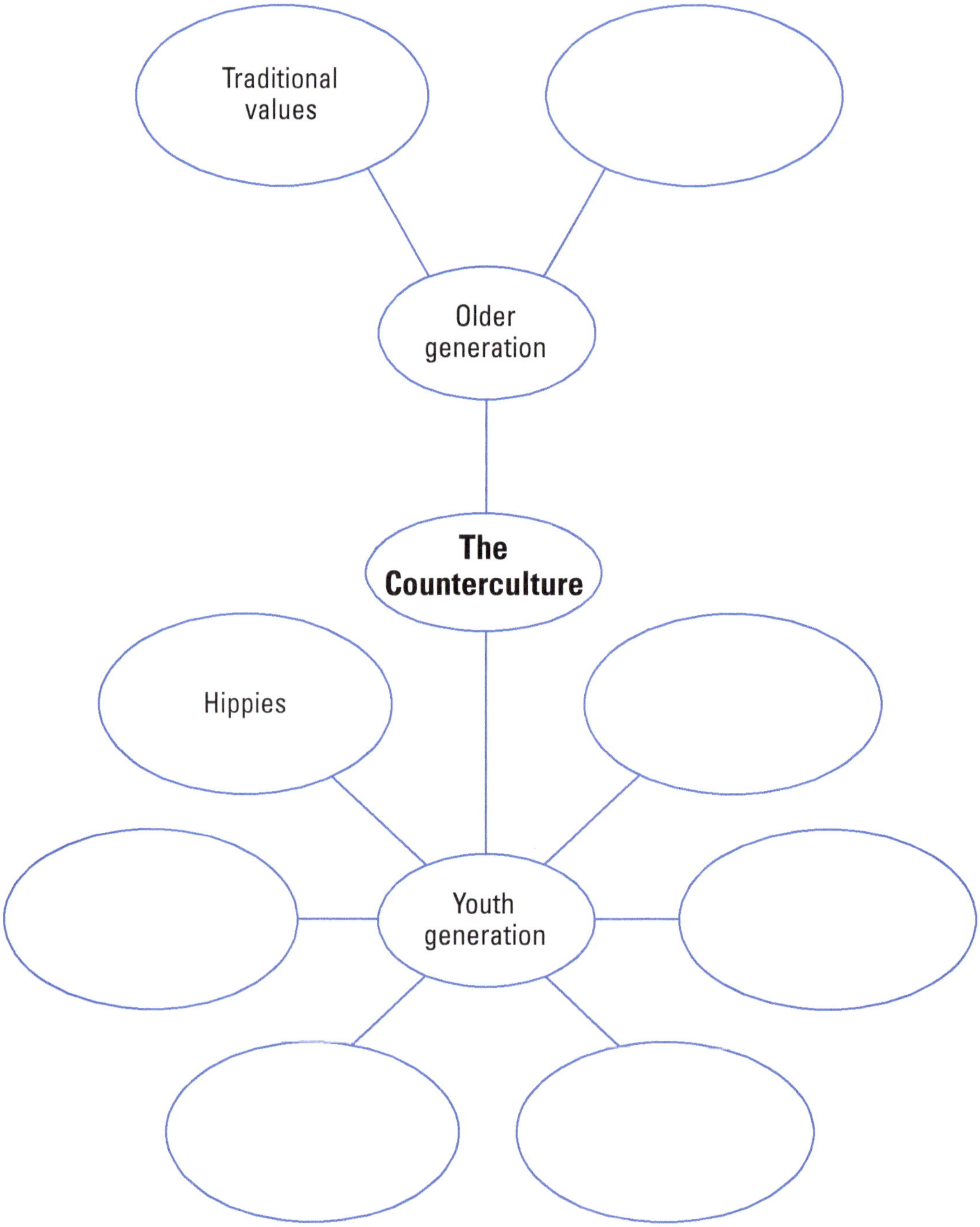

Section Summary
THE COUNTERCULTURE

The **counterculture** of the 1960s grew out of social and political changes, including the Beat movement, the civil rights movement, and opposition to the Vietnam War. Members of the counterculture were called hippies. <u>Hippies contradicted society's traditional restrictions.</u> They also promoted peace, love, and freedom. This created a **generation gap,** or misunderstandings between the older and younger generations.

Hippies had enormous influence on American society. Their style of dress, long hair, attitudes, art, and literature flavored the styles and opinions of the whole nation. Music of rock bands such as the **Beatles** defined the decade.

Hippies' rejection of society's restrictions on sexual behavior created a "sexual revolution." Some hippies also rejected traditional living situations. They lived together in small communities called **communes** where people shared their interests and resources.

The center of the counterculture was the **Haight-Ashbury** district of San Francisco. Many hippies came to experiment with drugs and listen to rock music and speeches by political radicals such as **Timothy Leary,** who encouraged drug use. Some hippies sought new avenues to spirituality, exploring Eastern religions or seeking to live off the land in harmony with nature. These beliefs made an impact on the growing environmental movement.

By the late 1960s, many hippies had become disillusioned with the excesses of the counterculture and had rejoined the mainstream, but their decade of rebellion continued to influence the growing "rights revolution."

Review Questions

1. What social and political events inspired the counterculture?

____

____

2. How did hippies explore their spirituality?

____

____

READING CHECK

What district in San Francisco was at the center of the counterculture?

____

____

____

VOCABULARY STRATEGY

Find the word *contradicted* in the underlined sentence. Look for clues in the surrounding words and phrases. Use these clues to help you figure out what *contradicted* means.

____

____

____

READING SKILL

Identify Main Ideas In what ways did the counterculture influence American culture?

____

____

____

CHAPTER 17

SECTION 2

Note Taking Study Guide
THE WOMEN'S RIGHTS MOVEMENT

Focus Question: What led to the rise of the women's movement, and what impact did it have on American society?

Record the causes, effects, and main figures in the women's movement in the chart below.

The Women's Movement		
Causes	**Proponents/ Opponents**	**Effects**
• Rights gained in the civil rights movement • • •	• Pro: Betty Friedan • •	• Can't legally discriminate based on gender • •

Section Summary
THE WOMEN'S RIGHTS MOVEMENT

The 1960s and 1970s saw a rise in **feminism.** Feminism is the theory of political, social, and economic equality of men and women. The successes of the civil rights movement encouraged women to challenge the ways in which society judged and discriminated against them.

The role of housewife was seen as the proper one for women, but many women found it deeply unsatisfying. **Betty Friedan** described this unhappiness in her 1963 book *The Feminine Mystique.* At the same time, women who worked were paid less than men. Friedan helped establish the **National Organization for Women (NOW),** which worked toward winning equality for women. The group wanted the **Equal Rights Amendment (ERA)** to pass. The ERA was an amendment to the Constitution that would guarantee gender equality under the law. NOW also worked to protect the right to an abortion. Radical feminists went further, protesting against discrimination. One radical feminist was **Gloria Steinem.** Steinem wrote about feminism and spoke out about it. She also helped co-found the feminist magazine *Ms.* in 1972.

Not all women supported feminism. **Phyllis Schlafly,** a conservative political activist, denounced women's liberation. She worked to defeat the ERA. Although the ERA did not pass, women did gain legal rights. New laws banned discrimination in education and made it illegal to deny credit to a woman on the basis of gender. The 1973 Supreme Court decision in *Roe* **v.** *Wade* assured women the right to legal abortions.

Changes in the workplace came slowly. Today more women work and many work in fields once denied to them, such as medicine and law. Despite these gains, the average woman still earns less than the average man.

Review Questions

1. What right would the Equal Rights Amendment have guaranteed?

____

____

2. What causes did the National Organization for Women work toward? Did its efforts succeed or fail?

____

____

Note Taking Study Guide
THE RIGHTS REVOLUTION EXPANDS

Focus Question: How did the rights movements of the 1960s and 1970s expand rights for diverse groups of Americans?

A. *Compare and contrast the Latino and Native American rights movements in the Venn diagram below.*

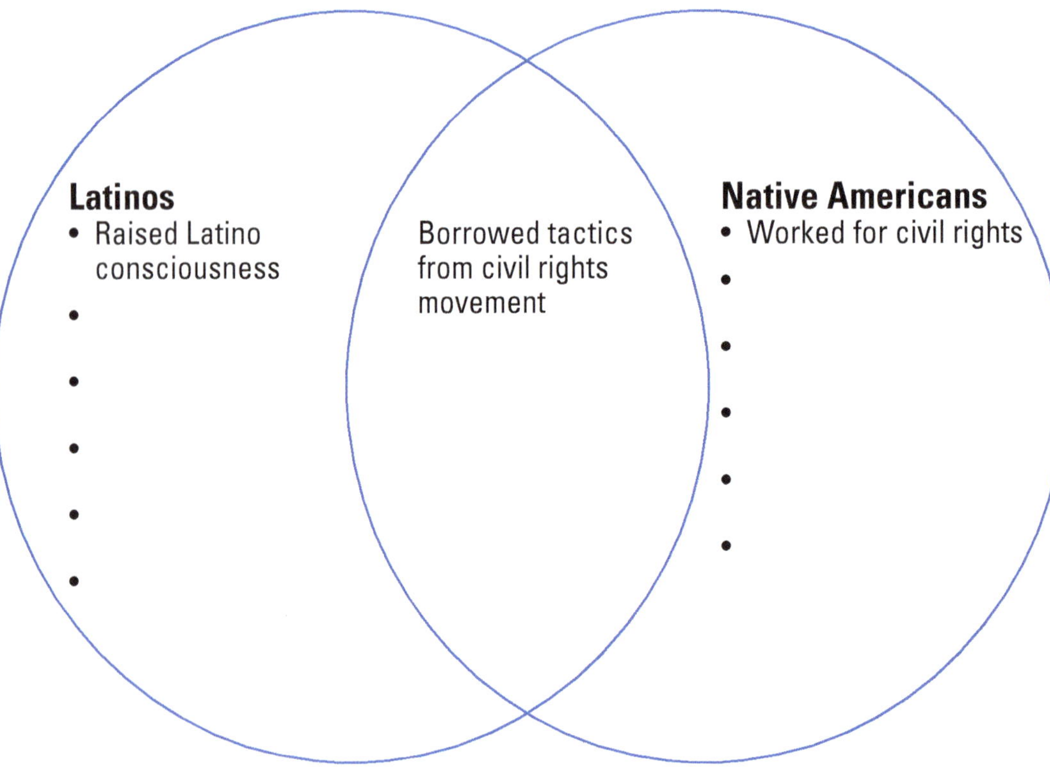

B. *As you read, identify causes of expanding rights for consumers and those with disabilities.*

Consumer Advocacy	Disabled Advocacy
• Ralph Nader published *Unsafe at Any Speed.* •	• •

Growing Movements Expand Rights

<table><tr><td>**CHAPTER**
17
SECTION 3</td><td>## Section Summary
THE RIGHTS REVOLUTION EXPANDS</td></tr></table>

Latin American immigrants came to the United States during and after World War II, filling the need for cheap labor. The *bracero* program allowed Mexicans to work on American farms. Later, the 1965 Immigration and Nationality Act Amendments led to a surge in immigration from Mexico. Other immigrants came from Puerto Rico, Cuba, and the Dominican Republic.

Like those in the civil rights movement, Latinos fought against discrimination. They also fought for better working conditions, salaries, and education. The most influential Latino activist was **Cesar Chavez.** He organized the **United Farm Workers (UFW).** <u>This union implemented a strike and consumer boycott.</u> It also secured safer working conditions for farmworkers. **Migrant farmworkers,** who moved from farm to farm to pick fruits and vegetables, were often treated poorly. The **Chicano movement** worked to reduce poverty and discrimination, and to gain political power for Latinos.

In 1968, the **American Indian Movement (AIM)** was founded to help secure legal rights and self-government for Native Americans. In 1969, a group occupied the island of Alcatraz and claimed it for the Sioux. Later, AIM took over the village of Wounded Knee, South Dakota, to protest living conditions on reservations. This led to the deaths of two AIM members. The government eventually agreed to reexamine treaty rights. Native Americans' efforts resulted in laws that granted tribes greater control over resources on reservations.

Other Americans also secured greater rights. **Ralph Nader** jump-started the consumer rights movement after his book *Unsafe at Any Speed* showed bad car design led to more accidents and deaths. The book prompted Congress to pass laws to improve automobile safety. People with disabilities also secured additional rights.

Review Questions

1. What factors encouraged Latinos to immigrate to the United States during and after World War II?

____

____

2. What changes did those fighting for Native American rights help bring about?

____

____

READING CHECK

What organization did Cesar Chavez help organize?

____

____

____

VOCABULARY STRATEGY

What does the word *implemented* mean in the underlined sentence? Look for clues in the surrounding words, phrases, and sentences. Circle the words in the underlined sentence that could help you learn what *implemented* means.

____

____

____

READING SKILL

Compare and Contrast Compare and contrast the results of the UFW's work and Ralph Nader's book.

____

____

____

Name ______________________ Class ____________________ Date ________

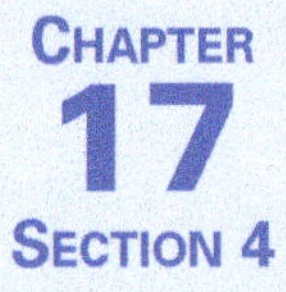

CHAPTER 17 SECTION 4

Note Taking Study Guide

THE ENVIRONMENTAL MOVEMENT

Focus Question: What forces gave rise to the environmental movement, and what impact did it have?

As you read, record major events in the environmental movement in the flowchart below.

Rachel Carson publishes *Silent Spring* in 1962.

↓

Americans celebrate the first Earth Day in 1970.

↓

↓

↓

Endangered Species Act passes in 1973.

Section Summary
THE ENVIRONMENTAL MOVEMENT

In 1962, a book by **Rachel Carson** inspired the modern environmental movement. *Silent Spring* described how pesticides were killing birds and other animals. Carson argued that people were changing the environment and had a responsibility to protect it. <u>The book sparked protests that compelled Congress to limit the use of the pesticide DDT.</u> Other environmental concerns included **toxic waste**—poisonous byproducts of human activity such as coal smog. In 1970, in response to growing environmental concerns, the first **Earth Day** was held. Close to 20 million Americans participated, and Earth Day became an annual event.

Public concern convinced President Nixon to support environmental reforms and laws. Under his leadership, Congress created the **Environmental Protection Agency (EPA)** in 1970. The EPA is responsible for environmental cleanup and protection. It also limits or eliminates pollutants that harm people's health. The **Clean Air Act** (1970) combated air pollution by limiting emissions from factories and automobiles. The **Clean Water Act** (1973) reduced water pollution by industry and agriculture. The **Endangered Species Act** (1973) helped protect endangered plants and animals.

In the late 1970s, several environmental problems alarmed the public. Toxic waste in the ground was blamed for high rates of birth defects and cancer in Love Canal, New York. Later, the core of a malfunctioning nuclear reactor at Three Mile Island in Pennsylvania began to melt.

These events caused some people to support environmental laws. Others opposed the government's actions. Conservatives complained that regulations took property rights away from individuals. Others argued that private property owners, rather than the government, should protect the environment. Industry leaders worried that regulation would harm business.

Review Questions

1. What environmental protection laws were passed under President Nixon?

____

____

2. What arguments did some people make against the U.S. government's role in environmental protection?

____

____

Note Taking Study Guide

NIXON AND THE WATERGATE SCANDAL

CHAPTER 18 SECTION 1

Focus Question: What events led to Richard Nixon's resignation as President in 1974?

A. *As you read, record Nixon's major domestic policies and goals in the chart below.*

Nixon's Domestic Policies and Strategies	
New Federalism	**Southern Strategy**
• Revenue sharing • • •	• Nominates conservative southerners to federal courts • •

B. *Use the chart below to record the causes and effects of the Watergate crisis.*

Watergate Crisis

Causes	Effects
• Break-in at Democratic Party headquarters • Senate investigation • • •	• Connections revealed between burglars and White House • Nixon refuses to turn over tapes to investigators, citing executive privilege • • •

<table><tr><td>

CHAPTER
18
SECTION 1

</td><td>

Section Summary
NIXON AND THE WATERGATE SCANDAL

</td></tr></table>

In 1968, Richard Nixon won the presidency. During his campaign, Nixon said he represented the **silent majority.** This term referred to the working men and women who made up Middle America. Nixon said that they were tired of "big" government. <u>However, he also said that they wanted the government to address social ills like crime and pollution.</u> He proposed **revenue sharing.** Under this system, the federal government gave money to the states to run social programs. Nixon's presidency was bothered by a combination of recession and inflation that came to be known as **stagflation.** The **Organization of Petroleum Exporting Countries (OPEC)** placed an oil embargo on Israel's allies, which caused oil prices to skyrocket.

In Nixon's **southern strategy,** he tried to get more white southerners, who had traditionally voted for Democrats, to support him. He appointed conservative southern judges and criticized busing school children to achieve desegregation. However, he supported **affirmative action** plans in employment and education. Nixon won the 1972 election easily. He was the first Republican presidential candidate to sweep the entire South.

In June 1972, burglars broke into the Democratic Party headquarters. After their conviction, one of them charged that administration officials had been involved. Nixon denied any wrongdoing. The scandal came to be known as **Watergate,** after the building where the burglary occurred. Nixon refused to turn over secret tapes he had made of Oval Office conversations. He claimed **executive privilege.** This principle claims that the President can keep certain information private. The Supreme Court ordered Nixon to turn over the tapes. The tapes proved that Nixon was involved in the coverup. Facing impeachment and conviction, Nixon resigned in August 1974. Gerald Ford became President. Ford had been appointed Vice President after Spiro Agnew's 1973 resignation.

Review Questions

1. What was Richard Nixon's attitude toward "big" government?

____

____

2. Why did Richard Nixon resign the presidency?

____

____

Note Taking Study Guide
THE FORD AND CARTER YEARS

Focus Question: What accounted for the changes in American attitudes during the 1970s?

As you read, use the outline below to record the political, economic, and social problems of the era and their impact on American society.

I. Gerald Ford's Presidency

  A. Major Domestic Issues

    1. Attempts to restore confidence in government

    2. _______________________________________

    3. _______________________________________

    4. _______________________________________

II. Jimmy Carter's Presidency

  A. As a Washington outsider, has trouble getting bills through Congress

  B. _______________________________________

  C. _______________________________________

  D. _______________________________________

III. Social and Cultural Changes in the 1970s

  A. _______________________________________

  B. _______________________________________

  C. _______________________________________

  D. _______________________________________

  E. _______________________________________

<table>
<tr><td>CHAPTER
18
SECTION 2</td><td>Section Summary
THE FORD AND CARTER YEARS</td></tr>
</table>

At first, President **Gerald Ford** had the support of Democrats as well as Republicans. He lost that support when he **pardoned** Nixon for any crimes Nixon might have committed as President. The pardon was meant to heal the nation's wounds. However, critics accused Ford of having made a secret deal. In the 1974 congressional elections, the Republicans lost 48 seats in the House of Representatives, displaying the public's disapproval of the pardon and the impact of Watergate.

In 1976, former Georgia governor **Jimmy Carter** won the presidency. He was a born-again Christian who won the support of many **Christian fundamentalists.** He was also a Washington outsider with no close ties to the Democratic leadership in Congress. His own party changed most of the bills he submitted to Congress. A day after his inauguration, he granted **amnesty** to Americans who had evaded the draft. He hoped to move the nation beyond the Vietnam War. Severe inflation continued, fueled by the ongoing energy crisis. <u>Carter contended with the oil crisis by urging Americans to conserve.</u>

Two trends continued during the 1970s: the migration of Americans to the Sunbelt and the growth of the suburbs. The Sunbelt's political power also grew. There were many new immigrants from Latin America and Asia. Other trends also continued. The divorce rate more than doubled between 1965 and 1979. The number of children born out of wedlock nearly tripled. The 1970s are sometimes called the "me decade." Many Americans appeared to be absorbed with trying to improve themselves. There was an increased interest in fitness and health.

The 1970s also witnessed a revival of fundamental Christianity. **Televangelists** preached to millions on television. Religious conservatives opposed many of the social changes that took place in the 1970s, forming alliances with other conservatives to create a new political majority.

Review Questions

1. What events troubled Gerald Ford's presidency?

____

____

2. How did Jimmy Carter deal with the oil crisis?

____

____

READING CHECK

Why were the 1970s called the "me decade"?

____

____

____

VOCABULARY STRATEGY

Find the word *contended* in the underlined sentence. Note that the word is a verb, which means it names an action. Ask yourself what kind of action President Carter was taking in relation to the oil crisis. Use this strategy to help you figure out what *contended* means.

____

____

____

READING SKILL

Identify Main Ideas How did being an outsider in Washington hurt Carter's presidency?

____

____

____

Focus Question: What were the goals of American foreign policy during the Ford and Carter years, and how successful were Ford's and Carter's policies?

Use the concept web below to record the main ideas and details about the foreign policies of Ford and Carter.

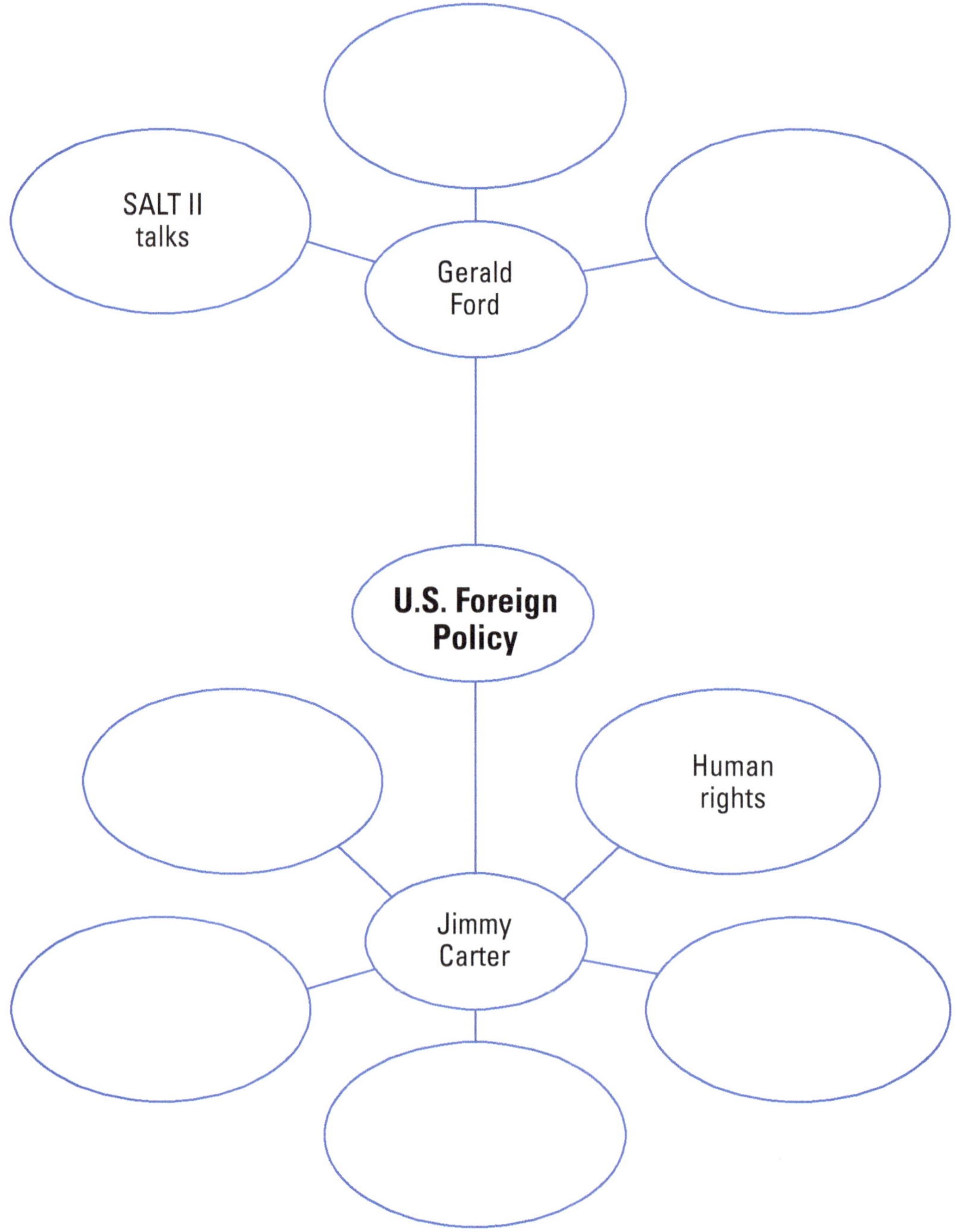

<table><tr><td>

CHAPTER

18

SECTION 3

</td><td>

Section Summary

FOREIGN POLICY TROUBLES

</td></tr></table>

During the Ford and Carter administrations, relations with the Soviet Union were at the center of foreign policy. President Gerald Ford met with Soviet leader Leonid Brezhnev to approve the **Helsinki Accords.** This document supported **human rights.** However, Ford's main concern was arms control, not making the Soviet Union give its people more political freedom. South Vietnam fell to the communists. Hundreds of thousands of Vietnamese **boat people** tried to escape in rickety boats.

Soon after becoming President, Jimmy Carter said that he would base his foreign policy on human rights. <u>He worked to end acts of political repression like torture.</u> However, Carter worked to relax tensions between the United States and the Soviet Union. In 1979, he signed the **SALT II** treaty to limit nuclear arms production. Relations between the two super-powers got worse after the Soviet Union invaded Afghanistan in December 1979. Carter responded by imposing **sanctions** on the Soviets. One sanction was a U.S. boycott of the 1980 Summer Olympics in Moscow. Carter also wanted to change U.S. relations with the **developing world.** He took away support of a number of dictators who did not respect human rights.

Carter had his greatest foreign policy success in the Middle East. He also had his worst setback there. Egypt and Israel had been enemies for a long time. In 1977, Carter invited the two nations' leaders to the presidential retreat called Camp David. The resulting **Camp David Accords** led to a peace treaty between Egypt and Israel. In January 1979, the U.S.-backed Shah of Iran was forced to flee his country. Fundamentalist Islamic clerics, led by the **Ayatollah Khomeini,** took power. Iranian radicals invaded the U.S. Embassy and took 66 Americans hostage. The Khomeini government defied the United States by taking control of the embassy and the hostages. Carter's failure to win their release was viewed as evidence of American weakness.

Review Questions

1. Compare Ford's and Carter's foreign policies.

____

____

2. What event of the Carter presidency was viewed as a sign of American weakness?

____

____

READING CHECK

Why did the United States boycott the 1980 Summer Olympic Games?

____

____

____

VOCABULARY STRATEGY

Find the word *repression* in the underlined sentence. What does *repression* mean? Look for context clues in the surrounding words and phrases.

____

____

____

READING SKILL

Identify Supporting Details
List two details that support the following statement: Carter's greatest foreign policy challenges were in the Middle East.

____

____

____

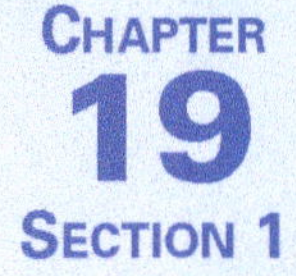

Note Taking Study Guide

CHAPTER 19 SECTION 1

THE CONSERVATIVE MOVEMENT GROWS

Focus Question: What spurred the rise of conservatism in the late 1970s and early 1980s?

As you read, summarize the rise of the conservative movement in the outline below.

I. Two Views: Liberal and Conservative

    A. Liberal ideas and goals

        1. Believed federal government should play active role in improving the lives of all Americans

        2. ____

        3. ____

    B. Conservative ideas and goals

        1. ____

        2. ____

        3. ____

<table><tr><td>CHAPTER
19
SECTION 1</td><td><h1>Section Summary</h1>THE CONSERVATIVE MOVEMENT GROWS</td></tr></table>

In the late twentieth century, Democrats and Republicans were the two major political parties in the United States. Many Democrats were **liberals** who believed that the federal government was responsible for improving the lives of all Americans. They supported social programs, regulation of industry, and international cooperation. Many Republicans were **conservatives.** They believed that private organizations and individuals, instead of the government, should care for the needy. Conservatives also favored tax cuts and supported a strong military.

The conservative movement, also known as the **New Right,** grew quickly during the 1960s and 1970s. The Vietnam War had divided the country, and many Americans had been alienated by the counterculture. Watergate, the oil crises of the 1970s, economic stagnation, and the Iran hostage crisis also weakened support for the government.

Conservatives blamed economic problems on liberal economic policies. They believed the government imposed too many taxes and spent money on the wrong programs. They disliked programs that the federal government required but did not pay for, known as **unfunded mandates.**

Reverend Jerry Falwell founded the **Moral Majority** in 1979, a political organization founded on religious beliefs. Members worried that traditional families were declining. They were also concerned that new freedoms brought by the counterculture would lead to the degeneration of youth.

The conservative movement helped former actor and California governor **Ronald Reagan** unseat President Jimmy Carter in the 1980 election. Reagan's conservative beliefs, charm, and optimism convinced Americans that he would usher in a new era of prosperity and patriotism.

Review Questions

1. What events contributed to the rise of the New Right?

____

____

2. What were the concerns of the Moral Majority?

____

____

CHAPTER 19 SECTION 2

Note Taking Study Guide
THE REAGAN REVOLUTION

Focus Question: What were the major characteristics of the conservative Reagan Revolution?

Identify the main ideas behind Reagan's policies.

Reagan Era		
Reaganomics	**Conservative Strength**	**Challenging Issues**
• Reduce taxes, giving people more money to spend	• Deregulation of industries	• Recession, 1980–1982
•	•	•
•		•
		•
		•
		•
		•
		•

<table><tr><td>**CHAPTER**
19
SECTION 2</td><td>## Section Summary
THE REAGAN REVOLUTION</td></tr></table>

President Reagan's economic policies, known as "Reaganomics," were based on the theory of **supply-side economics.** This theory assumed that reducing taxes would give people more incentive to work and more money to spend, causing the economy to grow. The Economic Recovery Act of 1981 reduced taxes by 25 percent over three years.

Reagan called for **deregulation,** or the removal of government control over industries. He also appointed conservative judges to the federal courts.

The economy experienced a recession beginning in 1980 but rebounded in 1983. Still, the number of poor increased and the richest grew even richer. Reagan increased defense spending but failed to win cuts in other areas of the budget. This led to a **budget deficit,** a shortfall between money spent and money collected by the government. The **national debt,** money the government owes to owners of government bonds, also rose. The deficit grew in 1989 when nearly 1,000 Savings and Loan banks failed. The government bailed out depositors during the **Savings and Loan (S&L) crisis.**

There were other problems as well. American students were scoring lower on standardized tests, prompting conservatives to further lobby for **vouchers,** or government checks that could be used to pay tuition at private schools. In addition, the nation faced a new disease—**Acquired Immunodeficiency Syndrome (AIDS).**

Despite these problems, Reagan remained popular and was overwhelmingly reelected in 1984. <u>However, his momentum did not lead to a triumph for conservatives in Congress.</u> Democrats kept control of the House of Representatives.

Review Questions

1. What occurred in the economy during the early 1980s?

____

____

2. What was the budget deficit, and what event made it worse?

____

____

READING CHECK

What new disease did the nation face in the 1980s?

____

____

____

VOCABULARY STRATEGY

Find the word *momentum* in the underlined sentence. What does *momentum* mean? Circle any words in the surrounding sentences that help you figure out what *momentum* means.

____

____

____

READING SKILL

Identify Main Ideas Describe the central idea of Reagan's economic policies.

____

____

____

CHAPTER **19** SECTION 3

Note Taking Study Guide
THE END OF THE COLD WAR

Focus Question: What were Reagan's foreign policies, and how did they contribute to the fall of communism in Europe?

A. *As you read this section, use the flowchart below to sequence major events related to the fall of communism in Europe and the Soviet Union.*

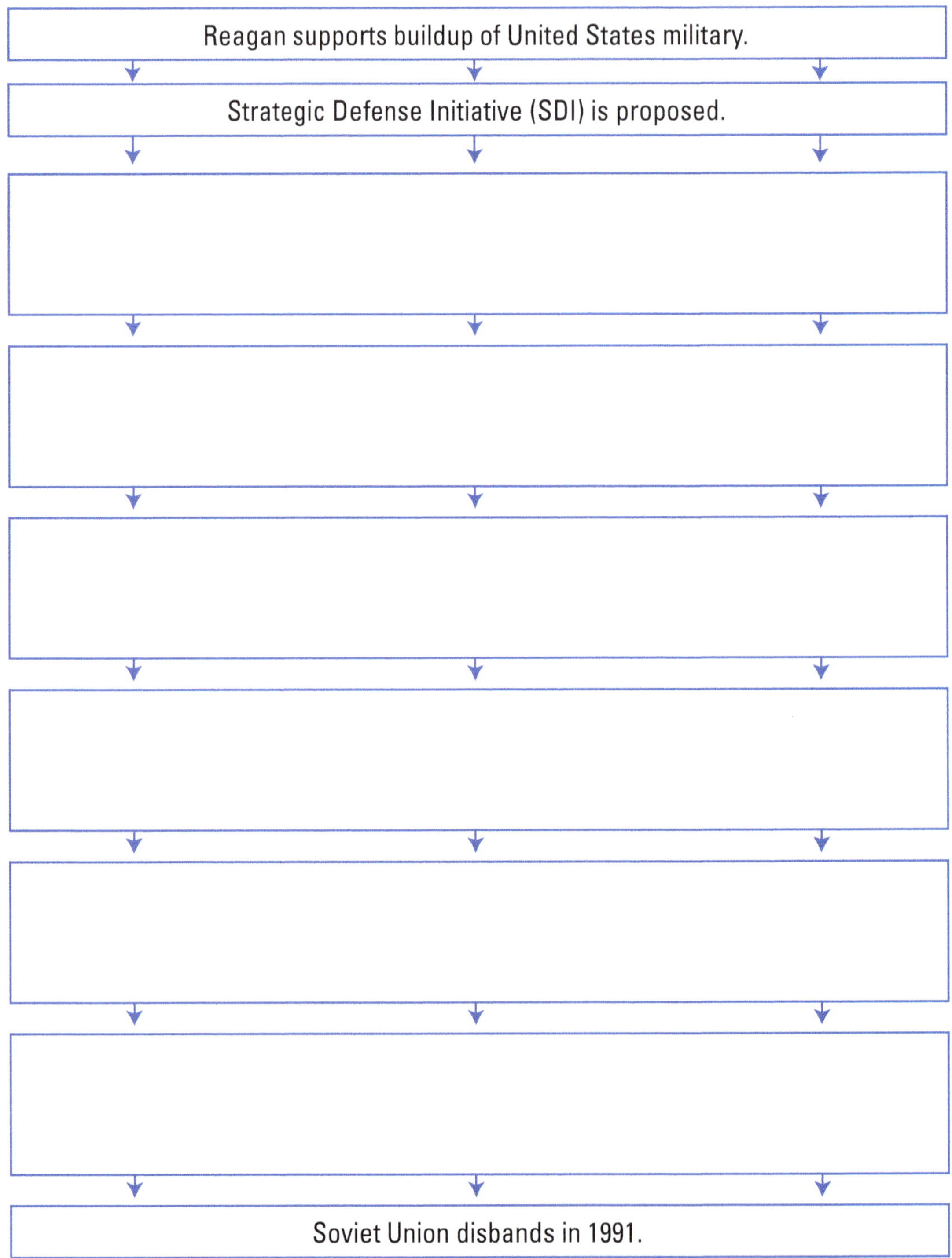

Note Taking Study Guide

THE END OF THE COLD WAR

Focus Question: What were Reagan's foreign policies, and how did they contribute to the fall of communism in Europe?

B. *Record the main ideas related to events in the Middle East during Reagan's presidency in the concept web below.*

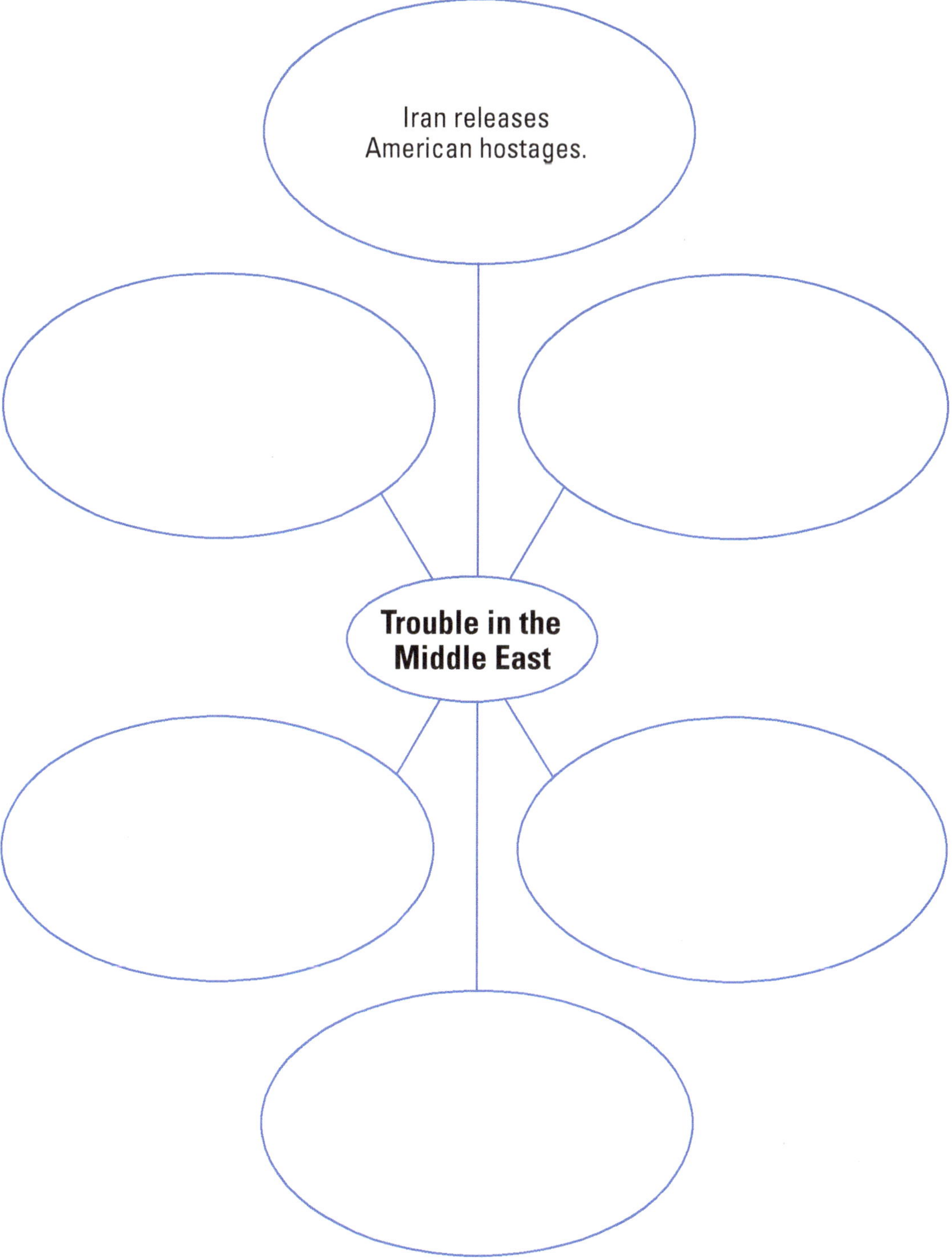

<table><tr><td>**CHAPTER**
19
SECTION 3</td><td>**Section Summary**
THE END OF THE COLD WAR</td></tr></table>

What country released American hostages early in Reagan's presidency?

____

____

____

Find the word *contradicted* in the underlined sentence. Use context clues to help you figure out the meaning of *contradicted*.

____

____

____

Sequence What policies did Mikhail Gorbachev pursue in the Soviet Union before the collapse of communism?

____

____

____

Under President Reagan, the United States worked to weaken communism and the Soviet Union by committing to the largest peacetime military buildup in U.S. history. Reagan proposed a program called the **Strategic Defense Initiative (SDI).** SDI would use lasers to destroy missiles aimed at the United States. Reagan also supported anticommunist rebellions worldwide. This included the **Contras,** anticommunist counterrevolutionaries in Nicaragua.

Mikhail Gorbachev, who became leader of the Soviet Union in 1985, pursued new reform policies. They were called *glasnost,* meaning a new openness, and *perestroika,* reforming the Soviet system. Relations between the United States and the Soviet Union improved. Eventually, both signed a nuclear arms pact. They also negotiated for a reduction of nuclear weapons. In 1991, communism collapsed and the Soviet Union split into 15 independent republics. The Cold War had ended.

In the Middle East, a truck bomb killed 241 United States Marines stationed in Lebanon. The United States also clashed with Libya, whose leader supported terrorist groups. On a positive note, all 52 American hostages held by Iran were released minutes into Reagan's presidency.

However, the **Iran-Contra affair** tarnished Reagan's second term. In 1985, the United States sold weapons to Iran in exchange for Iran's promise to pressure Lebanese terrorists to release American hostages. <u>This contradicted the administration's policy of not negotiating with terrorists.</u> Money from this sale was then used to fund Contras in Nicaragua, which violated a ban by Congress. Ultimately, several officials were convicted on charges from the scandal.

Review Questions

1. How did President Reagan weaken communism and the Soviet Union?

____

____

2. Why did the Iran-Contra affair tarnish President Reagan's presidency?

____

____

Note Taking Study Guide

FOREIGN POLICY AFTER THE COLD WAR

Focus Question: What actions did the United States take abroad during George H.W. Bush's presidency?

Use the chart below to summarize Bush's major foreign policy decisions.

Post-Cold War Foreign Policy	
America's new role in the world	**Persian Gulf War**
• Took a leading role in world affairs • • • • •	• Backed UN resolution after Iraq invaded Kuwait • • •

<table><tr><td>**CHAPTER**
19
SECTION 4</td><td>**Section Summary**
FOREIGN POLICY AFTER THE COLD WAR</td></tr></table>

What was the name of the oppressive system of segregation in South Africa that was dismantled in the early 1990s?

____

____

____

Find the word *tolerate* in the underlined sentence. The word *forbid* is an antonym of the word *tolerate*. *Forbid* means to prohibit or prevent. Use the meaning of *forbid* to figure out the meaning of *tolerate*.

____

____

____

Summarize What actions did President Bush and the United States take in the Persian Gulf War?

____

____

____

Under President George H.W. Bush, the United States took a leading role in world affairs. Bush continued the war on drugs and sent troops to Panama in December 1989. **Manuel Noriega,** Panama's dictator, was arrested and convicted of drug trafficking. He was sentenced to 40 years in prison.

Chinese students staged pro-democracy protests in Beijing's **Tiananmen Square** in the spring of 1989. China jailed many of the activists. President Bush suspended arms sales to China but kept up economic and diplomatic ties.

In the early 1990s, the oppressive South African system of segregation called **apartheid** ended, in part because of American economic sanctions. American firms **divested,** or withdrew investments, from the country. **Nelson Mandela,** the previously imprisoned leader of the antiapartheid movement, was elected leader of South Africa in 1994.

In the former Soviet Union, Yugoslavia was fighting a bloody civil war. Bush chose not to intervene with troops. However, later he did send United States Marines to Somalia on a humanitarian mission called "Operation Restore Hope."

In August 1990, Iraq invaded Kuwait. **Saddam Hussein,** Iraq's dictator, wanted to increase his power and control Kuwait's rich oil deposits.

President Bush made it clear that he would not tolerate Iraq's aggression against its neighbor. Bush worked to build an international coalition and backed a UN resolution demanding that Iraqi troops withdraw. Hussein did not comply. Under the name **Operation Desert Storm,** American, British, French, Egyptian, and Saudi coalition forces attacked Iraqi troops on January 16, 1991. On February 23, coalition forces attacked Iraqi forces in Kuwait. Within five days, Iraq agreed to a UN cease-fire. Iraqis left Kuwait, but Saddam Hussein still ruled Iraq. The entire conflict later became known as the Persian Gulf War.

Review Questions

1. Why did President Bush send troops to Panama?

____

____

2. What non-military actions did Bush take to help resolve conflicts in China, South Africa, and Somalia?

____

____

Name ______________________ Class ____________________ Date ________

CHAPTER 20 SECTION 1

Note Taking Study Guide

THE COMPUTER AND TECHNOLOGY REVOLUTIONS

Focus Question: How have technological changes and globalization transformed the American economy?

As you read, fill in the flowchart below to help you categorize technological changes and their impact.

Technology Revolution

Computers	Communications	Globalization
•	• Development of satellite technology	•
	•	
• 1954: IBM develops first commercially successful computer.		•
•	• Cellular telephones allow people to communicate away from their homes.	
	•	• Interconnection of world economies
• Development of personal computers		
•	•	

CHAPTER 20 SECTION 1	**Section Summary**
	THE COMPUTER AND TECHNOLOGY REVOLUTIONS

Technological change sped up rapidly in the twentieth century. New technology, particularly computers, changed many aspects of life. The first modern computer was developed in 1946. As technology improved, **personal computers** small enough to sit on a desk were introduced. By the 1980s, personal computers were changing the way people worked and communicated. So many people had access to new technology and information that the times were called the "information age."

Computers and new developments in **biotechnology** helped improve healthcare. **Satellites** orbiting Earth increased the speed of communications. Cellular telephones enabled people to communicate away from their homes. By the 1990s, the **Internet** made access to information almost instantaneous and changed commerce, education, research, and entertainment.

These technological changes had a dramatic effect on the American economy. Today, most workers need to have some computer skills even for low-wage jobs. Satellites and computers have made **globalization** much easier, so societies and economies around the world are linked. **Multinational corporations** operate in many countries at once, providing similar products and services to people around the world.

Some economists say that the United States now has a **service economy.** Rather than producing things as they once did, American workers provide services. Jobs in the service sector vary widely, from lawyer to fast-food worker. This radical change in the economy has taken power away from labor unions, and the average wages of workers have fallen.

Review Questions

1. How have recent developments in communications changed the way people live?

____

____

2. How has the rise of the service sector changed the American economy?

____

____

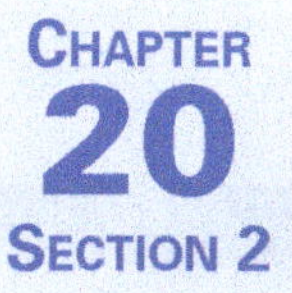

Note Taking Study Guide
THE CLINTON PRESIDENCY

CHAPTER 20 SECTION 2

Focus Question: What were the successes and failures of the Clinton presidency?

Complete the outline below as you read to summarize information about the Clinton presidency.

I. The 1992 Election

    A. Bush's popularity plummets.

    B. Clinton runs as "New Democrat."

    C. Clinton carries the election.

II. Clinton's Domestic Policies

    A. ____

    B. ____

    C. ____

III. The Republicans Galvanize

    A. ____

    B. ____

    C. ____

    D. ____

IV. Scandals, Impeachment, and Trial

    A. ____

    B. ____

    C. ____

    D. ____

<table>
<tr><td>CHAPTER
20
SECTION 2</td><td>## Section Summary
THE CLINTON PRESIDENCY</td></tr>
</table>

After 12 years of Republicans in the White House, Americans made a change in 1992. The Democrats nominated **William Jefferson Clinton,** governor of Arkansas, to run against President Bush. Texas billionaire **H. Ross Perot** ran as an independent. Clinton carried the election, and Democrats retained control of Congress.

Shortly after taking office, Clinton signed the **Family Medical Leave Act.** It guaranteed most full-time employees time off without pay for personal or family medical reasons. Clinton also signed the **Brady Bill.** That bill placed a five-day waiting period on sales of handguns. Clinton's wife, Hillary, led a task force that proposed a program to provide healthcare for all Americans. Her proposal never won congressional support and was ultimately dropped.

During the 1994 midterm elections, Georgia congressman **Newt Gingrich** introduced his **Contract With America.** It was a plan that attacked big government and emphasized patriotism and traditional values. Republicans won control of the House, the Senate, and most state governorships. Once in office, the Republicans passed much of Gingrich's program. In 1996, Clinton was reelected by a wide margin. However, Congress remained under Republican control.

President Clinton had dodged scandals from his first day in office. One scandal concerned investments the Clintons had made. Special prosecutor **Kenneth Starr** investigated the case. In seven years, he failed to uncover evidence of the Clintons' guilt. In the process, however, he began investigating the President's relationship with a White House intern. Clinton admitted he had lied about the affair, and Starr recommended **impeachment** proceedings. The House of Representatives impeached Clinton on charges of perjury and obstruction of justice. He was tried and acquitted on both counts by the Senate in February 1999.

Review Questions

1. What two bills did President Clinton sign after taking office?

____

____

2. What was the Contract With America?

____

____

Note Taking Study Guide

GLOBAL POLITICS AND ECONOMICS

Focus Question: What role did the United States take on in global politics and economics following the Cold War?

Complete the flowchart below to help you identify main ideas about global politics and economics.

U.S. Global Policy		
Free Trade	**Foreign Intervention**	**Middle East**
• NAFTA • •	• • NATO intervenes in Bosnia and Kosovo. •	• • • First al Qaeda terrorist attacks against United States

<table><tr><td>**CHAPTER**
20
SECTION 3</td><td>**Section Summary**
GLOBAL POLITICS AND ECONOMICS</td></tr></table>

In the 1990s, the United States was the world's sole superpower. The nation became involved in economic and political events around the world. One important issue in the 1990s was free trade. The **European Union (EU)** coordinates the monetary and economic policies of European nations. It is an example of a free trade bloc, and it challenged the economic leadership of the United States. The **North American Free Trade Agreement (NAFTA)** was a direct response to the EU. It created a free trade zone among the United States, Canada, and Mexico.

Clinton supported NAFTA, although many Democrats opposed it. Clinton also supported the revision to the **General Agreement on Tariffs and Trade (GATT)** aimed at lowering tariffs worldwide. A year later, the **World Trade Organization (WTO)** replaced GATT. The WTO has greater authority to negotiate trade agreements and settle disputes.

Although many Americans opposed military involvement in foreign countries, Clinton found it necessary to intervene in conflicts in Somalia and Haiti. After the fall of communism in Yugoslavia, civil war broke out in newly independent Bosnia. Bosnian Serbs attacked and murdered Muslims and Croats. This state-sanctioned mass murder became known as **ethnic cleansing.** In 1995, Clinton asked NATO to bomb Serbian strongholds. <u>This intervention brought about a cease-fire, but violence flared in another former Yugoslavian republic.</u> Once again, NATO responded. U.S. troops helped return some stability to the region.

In the 1990s, the conflict between Israelis and Palestinians grew. Clinton led negotiations that produced an agreement between Israeli and Palestinian leaders. That involvement in the Middle East made the United States a target of a terrorist group called **al Qaeda.** The group launched several attacks on U.S. targets at home and abroad.

Review Questions

1. How did the United States respond to the European Union?

____

____

2. What did Clinton do when violence broke out in Bosnia?

____

____

CHAPTER 20 SECTION 4

Note Taking Study Guide
BUSH AND THE WAR ON TERRORISM

Focus Question: What was the impact of Bush's domestic agenda and his response to the terrorist attack against the United States?

Record the sequence of events in Bush's presidency in the flowchart below.

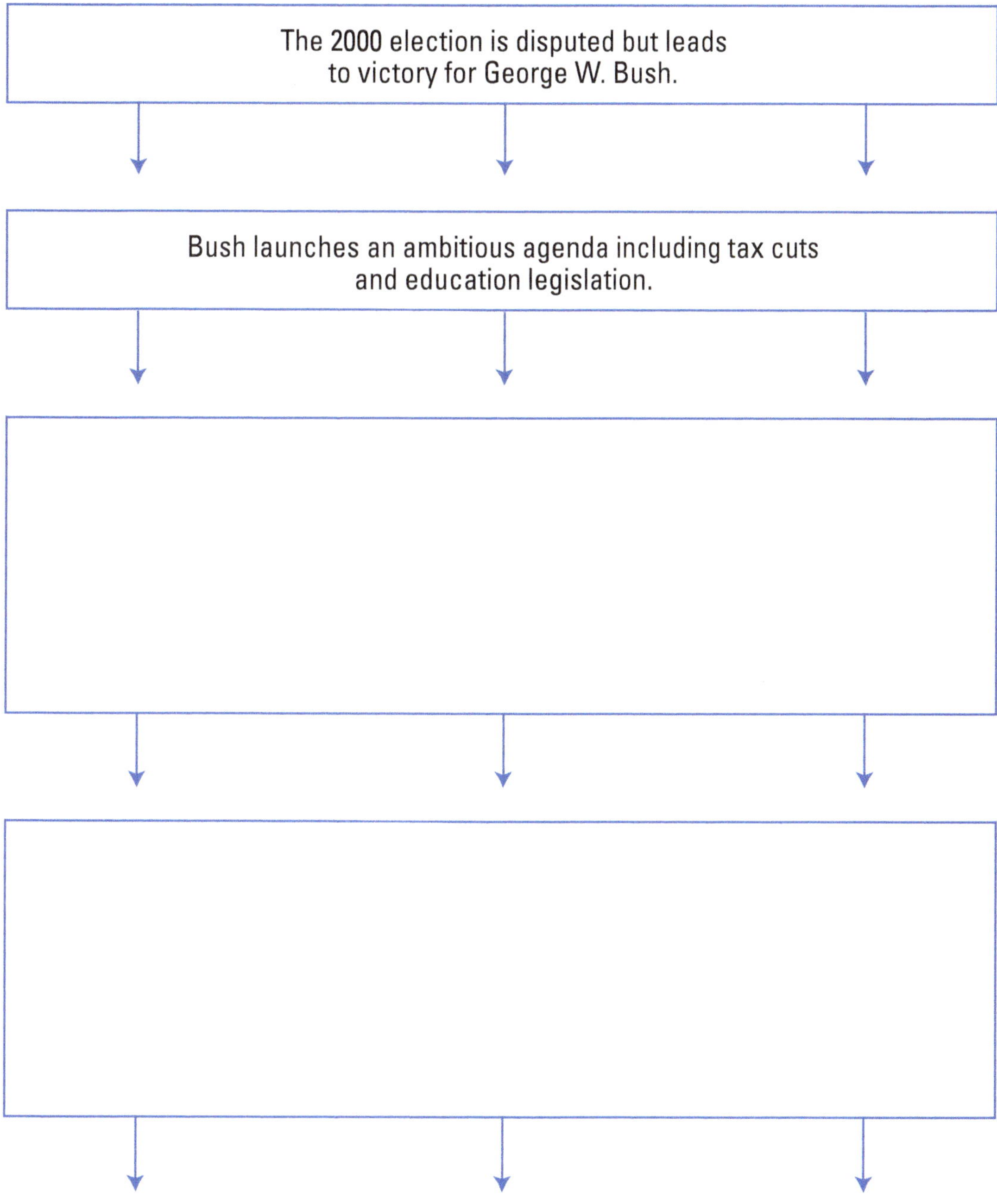

<table><tr><td>**CHAPTER**
20
SECTION 4</td><td>**Section Summary**
BUSH AND THE WAR ON TERRORISM</td></tr></table>

READING CHECK

What problems did President Bush face at home following the invasion of Iraq?

____

____

____

VOCABULARY STRATEGY

Find the word *priority* in the underlined sentence. The word *insignificant* is the antonym of the word *priority.* The word *insignificant* means "of lesser importance." Use context clues and the meaning of *insignificant* to figure out the meaning of *priority.*

____

____

____

READING SKILL

Recognize Sequence Which event in Bush's presidency has had the greatest influence on later events? Explain.

____

____

____

In 2000, the Democrats nominated Vice President Al Gore, Jr., to replace President Clinton. Gore faced Green Party candidate Ralph Nader and Republican candidate **George W. Bush.** The margin in the Electoral College vote was razor thin. The winner of Florida would win the election. Democrats demanded a hand recount. Republicans sued to prevent it. In *Bush* v. *Gore,* the Supreme Court decided to stop the recount and Bush won.

Bush's domestic agenda was overshadowed when the United States was attacked on September 11, 2001. Osama bin Laden's al Qaeda network was blamed for the attacks. Bin Laden and other al Qaeda leaders were believed to be hiding in **Afghanistan.** Bush demanded they be turned over, but the nation's Islamic fundamentalist **Taliban** government refused. Bush then sent American forces, which overthrew the Taliban and captured several al Qaeda leaders.

At home, improving national security became a priority. Congress passed the **Patriot Act.** It gave law enforcement broader powers to monitor suspected terrorists. Congress also created a Cabinet-level **Department of Homeland Security** to coordinate domestic security matters.

Bush next asserted that Iraqi dictator Saddam Hussein had **Weapons of Mass Destruction (WMD)** and was a threat to U.S. security. In March 2003, American and British military forces invaded Iraq. Later, Bush's popularity waned as violence against U.S. troops in Iraq escalated and the cost of the war increased. The 2008 election is historic. Barack Obama wins the election and becomes the nation's first African American President.

Review Questions

1. What role did the Supreme Court play in the 2000 presidential election?

____

____

2. How did the terrorist attacks on the United States affect domestic policies?

____

____

Note Taking Study Guide

CHAPTER 20 SECTION 5

AMERICANS LOOK TO THE FUTURE

Focus Question: How was American society changing at the beginning of the twenty-first century?

Record supporting details about the changing American society in the table below.

A Changing Society	
Immigration	**Demographics**
• Immigration policies relax. • •	• Family structures change. • Affirmative action provides opportunities for women and minorities. •

CHAPTER 20 SECTION 5

Section Summary

AMERICANS LOOK TO THE FUTURE

As the twenty-first century dawned, American society looked very different than it had a hundred years before. The **Immigration Act of 1990** had increased quotas and eased restrictions, making way for the greatest number of immigrants in the country's history. The largest group of immigrants is Latinos. The second-largest group is Asians.

Some people say immigrants make the American economy stronger. Others say they take jobs from native-born Americans. Opponents often dislike **bilingual education,** in which students are taught in English and in their native languages. Much of the debate concerns illegal immigration. The **Immigration and Control Act of 1986** penalizes businesses that hire illegal immigrants, but it has not stopped illegal immigration.

American demographics have changed, with many people moving from the Midwest and Northeast to the Sunbelt. The American family changed as well. Divorces and single-parent households are now more common than just 40 years ago.

<u>**Affirmative action** was created in the 1960s to help minorities and women overcome past discrimination.</u> It gives them preference in school admissions and job applications. Today, such programs are being challenged and in some cases, ended. Even so, women and African Americans continue to make social and political gains. Women are protected against unfair treatment in the workplace. The 1994 **Violence Against Women Act** increased federal resources to apprehend and prosecute men for violent acts against women.

Changing demographics are predicted to put a financial strain on the Social Security system. President Bush proposed **privatizing** Social Security. This change would allow younger workers to invest in individual retirement accounts. Opponents defeated his proposal and the debate continues.

Review Questions

1. What law led to the greatest number of immigrants in United States history?

____

____

2. How have American demographics changed in recent decades?

____

____

American Issues Journal

Global Interdependence

 **Essential Question:** Is global interdependence good for the American economy?

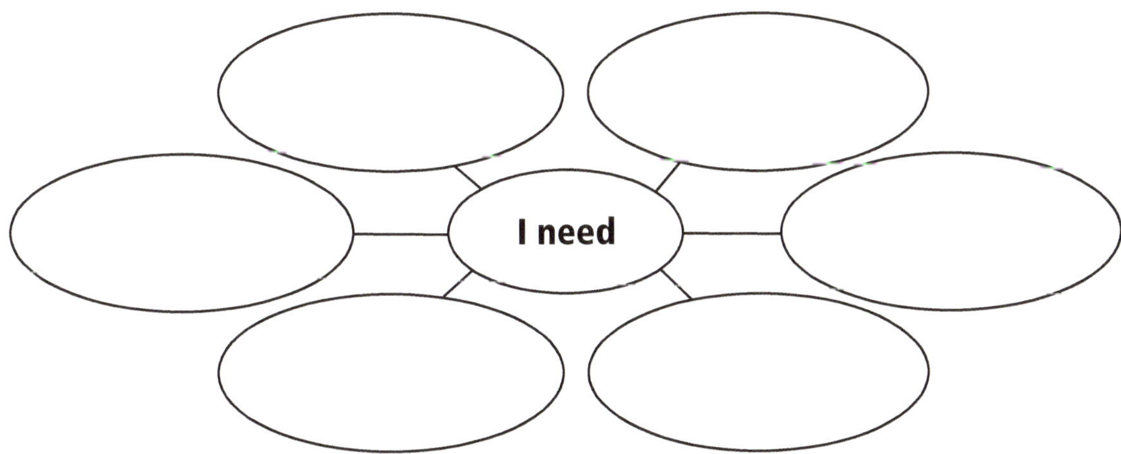

I. WARMUP

As nations have traded with one another over the centuries, they have become interdependent. Today, the United States economy depends on trade with countries around the world. The timeline on this page shows some key events in the development of this interdependence.

Global interdependence affects all Americans. For example, it affects the availability of products, prices of goods, costs of doing business, and the outsourcing of jobs.

1. How does this interdependence affect you? Fill in the concept web to show some of the products on which you depend in your daily life.

American Issues Journal

2. **a.** Which products on your list were produced in another country?
    b. Which products were produced in the United States?

Foreign Goods	**U.S. Goods**
___________	___________
___________	___________
___________	___________
___________	___________

3. How might global interdependence affect stores and restaurants in your community?

____

____

____

II. EXPLORATION

Now that you have explored the way global interdependence affects your life, consider the way global interdependence affects the nation.

A. World Trade Increases

In the chapter "Into a New Century" about the twenty-first century, you learned how technology has helped shape globalization.

What are three advantages of globalization? What are three disadvantages?

Advantages	Disadvantages
•	•
•	•
•	•

American Issues Journal

B. Find Out

1. Read the section about NAFTA in the chapter "Into a New Century." What is NAFTA?

2. Why was NAFTA created?

3. What does the term outsourcing mean?

4. Who would most likely support outsourcing?

5. Who would most likely oppose it?

C. What do you think?

Does NAFTA contribute to globalization? Explain.

You may wish to explore this issue further online. Go to:

Internet Research Activity

Transfer Your Knowledge
For: WebQuest **Web Code:** neh-6102

III. ESSAY

Bring together what you have read in your textbook with the information you have gathered online about this American issue. On a separate sheet of paper, answer the essential question: **Is global interdependence good for the American economy?**

American Issues Journal

Expanding and Protecting Civil Rights

Essential Question: What should the federal government do to expand and protect civil rights?

1791
Bill of Rights
First 10 Constitutional amendments

1868
Fourteenth Amendment
Citizenship for all native-born and naturalized Americans

1920
Nineteenth Amendment
Voting rights for women

1964
Civil Rights Act
Bans discrimination in jobs and public places

1990
Americans with Disabilities Act
Bans discrimination for disabilities

| 1820 | 1860 | 1900 | 1940 | 1980 | 2020 |

I. WARMUP

The scope of civil rights in the United States has grown along with the nation. Over time, the rights stated in the Constitution have been extended and supported by new legislation. The timeline on this page shows important milestones in this history.

Equal rights are guaranteed to all Americans. However, not all Americans enjoy the same privileges. What roles do rights and privileges play in your life?

1. How would you define the term "right"?

2. How would you define the term "privilege"?

What are three rights that matter to you?	What are three privileges that matter to you?
•	•
•	•
•	•

American Issues Journal

Expanding and Protecting Civil Rights (continued)

3. Why might healthcare or education be considered a right for all people?

____

____

____

____

II. EXPLORATION

Now that you have explored your civil rights, consider the challenges a nation faces in guaranteeing civil rights for all citizens.

A. Civil Rights Act

You know that the first rights guaranteed to Americans are in the Bill of Rights. However, it has taken more Constitutional amendments and many laws to ensure that these and other rights are extended equally. In some cases, the government has taken additional steps to ensure that some groups have really been able to exercise these rights.

1. Why do you think these groups have had to struggle so much for the rights they have won?

____

____

____

2. What are some ways you enjoy equality? Use the concept map to list four examples.

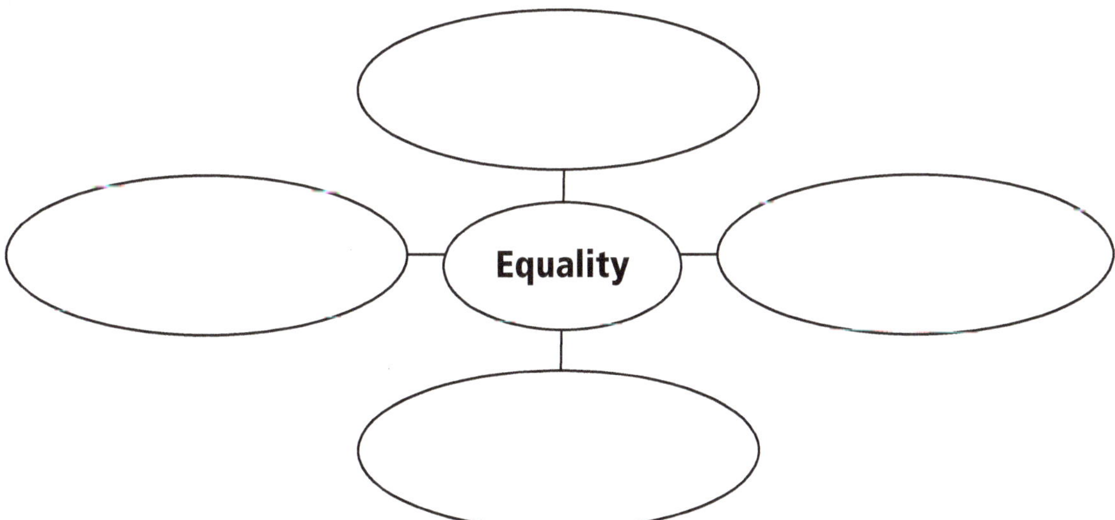

American Issues Journal

B. Find Out

1. Read Section 2 in the chapter "The Civil Rights Movement." How did the Civil Rights Act of 1964 address discrimination?

____

____

____

2. Read Section 3 in the chapter. Why were equal rights for all Americans still not fully enforced after the passage of the Civil Rights Act of 1964? List some of the barriers.

a.

b.

c.

d.

C. What do you think?

Do you think federal protection of civil rights is necessary? Explain.

____

____

____

You may wish to explore this issue further online. Go to:

Internet Research Activity

Transfer Your Knowledge
For: WebQuest **Web Code:** neh-6502

III. ESSAY

Bring together what you have read in your textbook with the information you have gathered online about this American issue. On a separate sheet of paper, answer the essential question: **What should the federal government do to expand and protect civil rights?**

American Issues Journal

Sectionalism and National Politics

Essential Question: How do regional differences affect national politics?

1812
War of 1812
Westerners and
Southerners for war

1861
Civil War
North and South at war

1948
Dixiecrats
Civil rights splits
Democrats

1820	1860	1900	1940	1980	2020

1787
Three-Fifths Compromise
Slaves counted
as three-fifths
of a person

1816–1832
Tariffs
North wants tariffs

2004
Presidential Election
Election confirms
division between
states

I. WARMUP

Throughout U.S. history, different regions or sections of the country have developed conflicting economic, social, political, and cultural interests. These interests have led to differences in views on national matters and have caused regions to respond to events in different ways. The timeline on this page shows the impact of regional conflicts on national politics.

1. Think about the neighborhood in which you live. How does your neighborhood differ from another one in your community?

My Neighborhood:	Other Neighborhood:
•	•
•	•
•	•

2a. How would you define the term "region"?

____

____

____

2b. In what region of the U.S. do you live?

____

____

____

American Issues Journal

3. How might economic factors in your community, such as household income or employment opportunities, affect the way you think about social or political issues?

____

____

____

____

II. EXPLORATION

Now that you have explored how local differences affect you, consider the ways in which regional differences might affect the nation.

A. Civil War

For more than 70 years, Americans were able to resolve sectional differences through negotiation and compromise. Looming behind many of these differences was the issue of slavery, an issue that had divided the country since its earliest days.

1. How would you define the term "compromise"?

____

____

2. What are some benefits of compromise? Some drawbacks?

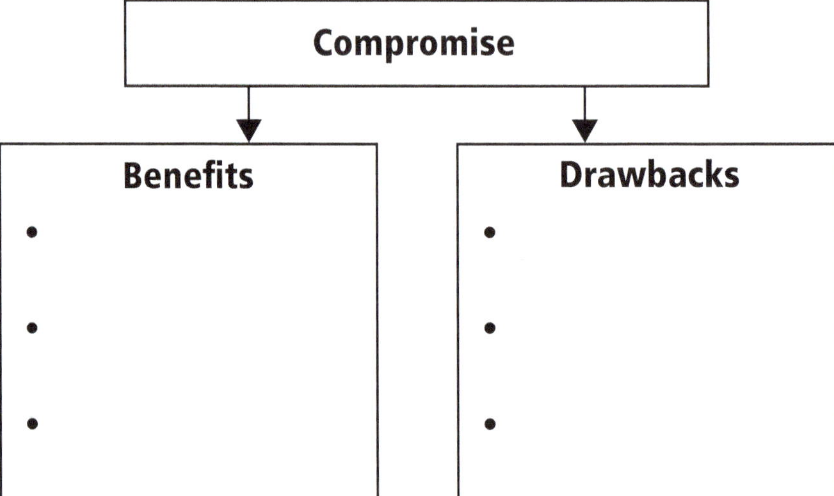

American Issues Journal

B. Find Out

1. Read the chapter "The Union in Crisis." Why did slavery become a more urgent problem as the nation grew?

____

____

2. What were some of the compromises made?

____

____

3. Why do you think that the South was willing to make compromises in the early and mid-1800s? Why was the North willing to make compromises? Fill in the speech balloons to show what a Southerner and a Northerner might have said.

North   **South**

C. What do you think?

Why did regional differences matter so much?

____

____

____

You may wish to explore this issue further online. Go to:

Internet Research Activity

Transfer Your Knowledge
For: WebQuest **Web Code:** neh-6702

III. ESSAY

Bring together what you have read in your textbook with the information you have gathered online about this American issue. On a separate sheet of paper, answer the essential question: **How do regional differences affect national politics?**

American Issues Journal

Church and State

 **Essential Question:** What is the proper relationship between government and religion?

1791
Bill of Rights
First Amendment

1840s
Sabbatarian Controversy
Debate over commerce
on Sundays

1984
Federal Equal Access Act
Religious clubs at
public schools

2000
**Mitchell v.
Helms**
Public funds for
private schools

| 1820 | 1860 | 1900 | 1940 | 1980 | 2020 |

1947
Everson v. Board of Education
Affirms separation of church and state

I. WARMUP

When Congress approved the Bill of Rights in 1789, it guaranteed freedom of religion to Americans, but it also made clear that Congress could not establish religion. Although the First Amendment set up a separation of church (religion) and state (government), questions have still arisen about the proper relationship between the two. The timeline on this page shows when these issues have come up.

When the government spends money, it is using tax money paid by Americans. The government uses this money to pay for or to support public needs.

1. How would you define the term "public"?

2. How would you define the term "private"?

____

____

____

____

3a. What are some public places or programs you use that are supported by the government?

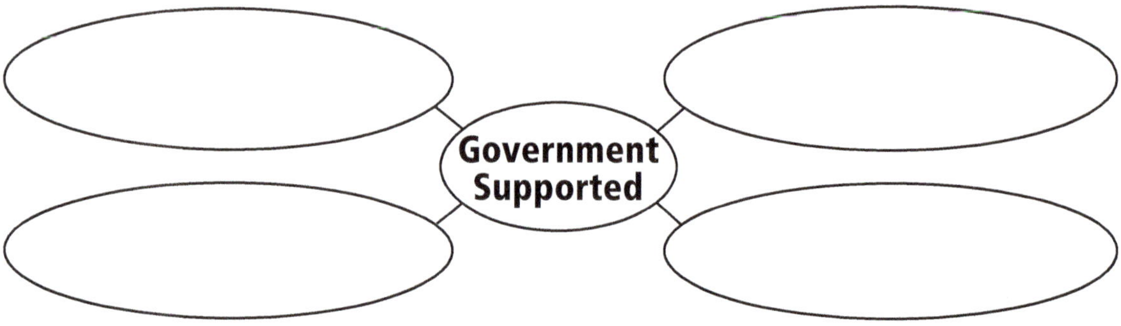

3b. What are some private places or programs that you use?

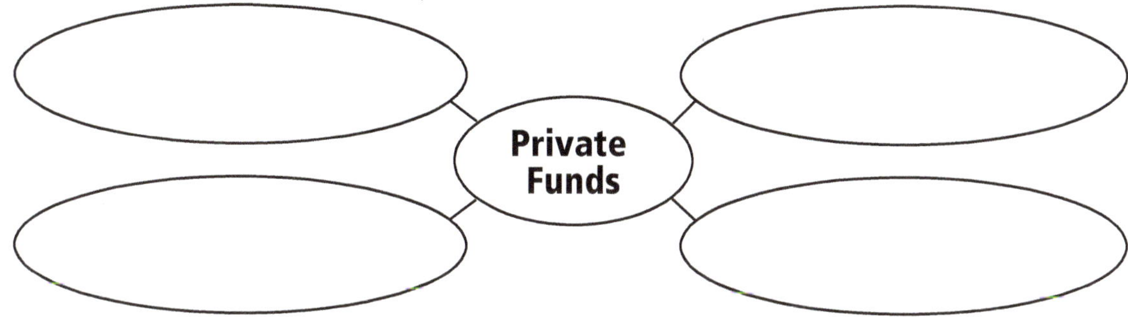

4. Should taxpayer's money be used for a program run by a private organization?

____

____

____

II. EXPLORATION

Now that you have explored the difference between private and public, consider how these differences might affect the role of religion in government.

A. Federal Equal Access Act

You know that not all people have religious freedom. In some nations, government supports or represents a particular religion. Sometimes people are persecuted or prohibited from practicing their religion.

1. As an American, what does religious freedom mean to you?

____

____

____

B. Find Out

1. Read the First Amendment. What does it say the government may not do regarding religion?

____

____

____

American Issues Journal

2. Read the section about the Equal Access Act in the chapter "The Conservative Resurgence." What does the act require?

____

____

____

3. How well do you think the Equal Access Act reflects the First Amendment? Explain.

____

____

____

C. What do you think?

Should there be an Equal Access Act? Why or why not?

____

____

____

You may wish to explore this issue further online. Go to:

Internet Research Activity

Transfer Your Knowledge
For: WebQuest **Web Code:** neh-6802

III. ESSAY

Bring together what you have read in your textbook with the information you have gathered online about this American issue. On a separate sheet of paper, answer the essential question: **What is the proper relationship between government and religion?**

American Issues Journal

Federal Power and States' Rights

Essential Questions: How much power should the federal government have?

1791
Bill of Rights
Tenth Amendment

1831
Nullification Crisis
Calhoun says states can overturn federal laws

1930s
New Deal
Federal government expands power

| 1820 | 1860 | 1900 | 1940 | 1980 | 2020 |

1798
Kentucky and Virginia Resolutions
States claim they can void federal laws

1857
Dred Scott *v.* Sandford
Federal government cannot outlaw slavery in territories

1965
Voting Rights Act
Federal officers register voters

I. WARMUP

The U.S. Constitution provides a federal system of government. One of its basic principles is that power is divided between the central government and the states. Over time, the distribution of power has created controversy. The timeline on this page shows some important events related to this issue.

When the federal government has expanded its power, the power of the states has been affected.

1a. How would you define the term "power"?

____

____

1b. What powers do you have?

____

____

2. Who are the people, organizations, or governments with power over you?

____

____

American Issues Journal

3. Do you think there should be equal power among the branches of government? Explain.

____

____

II. EXPLORATION

Now that you have explored how power affects you on a personal level, consider how the power of the federal government might affect your state.

A. The New Deal

You have learned that the New Deal implemented a series of programs to combat problems—unemployment, bank failures, hunger—caused by the Great Depression.

What are some ways that government helps you?

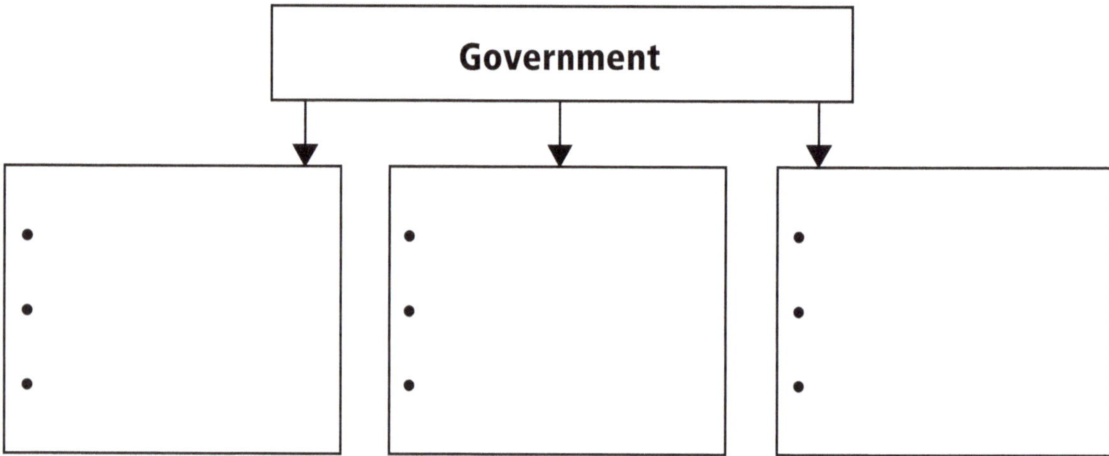

B. Find Out

1. Read the Tenth Amendment to the Constitution. What guarantee does it provide?

____

____

____

____

____

American Issues Journal

2. Fill in the thought bubbles below to show different points of view people held about federal power in the 1930s.

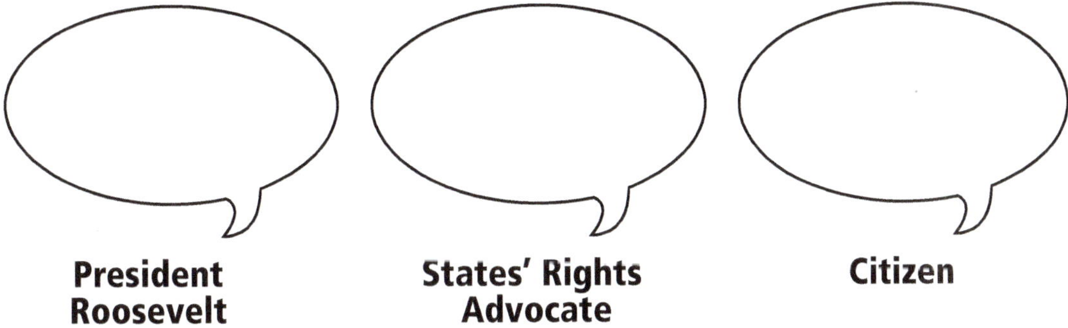

C. What do you think?

Is it sometimes necessary for the federal government to broaden its powers? Explain.

____

____

____

You may wish to explore this issue further online. Go to:

Internet Research Activity

Transfer Your Knowledge
For: WebQuest **Web Code:** neh-7002

III. ESSAY

Bring together what you have learned in your textbook with the information you've gathered online about this American issue. On a separate sheet of paper, answer the essential question: **How much power should the federal government have?**

American Issues Journal

Checks and Balances

 **Essential Question:** Does any branch of the federal government have too much power?

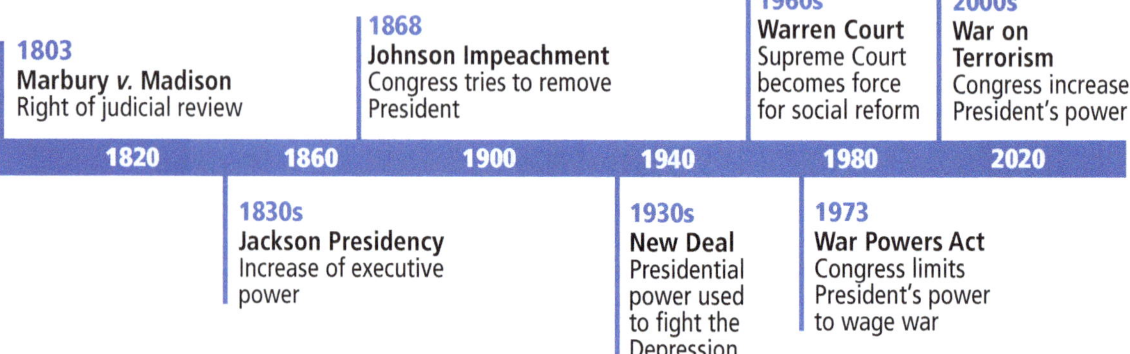

I. WARMUP

When the writers of the Constitution divided the U.S. government into three branches, they created a system of checks and balances. Under this system, each branch has the power to monitor and limit the actions of the other two, thus keeping any one branch from becoming too powerful. However, the balance of power has not always remained equal. The timeline on this page shows times when power has shifted.

Your life is full of checks and balances. For example, you may be able to drive a car, but there are laws that check or limit how you drive it. In this case, the resulting balance of power among drivers ensures safety on the road.

1. Fill in the chart to show other ways checks and balances work in your life.

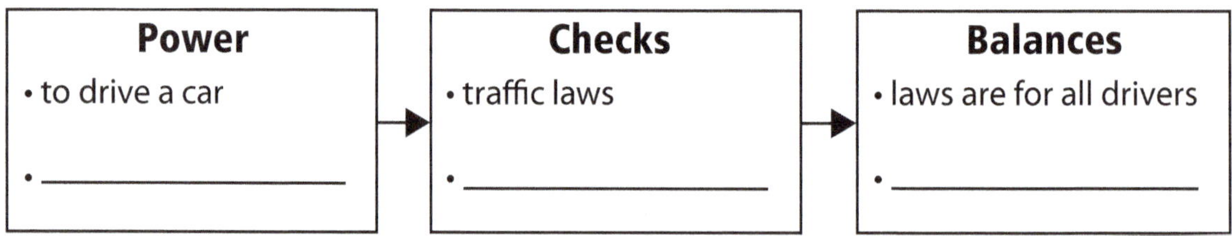

2. What would happen to the balance if some drivers did not have to obey the laws?

____

____

____

American Issues Journal

3. What are the benefits of checks and balances in your life?

____

____

____

II. EXPLORATION

Now that you have explored how checks and balances work in your own life, consider how they work in the federal government.

A. War on Terrorism

On September 11, 2001, the United States was attacked by terrorists. These attacks changed how Americans viewed terrorism and how the federal government viewed national safety.

How did you feel about the security of the nation before September 11? After it?

Before	After
•	•
•	•
•	•

B. Find Out

1. Read Articles I, II, III, and Section 4 of Article IV of the Constitution. How does the Constitution provide checks and balances?

____

____

____

American Issues Journal

2. What powers does the Constitution give the executive branch?

____

____

____

C. What do you think?

Did the War on Terrorism result in too much power for any branch of government? Explain your answer.

____

____

____

You may wish to explore this issue further online. Go to:

Internet Research Activity

Transfer Your Knowledge
For: WebQuest **Web Code:** neh-7202

III. ESSAY

Bring together what you have read in your textbook with the information you have gathered online about this American issue. On a separate sheet of paper, answer the essential question: **Does any branch of the federal government have too much power?**

American Issues Journal

Technology and Society

Essential Question: What are the benefits and costs of technology?

Late 1700s							1930s				2000s
Factory System Production increases; worker's conditions worsen							**Polymers** Plastics products; pollution increases				**Genetic Engineering** Benefits; Costs
1780	1800	1820	1840	1860	1880	1900	1920	1940	1960	1980	2000

1859
Oil Refining
Industrial growth;
pollution worsens

1940s
Nuclear Reactor
Nuclear energy; threats
of nuclear waste

I. WARMUP

Technology has played an enormous role in American life and has been responsible for many economic and social benefits. However, technological advances also have drawbacks or costs. The timeline on this page shows some technological advances that have had both benefits and costs.

1a. What does the term "technology" mean to you? How would you define it?

____

____

1b. How would you define the term "benefit"?

____

____

1c. How would you define the term "cost"?

____

____

2. Fill in the chart to show some ways that you use technology for your personal needs at home or at school.

Personal Uses of Technology
•
•
•

American Issues Journal

3. What kinds of costs might there be with the technology that you use for personal purposes?

____

____

____

II. EXPLORATION

Now that you have explored some ways that technology affects your life, consider how it might affect society.

A. Plastics

Plastics are long chains of molecules called polymers. Your home, school, and community are filled with these synthetic products. Plastics are useful materials that can be easily shaped. They often replace other materials such as metal, wood, stone, paper, ceramics, and glass.

1. What are some common plastic products that you use? Use the concept web to list four examples.

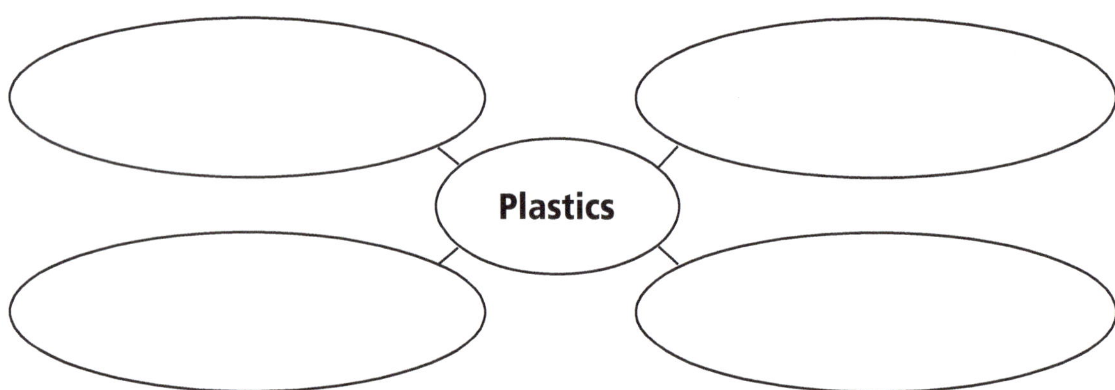

B. Find Out

Many people are concerned about the harmful effects of the disposal of plastic materials on the environment. Read Section Four in the chapter called "An Era of Protest and Change."

1. What is its main point about the impact of the Environmental Movement?

____

____

____

American Issues Journal

2. List four plastic items that you have thrown away or will throw away today.

1.

2.

3.

4.

3. How does your school or community address the problem of plastic items in garbage?

____

____

____

C. What do you think?

Do the costs of using plastics outweigh the benefits?

____

____

____

You may wish to explore this issue further online. Go to:

Internet Research Activity

Transfer Your Knowledge
For: WebQuest **Web Code:** neh-7302

III. ESSAY

Bring together what you have read in your textbook with the information you have gathered online about this American issue. On a separate sheet of paper, answer the essential question: **What are the benefits and costs of technology?**

American Issues Journal

Migration and Urbanization

Essential Question: How does migration affect patterns of settlement in America?

1862		1910–1930		1970s–Present
Homestead Act Free land brings settlers to Great Plains		**Great Migration** Southern blacks move north		**Sunbelt Growth** Movement to warmer, southern areas

1820	1860	1900	1940	1980	2020

	1889–1920		**1950s**
	Urban Migration Movement from farms to cities		**Suburban Flight** Movement from cities to suburbs

I. WARMUP

Since the first settlers arrived, Americans have been on the move. The settlement patterns of people have been shaped by several migration trends. The timeline on this page shows times when large migration trends changed settlement patterns.

1. Have you or members of your family ever moved? If so, what were the main reasons for moving?

____

____

____

2a. How would you define the term "migration"?

____

____

2b. How would you define the term "patterns of settlement"?

____

____

3. How might moving change a person's life?

____

____

____

American Issues Journal

II. EXPLORATION

Now that you have explored moving as it might affect you, consider how migration affected settlement patterns in the United States.

A. Suburban Flight

You have learned that millions of Americans migrated from rural to urban areas between 1890 and 1920. Thirty years later, large groups of people began moving again, this time to the suburbs.

How do suburbs differ from cities? How are the two areas alike? Use the Venn diagram to identify similarities and differences.

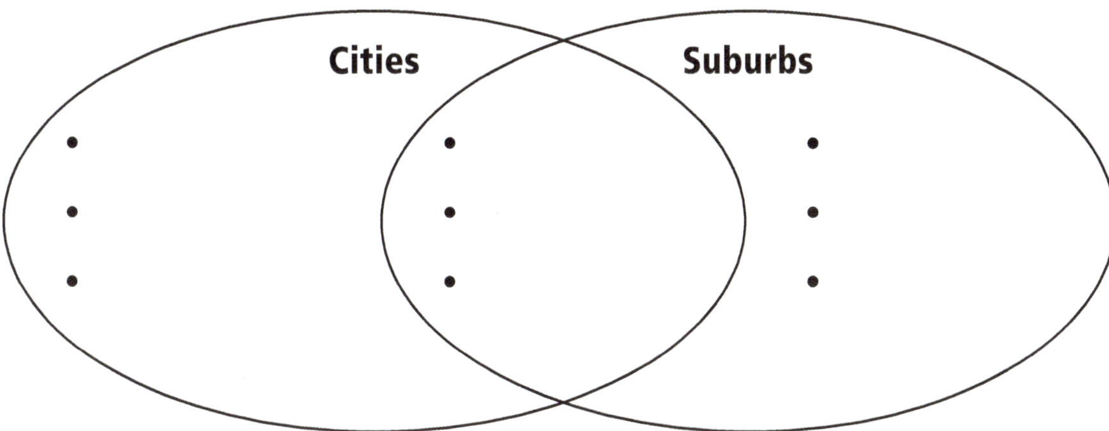

B. Find Out

1. Read Sections 1 and 2 in the chapter "Postwar Confidence and Anxiety." Why did so many people move to the suburbs after World War II?

____

____

____

2. What kinds of buildings and organizations did suburbs need to establish to support their growing populations?

____

____

____

American Issues Journal

3. What were the benefits of living in the suburbs? What were the costs?

Benefits	Costs
•	•
•	•
•	•

C. What do you think?

What are the social benefits of migration?

____

____

____

You may wish to explore this issue further online. Go to:

Internet Research Activity

Transfer Your Knowledge
For: WebQuest **Web Code:** neh-7402

III. ESSAY

Bring together what you have read in your textbook with the information you have gathered online about this American issue. On a separate sheet of paper, answer the essential question: **How does migration affect patterns of settlement in America?**

American Issues Journal

American Indian Policy

Essential Question: How should the federal government deal with Indian nations?

1787
U.S. Constitution
Gives government power to regulate trade with Native Americans

1887
Dawes Act
Reservations divided into individual holdings

1975
Indian Self-Determination Assistance Act
Indians get more control over schools and other services

| 1820 | 1860 | 1900 | 1940 | 1980 | 2020 |

1824
Bureau of Indian Affairs
Agency for handling relations with Native Americans

1934
Indian Reorganization Act
Tribal governments gain more control

I. WARMUP

Relationships between Native Americans and the federal government have often been characterized by confrontation, misunderstanding, and broken promises. Government policy regarding Native Americans has shifted several times since the country's early days. The timeline on this page shows periods when important changes have taken place.

Numerous treaties and agreements defined how the government has dealt with Indian nations. In the past, many of these treaties were broken or disregarded.

1. Why do you think treaties or contracts are important?

____

____

____

2. What happens when a contract is broken? For example, suppose a person signs a contract to buy a used car. What consequences might result if the contract is broken?

____

____

____

American Issues Journal

3. Is breaking a contract ever justified? Explain.

____

____

____

II. EXPLORATION

Now that you have explored how contracts affect your life, consider the challenges of how treaties affected the relations between the federal government and Native Americans.

A. Indian Self-Determination and Educational Assistance Act

You have learned about the struggles for rights of various groups in the United States. Successes in achieving rights by one group encouraged other groups to develop rights movements as well. One goal of the Indian nations was self-determination.

Define the term "self-determination."

____

____

B. Find Out

Review the material in Section 2 in "The South and West Transformed" chapter. Then, read Section 3 of the chapter "An Era of Protest and Change."

1. What conditions caused Native Americans to form the activist organization AIM?

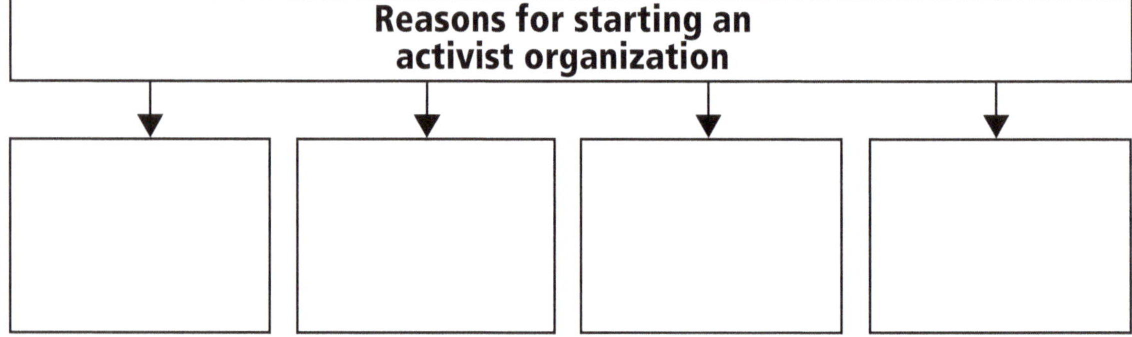

American Issues Journal

2. What tactics has AIM used to fight for equality and social justice?

____

____

____

3. What were some results of the protests staged by AIM in the 1970s?

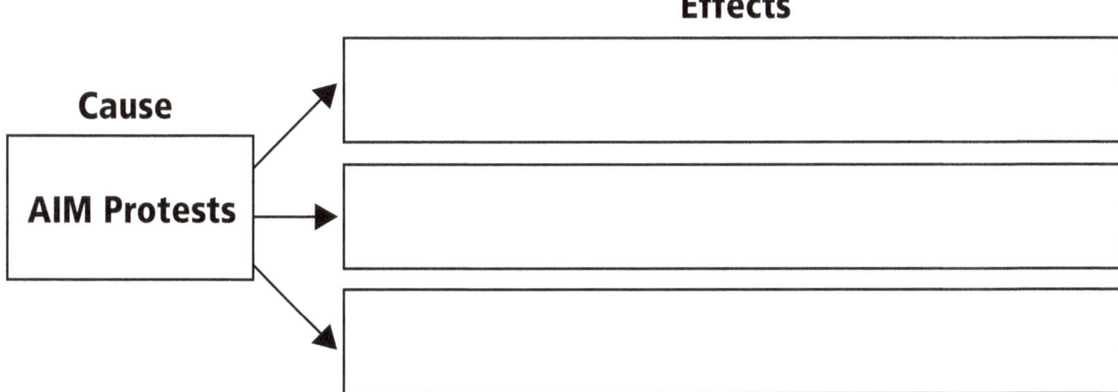

C. What do you think?

Are Native Americans justified in trying to reclaim land they believe still belongs to them? Explain.

____

____

____

You may wish to explore this issue further online. Go to:

Internet Research Activity

Transfer Your Knowledge
For: WebQuest **Web Code:** neh-7502

III. ESSAY

Bring together what you have read in your textbook with the information you have gathered online about this American issue. On a separate sheet of paper, answer the essential question: **How should the federal government deal with Indian nations?**

American Issues Journal

Women in American Society

Essential Question: Why do Americans disagree over women's rights?

1848
Seneca Falls Convention
Women meet to support
their rights

1869
**National Woman Suffrage
Association**
Anthony and Stanton fight
for women's suffrage

1920
Nineteenth Amendment
Women gain right to vote

1964
**Title VII of the
Civil Rights Act**
Protection against
job discrimination

1972
**Title IX of the
Education Codes**
Bans sex
discrimination
in schools

| 1880 | 1900 | 1920 | 1940 | 1960 | 1980 |

I. WARMUP

Women have always been a vital part of American society, but for much of the nation's history, they have not had the same rights as men. Women were denied basic legal rights such as voting, owning property, or holding public office. The timeline on this page shows when women finally won some of these rights

1. Who are some of the women you admire in today's society? Make a list of three or four women in different fields. The names you include might be people in your community or nationally known figures.

Name	Field

2. What stereotypes do you think these women had to overcome to succeed?

____

____

____

Name ______________________ Class ______________________ Date __________

American Issues Journal

Women in American Society (continued)

3. How can stereotypes about a group affect its rights?

II. EXPLORATION

Now that you have explored some aspects of rights for women, consider whether full equality for women exists today.

A. Title IX of the Education Codes

Traditional social arrangements do not always accord the same roles or rights to each gender. In the 1960s, a movement for women's rights challenged many of these traditional social arrangements. One piece of legislation that was passed was Title IX of the Higher Education Act. Until that time, most high schools and colleges spent nearly all their athletic funds for male dominated sports. With the passage of Title IX, however, women could demand equal spending for women's sports.

Check a box to show how you stand on spending for high school sports.

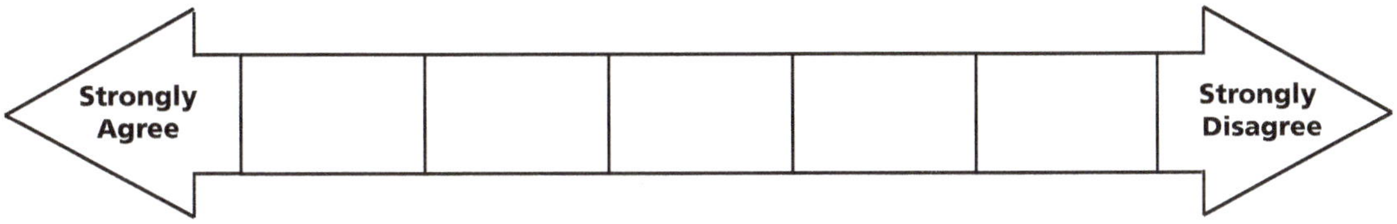

1. Why did you choose this rating?

American Issues Journal

B. Find Out

Read about the legal headway that women made in Section 2 of the chapter "An Era of Protest and Change."

1. Why was banning discrimination in education under Title IX important for women?

____

____

____

2. What are some arguments for and against equal rights for women?

For Equal Rights	Against Equal Rights
•	•
•	•
•	•

C. What do you think?

Should there be a law requiring equal spending for women's and men's sports in public schools? Explain.

____

____

____

You may wish to explore this issue further online. Go to:

Internet Research Activity

Transfer Your Knowledge
For: WebQuest **Web Code:** neh-7602

III. ESSAY

Bring together what you have read in your textbook with the information you've gathered online about this American issue. On a separate sheet of paper, answer the essential question: **Why do Americans disagree over women's rights?**

Social Problems and Reforms

Essential Question: What are the most pressing problems, and how can we solve them?

1990s–2000s
Healthcare Reform
High costs of healthcare challenged

1790s–1820s
Second Great Awakening
Christians start reforms

1890–1920
Progressivism
Reformers

| 1820 | 1860 | 1900 | 1940 | 1980 | 2020 |

1830s–1850s
Abolitionism
Antislavery forces

1950s–1960s
Civil Rights
Racial equality reforms

I. WARMUP

Throughout U.S. history, injustices and pressing needs have produced challenging social problems. In most cases, this has led to reforms. However, not all reforms have been equally welcomed; some have met with fierce opposition. The timeline shows periods in America's history when reform movements have occurred.

1a. How would you define the term "social problem"?

____

____

1b. How would you define the term "reform"?

____

____

2a. What are the most pressing social problems in your school? Use the chart to list them.

Social Problems in My School
1.
2.
3.
4.

2b. How do you think the social problems in your school might be solved?

____

____

____

American Issues Journal

3. Would these solutions be considered reforms? Explain.

____

____

____

____

II. EXPLORATION

Now that you have explored social problems and reform at your school, consider how social problems could be resolved by the federal government.

A. Healthcare Reform

Without insurance, few Americans can afford the high costs of healthcare. Two government healthcare programs are in place. One of them is Medicare, a program that supplies basic hospital insurance to people in the Social Security system who are age 65 and older. The other program, called Medicaid, provides basic medical services to poor and disabled Americans. Even so, millions of Americans do not qualify for these programs and have no health insurance.

Do all Americans have the right to health insurance? Show where you stand on this issue by checking one of the boxes below.

<table>
<tr><td>Strongly Agree</td><td></td><td></td><td></td><td></td><td></td><td>Strongly Disagree</td></tr>
</table>

1. Why did you choose this rating?

____

____

____

B. Find Out

1. Read the information about healthcare reform in Section 2 of the chapter "Into a New Century." Summarize its main idea.

____

____

____

____

American Issues Journal

2. What might be some pros and cons about a universal healthcare program or one that would guarantee free insurance coverage for all Americans?

Pros	Cons
•	•
•	•
•	•
•	•

C. What do you think?

Should the U.S. have universal healthcare coverage? Explain.

____

____

____

You may wish to explore this issue further online. Go to:

Internet Research Activity

Transfer Your Knowledge
For: WebQuest **Web Code:** neh-7702

III. ESSAY

Bring together what you have read in your textbook with the information you have gathered online about this American issue. On a separate sheet of paper, answer the essential question: **What are the most pressing problems, and how can we solve them?** Healthcare is one pressing problem. You can choose to discuss any other problem you have read about in your textbook, such as education or immigration.

American Issues Journal

Territorial Expansion of the United States

Essential Question: Should the United States expand its territory?

1803
Louisiana Purchase
Jefferson buys Louisiana without congressional approval

1848
Mexican Cession
U.S. gains Mexican lands after war

1893
Hawaiian Revolt
Americans overthrow queen; pave way to annexation

1820 — **1860** — **1900**

1845
Texas Annexation
Texas joins Union

1867
Alaska Purchase
U.S. buys Alaska

1898
Spanish-American War
U.S. control over Spanish lands

I. WARMUP

Throughout its history, the U.S. has increased the size of its territory many times and in various ways. While this territorial expansion has broadened the global power of the U.S., it has also caused considerable debate among Americans. The timeline on this page shows how the nation has expanded.

1. How would you define the term "expansion"?

____

____

____

2a. How would you feel if someone moved into your home without your permission? Use the thought bubble to explain your reaction.

American Issues Journal

2b. What actions might you take to reclaim your home?

____

____

____

3. What might be some benefits of one person taking over the property of another? Explain.

____

____

____

II. EXPLORATION

Now that you have explored the concept of territorial expansion on a small scale, consider the national and international effects of territorial expansion by the United States.

A. Mexican Cession

1. Read the chapter "Manifest Destiny." What does the term "Manifest Destiny" mean?

____

____

2. How did Manifest Destiny lead to war with Mexico?

____

____

B. Find Out

When the U.S. won a war with Mexico in 1848, it acquired a vast area of land known as the Mexican Cession. This territory now comprises the states of Arizona, California, Utah, Nevada, and part of Colorado and New Mexico.

1. There are always many points of view to consider when studying an historical event. Consider the reactions of a Mexican citizen and President Polk after the Mexican War. What might each one have said about the war and the Mexican Cession? Write your thoughts in the chart below.

Mexican Citizen	President Polk

American Issues Journal

2. Ralph Waldo Emerson predicted the United States would win the war against Mexico but said that "Mexico would poison us." How did the Mexican Cession "poison" the United States?

____

____

____

____

C. What do you think?

Was the U.S. justified in acquiring land from Mexico? Explain.

____

____

____

You may wish to explore this issue further online. Go to:

Internet Research Activity

Transfer Your Knowledge
For: WebQuest **Web Code:** neh-7802

III. ESSAY

Bring together what you have read in your textbook with the information you have gathered online about this American issue. On a separate sheet of paper, answer the essential question: **Should the United States expand its territory?**

American Issues Journal

America Goes to War

Essential Question: When should America go to war?

1812
War of 1812
Fought to stop Britain from
seizing American ships

1917–1918
World War I
Fought after
Germany violated
American
neutrality

1960s–1970s
Vietnam War
Fought to halt spread
of communism

1820	1860	1900	1940	1980	2020

1860s
Civil War
Fought over slavery, states'
rights, and saving the Union

1940s
World War II
Fought after Japan attacked
Pearl Harbor

I. WARMUP

The United States came into existence through a revolutionary war and has had many
reasons for going to war since then. The timeline on this page shows some of the
occasions when the nation went to war.

1. The list below shows some of the reasons America has gone to war. Rank the list from
1 to 6 to show what you think are the most important to the least important reasons.
Number 1 is the most important; number 6 is the least important..

__ protect itself

__ protect rights and freedoms

__ expand borders

__ gain economic benefits

__ aid allies

__ increase power and influence

2. Which of the reasons on the list do you think are worth fighting and possibly
dying for?

____

____

3. Are all wars equally justified? Explain.

____

____

____

American Issues Journal

II. EXPLORATION

Now that you have explored some reasons nations are willing to fight, consider the effects of one war in which the U.S. fought.

A. Vietnam War

Read the chapter "The Vietnam War."

1. Which President introduced the domino theory?

____

2. Define domino theory.

____

____

____

3. How was this theory used to justify sending troops to Vietnam?

____

____

____

B. Find Out

Opposition to the war lead to a strong anti-war movement. There were two groups—the Hawks and the Doves.

1. How did the Hawks and the Doves differ in their thinking about the war? Fill in the chart with your answers.

Hawks	Doves
•	•
•	•

American Issues Journal

2. Although not everyone fights in a war, a war affects a nation's citizens in different ways. The war in Vietnam had profound effects on the American people. Use the concept web below to show some of the ways the war impacted the nation.

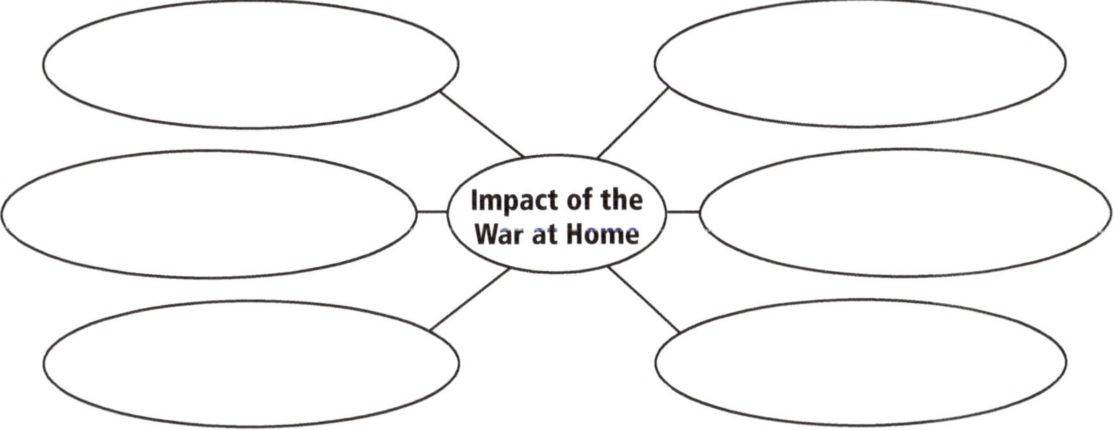

C. What do you think?

Should the U.S. have fought in Vietnam? Explain.

____

____

____

You may wish to explore this issue further online. Go to:

Internet Research Activity

Transfer Your Knowledge
For: WebQuest **Web Code:** neh-7902

III. ESSAY

Bring together what you have read in your textbook with the information you have gathered online about this American issue. On a separate sheet of paper, answer the essential question: **When should America go to war?**

American Issues Journal

U.S. Immigration Policy

Essential Question: How should the government regulate immigration?

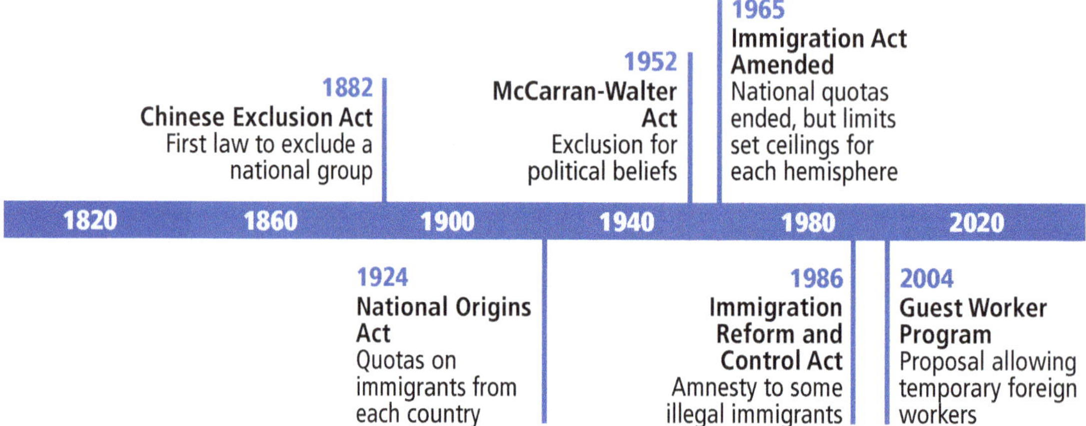

I. WARMUP

The history of immigration to America is long and complex. It began during the colonial era with both voluntary and involuntary arrivals. The timeline on this page reflects the national policy of immigration after 1850.

1. What are some reasons that immigrants have come voluntarily to the U.S?

____

____

____

2. Why did the U.S. begin to limit immigration?

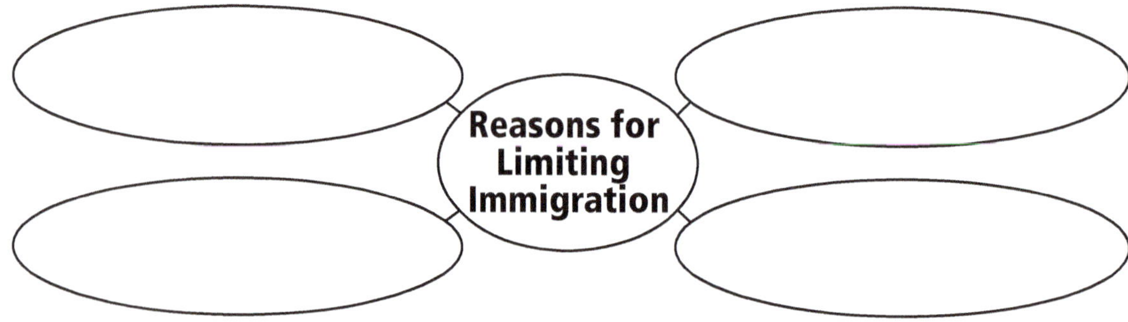

American Issues Journal

3. Is the U.S. right to limit immigration? Explain.

____

____

____

II. EXPLORATION

Now that you have started to explore the issue of immigration, consider how immigration continues to affect the nation.

A. Immigration Reform and Control Act

1. Read Section 5 of the chapter "Into a New Century." What was the purpose of the Immigration Reform and Control Act?

____

____

2. How did laws restricting immigrants contribute to an increase in illegal immigration?

____

____

____

3. Why do you think immigrants risked entering the U.S. illegally?

____

____

____

B. Find Out

Read the poem by Emma Lazarus in the Documents of Our Nation section at the back of your textbook.

1. How does its message differ from the Immigration Reform and Control Act?

Immigration Reform and Control Act	"The New Colossus" Poem

American Issues Journal

2. Based on what you have read, how do you think each of the following would feel about the Immigration Reform and Control Act?

C. What do you think?

Should there be an Immigration Reform and Control Act? Explain.

____

____

____

You may wish to explore this issue further online. Go to:

Internet Research Activity

Transfer Your Knowledge
For: WebQuest **Web Code:** neh-8002

III. ESSAY

Bring together what you have read in your textbook with the information you have gathered online about this American issue. On a separate sheet of paper, answer the essential question: **How should government regulate immigration?**

American Issues Journal

Government's Role in the Economy

Essential Question: What is the proper balance between free enterprise and government regulation of the economy?

1890
Sherman Antitrust Act
Curbs power of monopolies

1913
Federal Reserve Act
Controls money supply

2001
Tax Cuts
Taxes lowered to promote economic growth

1820	1860	1900	1940	1980	2020

1906
Pure Food and Drug Act
Regulates safety of food and medicine

1933
Agricultural Adjustment Act
Payments to farmers create high crop prices and farm profits

I. WARMUP

The U.S. economy operates under a free enterprise system. However, the role of the government has varied in response to different events. For example, during the 1960s and 1970s, demand for government protection of consumers and the environment led to the creation of new government agencies and regulations. The timeline on this page shows other periods in history when the government used regulation to control the economy.

The balance between regulation and free enterprise affects all Americans. How might the balance affect your life? One way is in protecting you as a consumer. For example, the sanitary conditions in which foods are produced are closely regulated.

1a. How do you define the term "free enterprise"?

1b. How do you define the term "regulation"?

2. Research, then list below three products you use that are regulated by consumer protection laws.

American Issues Journal

Government's Role in the Economy (continued)

3. Should the government be allowed to control items that might be dangerous to consumers? Explain.

____

____

____

II. EXPLORATION

You have looked at one way that government regulation can benefit the consumer. Now consider the steps the government takes to regulate the economy.

A. Tax Cuts

In the Constitution, the first power given to Congress is the power "to lay and collect taxes" to pay for debts, defense, and the common welfare.

You have read about the scope of the New Deal and how it increased the role of the federal government. For example, the government began taking taxes directly from the paychecks of workers. What does the government use tax money for? Use the chart to list four things.

TAXES

B. Find Out

Read the section in the Economics Handbook about Tools for Moderating the Business Cycle: Fiscal Policy.

1. What is fiscal policy?

____

____

American Issues Journal

2. Read Section 4 in the chapter "Into a New Century." Why did President Bush want a a tax cut in 2001?

____

____

____

3. What were the positive and negative effects of the tax cut?

____

____

____

4. Why do you think taxpayers are usually in favor of tax cuts and against tax increases?

____

____

____

C. What do you think?

Should the government raise and lower taxes to regulate the economy?

____

____

____

You may wish to explore this issue further online. Go to:

Internet Research Activity

Transfer Your Knowledge
For: WebQuest **Web Code:** neh-8202

III. ESSAY

Bring together what you have read in your textbook with the information you have gathered online about this American issue. On a separate sheet of paper, answer the essential question: **What is the proper balance between free enterprise and government regulation of the economy?**

American Issues Journal

Civil Liberties and National Security

Essential Question: What is the proper balance between national security and civil liberties?

| | | | **1940s**
World War II
Internment of Japanese Americans | **2001**
War on Terror
Patriot Act |

1790s
Undeclared War with France
Alien and Sedition Acts

| 1820 | 1860 | 1900 | 1940 | 1980 | 2020 |

1860s
Civil War
Habeas Corpus suspended

1950s
Cold War
Red Scare

I. WARMUP

Throughout its history, the U.S. government has faced moments when the safety of the nation seemed more important than preserving all the rights and liberties of its citizens. The timeline on this page shows when this issue surfaced in U.S. history.

The balance between national security and civil liberties affects all Americans. But how might the balance between safety and liberty surface in your life?

1. (a) How do you define the term "safe"?

1. (b) How do you define the term "freedom"?

____

____

____

____

2. Schools are places where students assemble to learn, discuss ideas, and acquire essential skills to become active citizens. Schools are also organizations with rules and regulations to ensure student safety.

A. What are three things that you think make your school safe?	**B. What three freedoms do you think students should have in school?**
•	•
•	•
•	•

American Issues Journal

3. How does the need for safety in schools affect students' freedom?

____

____

____

II. EXPLORATION

Now that you have explored the issues of safety and freedom in your school, consider the challenges of these issues for the nation.

A. Civil Liberties during the Civil War

In the chapter on the Civil War, you read about President Lincoln's response to Americans who sought to undermine the northern war effort. To keep the Union secure, Lincoln suspended the constitutional right of *habeas corpus* and empowered soldiers to arrest people suspected of disloyalty.

1. Civil liberties are freedoms that are or should be protected by the law. As an American, what three freedoms do you value most?

____

____

____

National security is the protection of a nation's citizens and institutions from threats.

2. What do you think makes a nation safe? Use the concept web to list four ways.

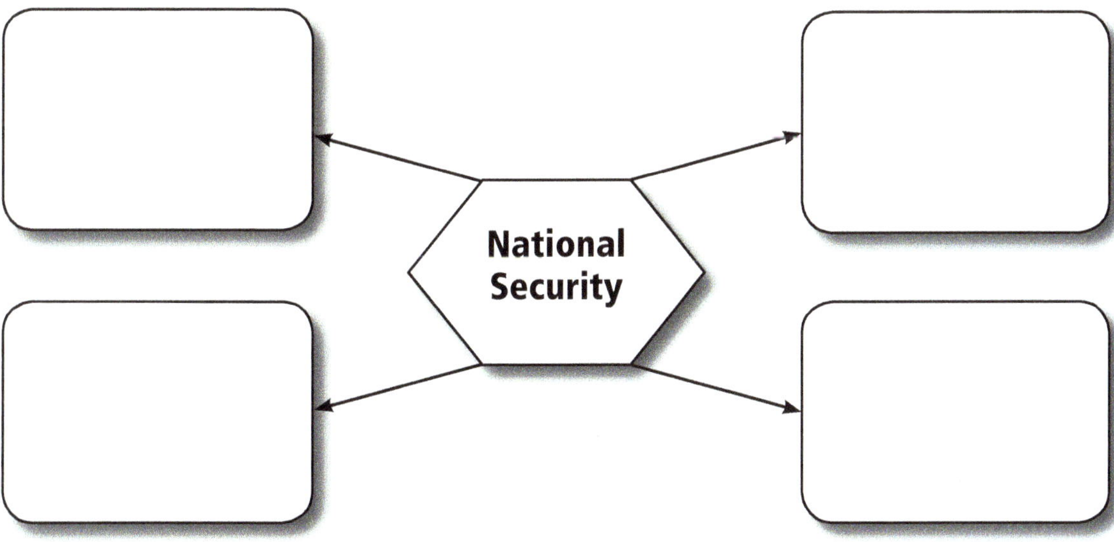

American Issues Journal

B. Find Out

1. Read Article II of the Constitution. What does it say about the powers of the President during time of war?

____

____

____

2. Read Article I, Section 9, Clause 2 of the Constitution. What does it say about habeas corpus?

____

____

____

C. What do you think?

Should Lincoln have suspended habeas corpus? Explain.

____

____

____

You may wish to explore this issue further online. Go to:

Internet Research Activity

Transfer Your Knowledge
For: WebQuest **Web Code:** neh-8502

III. ESSAY

Bring together what you have read in your textbook with the information you have gathered online about this American Issue. On a separate sheet of paper, answer the essential question: **What is the proper balance between national security and civil liberties?**

American Issues Journal

Voting Rights

Essential Question: What should the government do to promote voting rights?

| 1820 | 1860 | 1900 | 1940 | 1980 | 2020 |

1820s–1830s
Age of Jackson
Move toward universal white male suffrage

1920
Nineteenth Amendment
Vote for women

1971
Twenty-sixth Amendment
Voting age lowered to 18

2000
Presidential Election
Polling-place irregularities lead to some reforms

1870
Fifteenth Amendment
Vote for African American men

1965
Voting Rights Act
Strengthening of African American voting rights

I. WARMUP

As you have learned, ensuring voting rights for all American citizens has been a long and sometimes embattled process. Over time, however, more and more Americans have gained suffrage. The timeline on this page shows some key events in the struggle for voting rights.

1. How would you define the term "voting rights"?

____

____

2. In a democracy, people vote all the time to make choices about things. Often, these choices are about leaders of a group, actions that a group will take, or rules that a group will follow. As a student, you probably voted for class president. What other school issues did you vote for?

____

____

____

American Issues Journal

3. What are two important responsibilities of a voter?

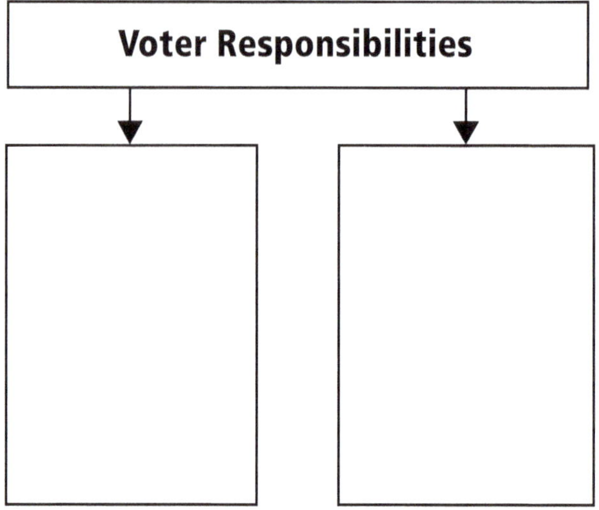

4. Why do groups use voting as a way of deciding things?

____

____

____

II. EXPLORATION

Now that you understand the importance of voting, explore the efforts of different groups of citizens to obtain this right.

A. Twenty-sixth Amendment

The U.S. government has lifted voting restrictions several times throughout its history to broaden the number of citizens who can vote.

Look at the amendments listed on the timeline. Identify any amendments that have helped to make you eligible to vote in the next Presidential election.

____

____

____

B. Find Out

Read Section 3 of the chapter "The Vietnam War Era" and the Twenty-sixth Amendment to the Constitution. The amendment was in part a response to student protests during the Vietnam War.

American Issues Journal

Not everyone thinks that eighteen-year-olds should be allowed to vote. What might be some arguments for and against the Twenty-sixth Amendment?

Arguments for 26th Amendment	Arguments Against 26th Amendment
• • •	• • •

C. What do you think?

Should the government raise the voting age to 21? Explain.

____

____

____

You may wish to explore this issue further online. Go to:

Internet Research Activity

Transfer Your Knowledge
For: WebQuest **Web Code:** neh-8702

III. ESSAY

Bring together what you have read in your textbook with the information you have gathered online about this American issue. On a separate sheet of paper, answer the essential question: **What should the government do to promote voting rights?**

American Issues Journal

Poverty and Prosperity

Essential Question: How should Americans deal with the gap between rich and poor?

1800s
Community Aid
Private charities aid poor

1900
Poverty Level
About 40% of Americans living in poverty

1964
War on Poverty
Programs to reduce poverty

1996
Welfare Reform
Limit on welfare programs

| 1820 | 1860 | 1900 | 1940 | 1980 | 2020 |

1933
New Deal
Federal government aids poor

1980s
Reaganomics
Business growth to reduce poverty

I. WARMUP

From the earliest days of the nation, Americans have not been equal in wealth. To balance the extremes between wealth and poverty, some people have supported federal government policies to distribute wealth. Others believe the role of helping needy people should be left to nonprofit charitable organizations. The timeline on this page shows when various efforts to close the gap between rich and poor have occurred.

1. Have you ever worked with a community, religious organization, school, or other local group to help people in need? How did you help? Check the ones that apply.

__ soup kitchen   __ food bank   __ clothing drive

__ recycling toys   __ holiday gifts   __ fuel drive

__ other

2. If you have not joined in these efforts to help the poor, what other ways would you suggest helping those in need in your community?

____

____

3. What do you think? How effective are community-level organizations in addressing poverty?

____

____

____

American Issues Journal

II. EXPLORATION

Now that you have started exploring local ways to help those in need, consider these issues on a national level.

A. War on Poverty

1. What are some things that poor people have to struggle for?

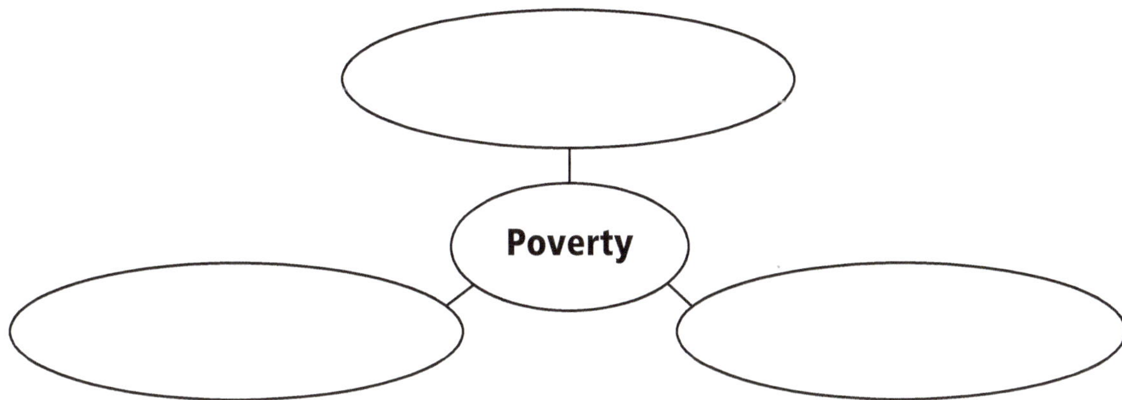

2. Michael Harrington wrote about poverty in the cities, or urban poverty. Do you think urban poverty still exists? Explain.

____

____

____

____

B. Find Out

1. Read Section 3 of the chapter on "The Kennedy and Johnson Years." What was the goal of the War on Poverty?

____

____

2. Why do you think the word "war" was used to name this program?

____

____

____

____

American Issues Journal

3. What were three important programs set up during the War on Poverty? What issue did each program address?

Program	Purpose

C. What do you think?

Should the government be responsible for creating social programs to help the poor? Explain.

____

____

____

You may wish to explore this issue further online. Go to:

Internet Research Activity

Transfer Your Knowledge
For: WebQuest **Web Code:** neh-8802

III. ESSAY

Bring together what you have read in your textbook with the information you have gathered online about this American issue. On a separate sheet of paper, answer the essential question: **How should Americans deal with the gap between rich and poor?**

American Issues Journal

America and the World

Essential Question: What is America's role in the world?

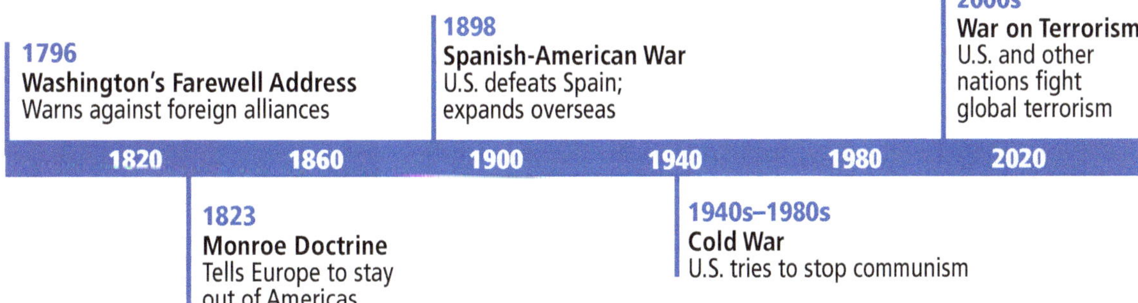

1796
Washington's Farewell Address
Warns against foreign alliances

1898
Spanish-American War
U.S. defeats Spain;
expands overseas

2000s
War on Terrorism
U.S. and other
nations fight
global terrorism

| 1820 | 1860 | 1900 | 1940 | 1980 | 2020 |

1823
Monroe Doctrine
Tells Europe to stay
out of Americas

1940s–1980s
Cold War
U.S. tries to stop communism

I. WARMUP

As he left office in 1796, George Washington warned the nation against foreign alliances. For many years, the U.S. did try to avoid involving itself in the affairs of other nations. However, much has changed since the late 1700s, and the U.S. has played an active role in more and more world affairs as the timeline on this page shows.

Have you ever been in a position where you were the strongest or most able member of a team or group? Because of your status, perhaps you helped the group by using your strength or ability in some way such as scoring a winning point or proposing a plan.

1. Use the graphic below to show what happened.

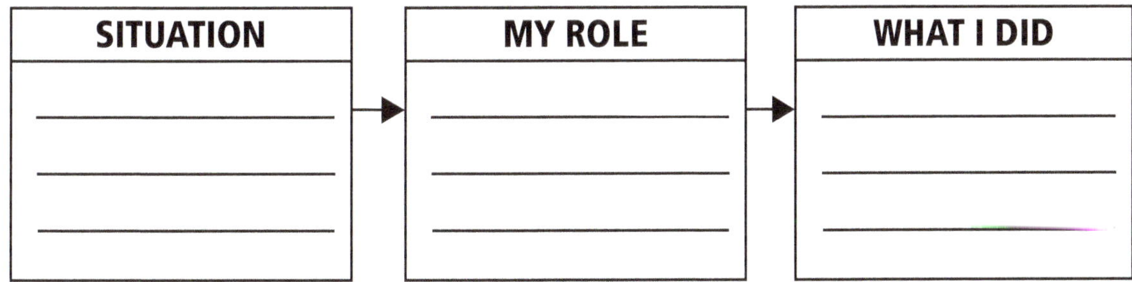

2. How do you think the other members of the group might feel about your role?

____

____

____

American Issues Journal

3. Should it be your responsibility to help others because of your status?

____

____

____

II. EXPLORATION

Now that you have explored roles you might play as the strongest member in a group, consider the roles the U.S., as a superpower, plays in the world.

A. War on Terrorism

The United States has for many years been one of the most powerful nations in the world. It is also one of the wealthiest. What are some leadership roles you think a nation such as the U.S. should play in the world? For example, should the United States try to settle international disputes?

Show your ideas by filling in the concept web below.

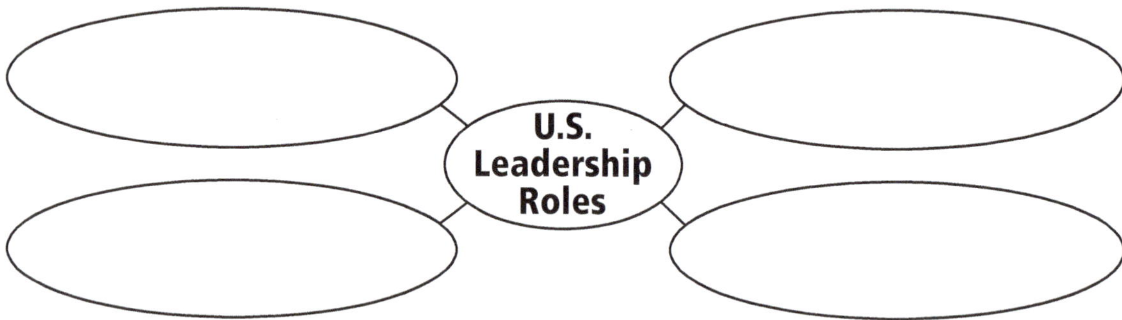

B. Find Out

1. Read the end of Section 3 in the chapter "Into the New Century." What did Americans learn about terrorism?

____

____

____

2. Read the speech on terrorism by President George W. Bush in the section of your textbook entitled Documents of Our Nation. Summarize his main point about the U.S. role in world affairs.

____

____

American Issues Journal

3. Read Section 4 in the chapter "Into the New Century. " Why did the U.S. invade Afghanistan and Iraq?

Afghanistan	Iraq

C. What do you think?

Should the U.S. get involved in the affairs of other nations?

____

____

____

You may wish to explore this issue further online. Go to:

Internet Research Activity

Transfer Your Knowledge
For: WebQuest **Web Code:** neh-8902

III. ESSAY

Bring together what you have read in your textbook with the information you have gathered online about this American issue. On a separate sheet of paper, answer the essential question: **What is America's role in the world?**

American Issues Journal

Interaction with the Environment

 **Essential Question:** How can we balance economic development and environmental protection?

1820	1860	1900	1940	1980	2020

1872
Yellowstone
First national park

1962
Silent Spring
Carson's book
exposes pesticide
dangers

1973
**Endangered
Species Act**
Protection for
threatened species

1916
**National Park
Service**
National Park
system created

1970
**Clean Air
Act**
Air quality
standards
established

1997
Kyoto Protocol
U.S. fails to ratify
global treaty on
greenhouse gases

I. WARMUP

Although the government has long worked at conserving public lands and parks, concern about protecting the environment was not an important issue until the 1960s and 1970s. Rachel Carson's book *Silent Spring*, published in 1962, helped make people aware of how human actions were altering the environment in harmful ways. Her book not only inspired the modern environmental movement; it also exposed the connection between economic growth and environmental protection.

1a. How would you define the term "economic development"?

____

____

____

1b. How would you define the term "environmental protection"?

____

____

____

2a. What are some ways that you help to protect the environment? Use the concept web below to list four things you do.

American Issues Journal

2b. Why might some industries have unfavorable views of environmental controls?

____

____

____

3. Why should people try to protect the environment?

____

____

____

II. EXPLORATION

You have started exploring the interaction between economic development and the environment. Now consider what role the government should take.

A. Kyoto Protocol

In the chapter "An Era of Protest and Change," you read about the development of the environmental movement. Although many people supported the government's actions, critics felt that it had gone too far in environmental regulation. Some said it hampered U.S. business by diverting funds to clean up projects.

1. List two or three federal or state environmental laws.

____

____

____

2. What impact have these laws had?

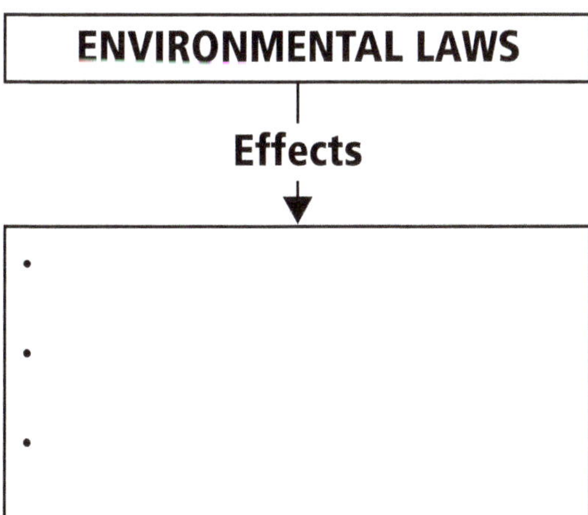

American Issues Journal

B. Find Out

In 1997, more than 170 nations met in Kyoto, Japan, to draw up a treaty about global climate change. The resulting Kyoto Protocol addressed the issue of reducing greenhouse gases, a cause of global warming. Although these gases occur naturally, they are also created by human activities such as burning oil and gas. The treaty called for industrial nations that have emitted the most greenhouse gases to take the lead in reducing emissions. Less was expected of developing nations such as China and India.

President Bill Clinton signed the Kyoto treaty, but the U.S. Congress has never ratified it. What might be some of the pros and cons of the Kyoto Protocol for the U.S.? As you complete the chart, think about the effect of the treaty on the U.S. industry as well. Would it hamper or help industry?

Pros	Cons
•	•
•	•
•	•

C. What do you think?

Should the U.S. ratify the Kyoto Protocol? Explain.

____

____

____

You may wish to explore this issue further online. Go to:

Internet Research Activity

Transfer Your Knowledge
For: WebQuest **Web Code:** neh-9002

III. ESSAY

Bring together what you have read in your textbook with the information you have gathered online about this American Issue. On a separate sheet of paper, answer the essential question: **How can we balance economic development and environmental protection?**

American Issues Journal

Education and the American Society

Essential Question: What should be the goals of American education?

1600s–1700s
Colonial Education
Emphasis on religious study

1903
Du Bois-Washington Debate
Role of education in lives of
African Americans debated

2001
No Child Left Behind Act
Federal law to raise student performance with standardized testing

1600	1820	1860	1900	1940	1980	2020

1852
Public Schools
Massachusetts has first compulsory school attendance law

1926
Scholastic Aptitude Test
First SAT given

I. WARMUP

Education has long been an important element in American life. While schools in colonial times had a religious focus, schools in later times have promoted democratic values. Today, public schools place an emphasis on performance standards. The timeline on this page shows some key events in American education.

1. What are your goals for your education?

____

____

____

2. How successful do you think you have been so far in achieving these goals? Show your progress by checking one of the boxes below.

Very Successful ← | | | | | → Not Very Successful

3. Explain your choice.

____

____

____

American Issues Journal

Education and the American Society (continued)

4. Why is education important?

____

____

____

II. EXPLORATION

Now that you have explored your own goals in education, consider what goals the government should set for American education.

A. No Child Left Behind Act

As a student, you have no doubt taken many quizzes and tests during your school years. You also know that two teachers of the same subject may give very different tests. A good mark on one test may not be as good on another test.

1. What is the purpose of a test?

____

____

____

2. What other ways are sometimes used to measure what you have learned? List three ways.

____

____

____

3. Does test preparation help you better understand a subject? Explain.

____

____

____

B. Find Out

1. Review the section in the chapter "Into a New Century" on the No Child Left Behind Act. What was the purpose of this?

____

____

____

American Issues Journal

Education and the American Society (continued)

In the U.S. each state has its own school system paid for by state and local taxes. The states also receive federal funds to help support their educational systems. Traditionally, the quality of education has varied significantly from state to state.

1. Do you think federal programs would improve the quality of education? Explain.

____

____

____

2. How does standardized testing affect what is taught? List a possible positive and negative result on the chart.

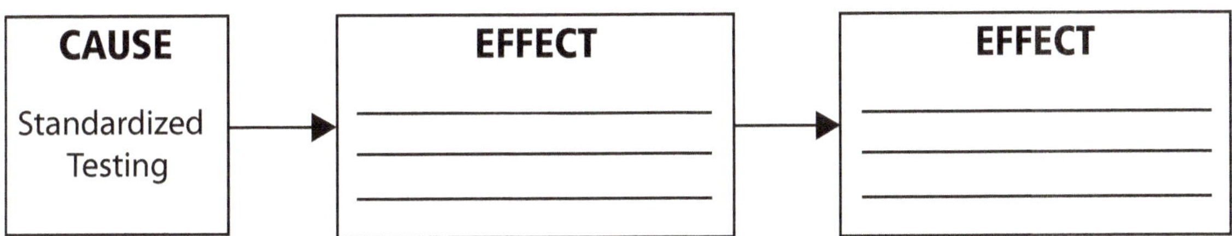

C. What do you think?

Do the advantages of the No Child Left Behind Act outweigh the disadvantages? Explain.

____

____

____

You may wish to explore this issue further online. Go to:

Internet Research Activity

Transfer Your Knowledge
For: WebQuest **Web Code:** neh-9302

III. ESSAY

Bring together what you have read in your textbook with the information you've gathered online about this American issue. On a separate sheet of paper, answer the essential question: **What should be the goals of American education?**